So Many Fragile Things

On May 13, 1900, Samuel Moser murdered his wife and children. Was he a murderer or a martyr?

D1523287

Amy Steidinger

ISBN 978-1-64670-586-3 (Paperback)
ISBN 978-1-64670-587-0 (Digital)

Covenant Books, Inc.
11661 Hwy 707
Murrells Inlet, SC 29576
www.covenantbooks.com

Acknowledgments

To my high school writing teacher, Ann Nussbaum, for making me think of myself as a writer.

To my college thesis advisors, Anthony Crubaugh and Stewart Winger, for their extreme patience and teaching me that you have to push print at some point.

To Darrel Sutter, for your inspiring love of all things history and teaching.

To my mother, Denise Erickson, for being my absolute biggest fan and supporter.

To my brother, Adam Kinzer, for his writing feedback and amazing photography.

To my amazing kids, my joy and inspiration.

To my husband, Jay—for being excited about growing old together.

To all of my family and friends in the Apostolic Christian Church (and its many branches). Thank you for accepting us, loving us, and embracing our differences. I pray that the telling of this story challenges us as Christians but honors the precious people that I know and love.

Here's a strange
mixture of religion
and fanaticism,
love, and murder...

Deep within the pages of the Moser family book lies a secret. The leather-bound book sits high upon a shelf, quietly gathering dust because most of the Mosers aren't very interested in what's gone on long ago. They're busy going to work, raising their children, and living their lives. They go to the Moser family reunion in the summers. They eat watermelon, laugh with cousins they grew up with on the farm, and stroll over to watch their children in the swimming pool next to the park pavilion. The elderly Moser aunts sit at the picnic table, telling family stories as they leaf through the family photo albums. They know the secret. But they won't admit it. They've shoved it to the back of the closet for too many years. They have no intention of letting it out now.

Chapter 1
Discovery

There is a strange moment in time, after something horrible happens, when you know it's true, but you haven't told anyone yet.

—Barbara Kingsolver,
The Poisonwood Bible

1900
Tremont, Illinois

Noah pulled the wagon to a stop in front of his brother's house, his errand to deliver a load of hay forgotten. He realized that he had known something was wrong before he'd even left his farm, down the road. What was it Sam had said as he was leaving, after dropping Hanna and the boys off after church the other day? Nothing. Something about the way Sam looked at him made him pause for a moment and look back questioningly. The set of his jaw. The way he sat stiffly in the rocking chair, watching the boys and Hanna pile out of the wagon, coming home from church. Sam sat there, watching them. Removed somehow. Noah suddenly remembered that he'd thought for a second that Sam had fallen asleep there—but no, he was awake, just watching. He usually called to them, smiled down at his boys, tousled their hair, and listened to their stories patiently. Sam was always like that with his boys, but not that day. Now the rocking chair sat empty and seemed to mock him for not realizing sooner—Sam was having a bad spell.

He'd meant to help his brother by taking his wife and children to church. Sam had argued with the elders and refused to apologize. He hadn't gone to church for years now. But Noah's wife was always wondering if Sam wasn't mad at them for intruding; helping Hanna to go, when Sam clearly wanted her to stay with him. He always thanked him, but sometimes it seemed that he didn't like being indebted, was tired of the situation. Noah often wished that Sam would just swallow his pride and go back to church, move past his unforgiveness.

Noah had finished loading the straw and was about to leave when Hanna's parents drove into the lane. As he pulled the wagon up next to them, he noticed that they too were worried. They had come down from Goodfield to spend a short visit with their daughter, they told him. Did he know where Sam and Hanna had gone? They'd been unable to rouse anyone or get into the house, so they'd left a short while earlier. So much was unspoken in that. He told them he didn't know, but would investigate. He didn't have to tell them to stay in the wagon. They just did.

He climbed down from the wagon and slowly walked toward the house. The very house seemed to be holding its breath. It was so still, so quiet. His heart was beating fast, and something seemed to whisper to his feet to run. It felt like someone was watching him, but clearly no one was home. For some reason, he looked over his shoulder. What did he think he would see there? He told himself he was being foolish. He should just dump the load of hay and come back later when Sam and his family had returned. Yet he kept walking toward the door. Later he thought, It was as if I knew. *Then the guilt came crushing down on him. If he'd known then, why didn't he know sooner? Why didn't he do something—anything—to stop what had happened, anything to keep those worried parents from looking as they did? Oh, God, what happened here?*

He realized suddenly that Sam and Hanna must have left again. That was it; they'd gone away. The animals had been turned out to pasture. The windows were covered up with something, all of them. Newspapers, he realized as he got closer. Someone had covered the insides of the windows with newspaper. His heart leapt at the simple explanation that they'd gone, but the sinking feeling in his stomach reminded him that they'd never covered the windows like that when they'd moved away before. They'd never gone without telling Hanna's parents, who were beside themselves with worry. Their questions rang in his ears. When had he last seen Hanna and the boys?

Sunday night, he'd dropped them off after church, and now it was Tuesday. Had he ever gone that long without seeing his brother or his family? Had he been avoiding coming down here? He thought again that he should have brought Hanna and the boys home with him on Sunday night. Elizabeth would have loved to look after them for a few days. Joseph was three years old and enjoyed spending time with his cousins. Sam would have been angry at him for meddling, but he'd agree that something must be done. They were family.

He found himself at the door and tried the knob. Locked. He tried the others, though he knew the parents had done the same. He realized suddenly that he was stalling, plain and simple. He was hoping that they'd pull in the drive, or he'd wake from this dream before it really began. Finally, he walked around to the cellar door and peered in through a small space between the edge of the newspaper and the windowsill. If he turned enough, he could just barely see down the stairs...there. What was that? He squinted in the light, put his hand up to shade his eyes some, and looked more closely. Oh, God. No. Hanna. She lay on the floor in a puddle of blood. She'd clearly been dead for a while.

He turned back to her parents, willing his voice to be steady, his hands to be still. "We'll go to the neighbors." Hanna's mother clutched at him. "They wouldn't go away without telling us, would they?" He tried to be reassuring as he shook his head no but knew he looked shaken. She searched his eyes and then looked to her husband quickly. Hanna's father still stared at the house. It was painfully awkward as they drove the quarter mile to Henry Hoffman's farm, but Noah didn't trust himself to speak.

At first, when Henry Hoffman opened his door to find Noah Moser standing on his porch, he couldn't understand what was happening. His former neighbor was babbling almost incoherently about how his nephews didn't run to help him as they usually did. "Slow down, take a breath, what's happened?" But soon the old man got enough information to know what was needed of him and stepped out to the wagon. When he saw the parents of Hanna Moser waiting there, he sent them into the house to wait with Mrs. Hoffman. As he rode with Noah back to the farm, he heard the story in fits and starts. A sinking feeling began in the pit of his stomach. He too felt that he'd somehow known this day was coming.

Chapter 2

The Family Tree

Other things may change us, but
we start and end with family.

—Anthony Brandt

1994

Forrest, Illinois

I didn't start out looking for Sam. I suppose it was ironic that I found him at a family reunion. My husband's maternal grandmother's family—the Mosers. They had planned it at a local park, which just happened to have the largest public swimming pool in America (which probably means the world?). It kind of takes your breath away, all that sparkling blue water in the middle of a small town park. It is staggeringly huge, and it's like a lake. It is shallow around the outside and gets deeper in the middle. Moms can pull their beach chairs right up into the water and sunbathe near their little ones playing. So it was a great place for a reunion, in a sense. There was plenty to do: volleyball, swings, swimming, baseball. But on the other hand, that was its downfall. The moment the food was devoured, everyone ran in a dozen directions.

But under the pavilion, sitting at a picnic table, the elderly aunts remained. Their little old bodies didn't allow for the physical activity that the younger ones ran toward. Their religious traditions kept them from donning swimsuits. Or maybe the wisdom of their years told them that the meaningful moments of reunion were found here, at the tables, over the photo albums.

The two sisters and a brother who was in a nursing home were all that was left of ten siblings. They lived together in a small house a few blocks from Main Street. They had worked at the Walton's department store downtown before they'd retired many years back. Aunt Lavina worked in the shoe department upstairs, and Viola was a bookkeeper in the basement offices. They were an entertaining duo, quick to laugh and finish each other's sentences.

My own grandmother had passed away just as I was having my babies. My first two were toddlers and my third on the way. Grandma Delores had gone way too soon. There wasn't time for me to realize what a wealth of knowledge she was, what all those family heirlooms and photographs in the boxes under the stairs really represented. And so she left us, and no one knew who was in those pictures, who'd sent those letters from France during the war. No one knew the answers to those questions that used to be answered with, "Grandma will know."

And so, though I was only twenty-three, I was drawn to those little elderly aunts sitting under the pavilion. I pulled up a lawn chair and listened while they reminisced over the photo albums. I laughed at their childhood memories, and I asked questions about the good old days. They were precious. Their wrinkles seemed to melt away, and you could catch a glimpse of the little girls they had been. I loved that they seemed to appreciate my listening. I watched the activities going on around the park and treasured it as a different kind of family bonding, but I wanted to yell to everyone, "You're really missing out on something here! You should be listening to these ladies tell their stories! They won't be around much longer, you know!" I thought it was a shame that so many would leave that day, having had such a good time swimming and grilling out but not knowing anything more about their family roots.

Soon it was time to pack it up. The heat was getting to them. They tired quickly these days, they told me. I felt something slipping away. I didn't want them to go, like grandma had gone, taking their stories with them. I didn't trust myself to remember. So I asked them if we could work together and make a Moser family book—preserve the history and tell their stories.

They were thrilled and chattered excitedly about information they had at home. They had a notebook of dates and newspaper clippings that could get us started. They had some ideas of what they would like to see included. They seemed renewed with a sense of purpose and enthusiasm for our common task.

It was a great partnership. I was a teacher who was home with my little ones for the summer. It seemed that nothing stayed done for five minutes. Diapers needed to be changed again and bottles filled. It seemed I'd no sooner finish the dishes, and they needed to be done again. Yes, I was busy. But a project that would challenge my brain and focus my writing skills sounded like a welcome relief. A few stolen hours during nap time, an hour or two in the early morning was valuable quiet time, something that spoke to my spirit. The work I put in on the Moser book was different—it would stay done. I could feel the progress, and it was gratifying. It also felt like something that would be passed on to my children someday, a labor of love.

A more obvious reward was that the aunts were thrilled at each step of the progress. They supported the project whole-heartedly and called to check on me regularly. They submitted to interviews, wrote memories, questioned one another, and returned my calls. They were fantastic sources of information and encouragement. Then they gave me the book where I found Sam—there on a page with Hanna and their children.

I turned the page, and there they were. Just a few lines of simple typed letters at the top of a blank page—but the question marks jumped off the page at me. The Moser family is of the Apostolic Christian faith. If you think Amish or Mennonite, then you're in the right neighborhood. They are similar in many ways, but they were much more so in 1900, which is when Samuel Moser's wife and three children all died on the same day.

Samuel Moser (1868–1910)

He married Hanna Hohulin in 1892 (b. 1863, d. May 13, 1900)

They had three children:

Ezra, b. 1895, died May 13, 1900

Benjamin, b. 1897, died May 13, 1900

Baby, b. 1899, died May 13, 1900

Back then, Apostolic Christians usually had huge families with lots and lots of children, so before I even noticed the death dates, the page struck me as strange. All the other pages containing the names and dates for Samuel's siblings were covered from top to bottom with children, their spouses, their children and their spouses, and so on. But here was Samuel's family—obviously cut short in some tragic way—all on the same day. And he lived on, without them. I could imagine his devastation. How could he go on after losing his entire family? What would have taken them so suddenly? Probably not disease, the first thing you think of with death all those years ago. It wouldn't have taken them all in one day, surely. I thought about a buggy accident, a tornado. I remembered hearing stories about immigrant families traveling west who would load all of their possessions on a raft to go across the river. Something like that maybe? I couldn't imagine the father's grief. Did he blame himself for what happened?

Curiosity flooded me. I tried to imagine the possibilities, the ones that seemed likely for the time period. Well, I was sure the Moser aunts would know. Sam would have been their uncle, a brother to their dad. I could give them a call.

I checked the clock on the wall and decided it was probably an okay time to call. These conversations had been frequent the past few weeks. Sometimes I called. More often, I'd stop by with folders of information and computer printouts, and we'd discuss the structure of the book, questions about photographs, and lists of descendants that needed updating. It was a very large family. The phone rang a few times, and I heard Viola's signature greeting on the other end, "Ye-eh-lo."

I hesitated. There was a twinge of uncertainty. I cautiously described what I'd found and asked what had happened to their uncle's family. It was quiet for a few seconds before she replied, "We don't talk about that."

There was a click, and I was listening to dial tone.

She'd hung up. Whoa. I sat back, stunned. It hadn't occurred to me that it could be something they didn't want to talk about. If I'd been curious when I'd called, this certainly wasn't helping matters. Part of me wanted to respect her wishes. Really, I did. And of course, I didn't talk to them about it again or put anything about it in the Moser book, which eventually was finished and delivered to them. But part of me couldn't accept their direction to leave it be, obviously.

I asked my husband to watch the kids for a while and drove in to our local public library. These were the days before easy internet searches, so I had to fire up a microfiche machine. I didn't think about them being from somewhere else, so I looked in our little small town paper's archives. I pulled out the file drawer and located the correct reel of film. The reel fitted onto the mechanism, and I stretched the film across the glass to the other side. Looping the end through the crank and turning, I watched as images from 1900 flashed across the screen. Ads from the Walton Brothers Department store, where the aunts had worked, classified ads for livestock, weather reports, and news articles. The pages flashed by in a blur as I turned the electric knob to sort through the information on the screen. I stopped periodically to check my progress. Soon I was in the right month. As I watched the dates roll by at the tops of the pages, I realized the paper didn't come out every day. I estimated, looking through the week following the death dates.

Getting close…no, too far…back a little bit. Finally, there it was: May 15, 1900. The first article I found brought things into crisp focus—why the aunts wouldn't want to talk about it.

The Blade

Fairbury, IL

Friday, May 18, 1900

Family Butchered

Mother and four children found dead in their home near Tremont, IL—Father is missing

Peoria, IL.—May 16—Mrs. Thomas Moser, wife of a farmer living three miles north of Tremont, Ill, and her four small children were found dead in their home Tuesday. All had apparently been dead since Sunday. Their throats were cut from ear to ear. Mrs. Moser's body was found in the cellar, covered with old carpet. The children lay in their beds upstairs, apparently having been killed as they slept. Moser has disappeared, but there is no known evidence pointing to him having committed the terrible crime. Nothing has been seen of the family since Sunday, and Tuesday neighbors broke open the doors of the farmhouse. They spread the alarm, but no trace of the murderer has yet been found, although some of the neighbors are convinced that Moser wiped out his family in a fit of insanity.

I could see why someone would want to keep that in the closet.

That first article was wrong. Several of the details were off: he was named incorrectly, the boys' ages were wrong. The crime happened in Tremont, Illinois, and this was the small town paper of Fairbury, about seventy miles away. The news must have spread from mouth to mouth, something like the telephone game. Sam became Thomas (a huge problem if you're Thomas Moser, I would imagine), three kids became four, and the details became more grisly. I tried to think of what things would have been like in 1900. Did they have phones? Use cars? I needed to investigate further.

I looked up which newspapers would have been published in that time period closer to Tremont and tried the *Bloomington Pantagraph*, which was also available at this library. I soon discovered that while the results were just as tragic, at least no throats had been cut. Same story, but this time, the correct name: Samuel Moser.

Three Little Boys and Their Mother
Victim of Father's Pistol

Still there was so much more I wanted to find out. What drove him to this act of insanity? How could this happen within the Apostolic Community—a religious group known for being nonviolent to the point of pacifism?

Well, the Moser aunts didn't want to talk about it. That was for sure. But what about the wife's family? I looked back at the original notation in the Moser information. Her name was Hanna Hohulin. I didn't imagine that the story would have the same stigma for the family of the victim that it would have for the family of murderer. I called information and asked for someone by the name of Hohulin in Tremont, Illinois. The operator gave me a few options, and I chose one who seemed like a good bet.

I called the number and introduced myself. It felt so awkward to tell the man who answered what I was looking for. It suddenly seemed so intrusive and maybe inappropriate. Thankfully, he knew what I was talking about, and he seemed okay with talking about it.

He said he couldn't tell me much about it, but his Uncle Ben would absolutely talk my ear off, given the chance. He gave me Ben's phone number and wished me luck. I called and talked briefly with Ben, who just said "Sure, when do you want to come over?"

I drove to Goodfield that afternoon to meet with Ben and Esther Hohulin. They lived just off a main thoroughfare, their little cottage set back within a white picket fence. Completely surrounded by rosebushes, it looked like the cover of *Better Homes and Gardens*. They were such a nice couple, and we made small talk about acquaintances we had in common. My husband's grandmother had been a nanny in the same neighborhood with Esther in Peoria many years before. Some of my brother and sisters-in-law were friends of Ben's family. He wondered about my husband's connection to the church and what I thought about it all. Finally, it seemed that Ben had made up his mind about me. He left me visiting with Esther and went down to the basement. Moments later, he returned, carrying a brown paper tube, like you might mail a poster in.

He popped the plastic cap out of the end of the tube and dumped its contents on the kitchen table. Dozens of newspaper articles spilled out, each one carefully clipped and laminated. Many of them had the dates carefully written at the top in pencil. The loopy delicate handwriting made me wonder about the woman that had carefully assembled this collection. Was it Ben's mother? She would have been Hanna's sister-in-law. I could see her in my mind's eye, bent over these articles at this very kitchen table, reading through her tears. It made what this family had gone through so very real.

Of course, Ben carried the story inside of him. He'd witnessed his parents' grief. He'd felt their loss. He was surrounded by family throughout his life, but someone was missing. He'd wondered about them and searched for answers. He began to tell the story.

He'd traveled a lot in search of answers. He'd gone to libraries, archives, and repositories. He'd gone to courtrooms and the house where it had happened. He'd driven the road to the train station. He had gone to the jail, the prison, and the cemeteries. He had found lots of answers, but he'd come to many dead-ends. He was excited for new technology that might help to make connections, but he didn't know where to begin. He seemed happy to pass the torch. He hoped someone would write a book.

We visited for a long time. My brain was crowded with details that didn't yet fit into any framework. I was ready to go when Ben asked, "Would you like to see the clothing they were wearing when it happened?" I wasn't too sure about that. What I imagined was, Why would anyone keep them? It made me feel differently about him for a moment, like it was a slightly inappropriate invitation. And yet, he'd been so open—so generous with his time and years of research. He looked hopeful. I couldn't bear to disappoint him.

We drove a few blocks across town to a beautiful Victorian home. The aunt and uncle who had lived there, Ben explained, had moved to the nursing home. He unlocked the large wooden door and swept his arm forward to invite me in. A grand foyer stood before us with beautiful wooden pillars and built-in shelves to the side. Soft light fell through the cut glass in the arched windows above us. There was a hush; it seemed like a warm, cozy museum, everything perfectly placed to look as it would have a hundred years before. There was a reverence; it felt like we were standing on holy ground.

Ben gestured to the top of the stairs, where a giant armoire stood with its doors spread wide. Inside the cabinet were the delicately placed shirts and pants that the children had been wearing. I felt pulled and climbed the stairs. Later I wouldn't remember if Ben came with me. Reaching the landing, I felt unsure. Was it okay to be here? Was I trespassing? But even as I questioned,

I felt assured. It felt like I was standing at the altar—there was a strong feeling of presence. It was warm and loving. I felt welcomed, and I felt a connection as a mother. I almost want to say now, all these years later, that I felt that Hanna wanted to show me, wanted me to write their story, to bring them to life for others on the page. To make sure they weren't forgotten. To explain.

On ancient hangers, the little shirts and dressing gown were hung. They were so beautiful, so perfect—without spot or wrinkle but golden with age. I wished I had brought my camera. Couldn't imagine I didn't have it. Yet I knew that what I was seeing couldn't really be captured on film. There was such a sense that the children had just stepped away for a moment. Gone and put on their playclothes. I had to remind myself that it had been ninety-four years.

After a few moments, I pulled myself away. I realized suddenly that I'd been wiping tears. I had to concentrate to go back down the stairs. I felt a little woozy, a little sad. When I got back to the door, Ben was waiting for me. The look on his face said that he knew what I was feeling. He had felt it himself. I thanked him, and we said our goodbyes.

The next few weeks, I spent every free moment—while my kids napped or once they'd gone to bed, mostly—reading and transcribing the newspaper articles that Ben had loaned me. Many of them were so difficult to read that almost the only way to get their meaning was to laboriously type them and piece together the clues to decipher the smudged words. I was obsessed with putting it all together. Each article answered questions, yet left me with so many more. There were clues everywhere. Characters being introduced, whole new lines of research suggested. I sent inquiries to the state archives and waited by the mailbox for a response.

But being immersed in the story was also very difficult for me. I was almost the same age that Hanna had been when she died, and I had three small children. Hanna's children were five, three, and ten months. My children were four, three, and five months. Sometimes I got a serious case of the creeps. One night I decided I needed a break. I packaged up the articles that had been spread all over my desk and put them back in the poster tube. I set it on the floor next to my desk and went to bed. In my dream that night, Sam was there in that space next to my desk where I'd left the poster tube. He crouched in the dark, watching us. That was it. I was done for a while.

The school year began that fall, and I was back to work. My husband worked nights and watched the kids. We were busy and trying to find ways to make it all work. I looked forward to getting back to my research in the summer, but for now, it would have to wait.

My progress on the book was slow for a few years. I had so little time. I continued to teach, and when I'd finally get some time off, my kids were the priority. Still the story pulled at me.

Nine years before, in February of 1891, Hanna Hohulin was married to Samuel Moser in the village of Congerville, which was then her home. Samuel was twenty-three years old, and Hanna twenty-eight years old. They were young people from good families, both raised in the church. It seemed to be a good match. The early years of married life passed, and two baby boys came to the home: Ezra in March of 1893 and Bennie in June of 1895.

At first, they lived on a farm two miles northeast of Goodfield and five miles south of Eureka. They seemed happy there, until Sam had a falling out with the church when Benjamin was just a baby. He'd bounced him on his knee during the church service and been reprimanded from the pulpit for idolizing his child. Embarrassed in front of the congregation, Sam had tried to talk to the elder, and they'd argued. The heated exchange ended with Reverend Witzig placing the ban on Samuel: he would be excommunicated from the church until he apologized and repented. Samuel felt he'd done no wrong and refused. He had been shunned by the other members for about five years.

I ached to put it together on paper. I saw it everywhere I looked. I would hear a news report and think of Sam. I'd read a book about the Amish and think of what Sam and Hanna's life together would have been like. I kept researching and writing, but time slipped away.

In 1898, Sam moved his family to Minnesota. He was desperate to get out from under the control of the church and start a new life. There was a new settlement of Apostolic Christians there. Hanna's brothers, Joseph and Timothy, had moved out the year before and said that there were plenty of opportunities for work. The church leaders in the new community were younger and not as strict. It was thought that Samuel could get along better there.

After only a short time, however, it became clear that Minnesota was not far enough away. They didn't tell him outright, but it was obvious that his neighbors had been made aware of the ban against Samuel. People who only the week before had been cordial and friendly were suddenly silent, their lips pursed together in disapproval. They looked away into the distance when he tried to speak to them. It was all starting to feel very familiar.

One thing I was realizing, though, was that I felt very underqualified to tell the story. Here and there, some aspect of the research would just overtake me, and I'd suddenly have the feeling that there was so much I didn't know. There was a larger framework of history and religion that Sam's story fit into. I had to wrap my head around it before I could articulate it to a reader. Could I really do that?

They were there for several months when Hanna became sick. As difficult as it had been to deal with Samuel's excommunication in Illinois, it was so much harder when they were far away from Hanna's family and friends. They at least could lend her support, even if they did enforce the ban against Samuel. Hanna's parents traveled to Minnesota and brought her and the children back. There was speculation about whether she was actually ill or simply homesick. Soon it was obvious what had caused her symptoms—she was expecting their third child. She wrote to Sam in Minnesota, hoping the news would help him seek restoration with their home church. With three young children, she wanted to be closer to her mother and sisters. She wanted her sons to grow up with their cousins, as she had done.

Samuel soon returned, and their third son was born in October of 1899. In January, they moved to the Jenks farm, three miles northeast of Tremont and about the same distance south of Morton. The land was owned by his father, Benedict Moser, so they felt blessed that he saw through to rent to them even with Sam's membership status unchanged. The house was a two-story frame structure, comfortably furnished, and it seemed to Hanna a good place to make a new start.

But the rumors about Sam persisted.

In 2003, I suddenly found myself facing a life-threatening illness. An emergency surgery left me in ICU for three days, fighting for my life. I got better but was in the hospital for fourteen days before being sent home to recover. I was off work for months and then on light duty. By this time, my kids were all in school, and so I had a lot of time to myself. I read and I wrote, but mostly I grappled with the realization that I'd gone through a truly life-altering event. I found myself reevaluating my life, my goals, and my bucket list. Some people jump out of planes, I guess. Me? I applied to grad school. I wanted to study religious history. I needed to prepare myself to tell the whole story.

Chapter 3

Sorrow

There are certain clues at a crime scene which, by their very nature, do not lend themselves to being collected or examined. How does one collect love, rage, hatred, fear?

—James Reese

1900
Tremont, Illinois

When they reached Tremont, Henry Hoffman took charge of contacting the sheriff and explaining the situation. Noah seemed to be in shock. He was no longer trying to explain things and had gone very quiet. The coroner and state's attorney in Pekin were telephoned. Soon, a buggy was filled with men who would drive out to the Moser farm: editor Cottingham of the *Tremont News*, F. J. Davis the banker, Ernest Abbot the liveryman, and Robert Markham, a Chicago traveling man.

The house and yard were eerily quiet when the men arrived. They climbed down from the wagons and stood in groups looking up at the house. None of them were eager to step forward. They were uneasy, hopeful that someone else would take charge or somehow know what to do first. Finally, it seemed that everyone who was coming had already arrived, and they might as well get it over with.

Someone suggested that the murderer might still be on the property. Another advised caution, pointing out that he might be in one of the upstairs rooms. A ladder was raised from the outside so that they might look in through the windows. Reassured, they began to look for a way into the house. Everyone seemed to think of a different course of action as they tried to look knowledgeable and assured, or at least not cowardly. Someone found a window unlatched, although a curtain was nailed down over it. Opening this, he was able to crawl through into a bedroom. He went through to open the door, allowing the others to enter more easily. They stopped quickly as they entered; for there, at the entrance to the sitting room, lying side by side on the floor—partially covered by garments thrown over them—were the bodies of Samuel Moser's three children. They wore their Sunday clothing but were barefooted, having evidently taken off their shoes and stockings after returning from church.

Each had been shot one or more times. Ezra, the oldest, had two bullet wounds in his head. From a streak of blood leading from his body, it was supposed he had been shot in the kitchen and then either walked or was dragged into the bedroom. Benjamin, the second boy, had a bullet hole almost in the top of his head—so close that his scalp was powder-burned. The baby, whom relatives said had not yet been named, had been shot three times: twice in the head and once in the breast, just over the heart. There were powder burns there also.

The bodies of the children had evidently been carefully placed side by side on the floor after they were killed. A child's dress lay over the oldest, a blanket over the other two, their feet protruding from the edge of the covering. A bullet hole in the wall showed where one shot had gone wild. An empty cartridge box and a loaded shotgun were found in the same room. A blood-spattered suit of clothing was found on the floor, and it was presumed that the murderer had exchanged it for another suit before departing.

The cellar door was open, so the men cautiously descended the stairs. It was close and damp, the putrid stench almost over-whelming. The body of Mrs. Moser lay on the brick floor, just as it had fallen, and covered with a blanket. She had clearly been there awhile. Her face was turned upward, a bullet hole in her right temple. They agreed her death had probably been instant.

In her right hand, she grasped a common case knife. Near the left was a dish, which had broken as she fell to the floor. There was no sign of a struggle, aside from the fact that the right hand had been cut by the knife which it held, and the knife was broken close up to the handle. But these things might have been caused by the fall. She wore the dress which she had worn to church on Sunday.

On a shelf nearby was a large dish of cooked potatoes. A second potato had been cut into the contents of the dish, and it was presumed Mrs. Moser was shot as she was getting supplies from the cellar to prepare them for supper. Such an ordinary thing. The men thought of their own wives. They thought of their own bare-footed children. They wished to be anywhere but this place.

Gratefully returning to the fresh air of the backyard, they awaited the arrival of the county officials. Neighbors who were milling about in the yard looked to them with questioning eyes. The men solemnly reported their discoveries. It was noted that the man of the house was nowhere to be found.

While there was not yet solid evidence pointing to his having committed the terrible crime, some of the neighbors were convinced that Moser wiped out his family in a fit of insanity. They said that he was not a drinking man but was known to be difficult and bad-tempered at times. He had been expelled from the Amish church some years before.

The crowd was growing larger by the minute, with wagons arriving regularly. Voices raised with excited talk of what would be done to Moser if he were found. Dozens of men bragged that they would shoot him full of holes if he were discovered. Knowledge of the crime spread throughout the small community—from mouth to mouth and home to home—and the horror only intensified with the telling. A murderer was on the loose.

It was nearly noon when a buggy arrived from Pekin containing Coroner Bailey, State's Attorney Cunningham, and Deputy Sheriff Ball. These officials took charge of the investigation. They confirmed the earlier observations and added some of their own. All the wounds were from a .32 caliber revolver. It was not found.

Some men were gathered to act as the coroner's jury: Edward Rollins (foreman), M. L. Cottingham, John P. Hurley, Frank J. Davis, Ernest Abbott, and T. H. Harris. They viewed the bodies of the dead, took notes of the surroundings, indicated the details of the tragedy, and instructed undertaker J. W. Winzeler to prepare the bodies for burial.

The coroner noticed a crumpled piece of paper on the floor. He found upon opening it the following, written in plain but shaky characters:

Tremont, Ill., May 13, 1900

Inform the postmaster by wire that my woman and three boys can be found dead in my house. Sam Mo—

The men passed the note around and speculated about why it was unfinished, why Sam had changed his mind about writing it or leaving it. Finally, the coroner and the jury adjourned to Tremont for the inquest. Witnesses before the jury were Samuel's father, Benedict Moser; Hanna's brother-in-law, Herman Stoller; the neighbors Henry Hoffman and William Gerstner.

When Coroner Bailey and his jury had heard the testimony of these witnesses and had noted all the circumstances of the case, a verdict was returned for each of the victims: "We, the undersigned jurors, sworn to enquire into the death of Hanna Moser, Ezra Moser, Benjamin Moser, and Baby Moser, on oath do find that they came to their deaths by the effects of the pistol ball fired by Samuel Moser."

Sheriff Mount sent word all over the country to be on the lookout for him.

The next morning, the women from Hanna's church descended upon the house, each filling a particular role in its redemption. These were Hanna's sisters, some of them literally but all of them sisters in Christ. These were the women that she'd talked to, prayed with, leaned on, asked advice of, taken food to, trusted. She'd known many of them her entire life. They'd gone to Sunday school together; many of them had attended each other's weddings. They'd been pregnant at the same time; they'd tended one another's children.

These women had felt the news of Hanna's death; they'd taken it in as a shocking physical blow. Hanna and her precious little boys...the loss was their own. Each of them felt terrible guilt, as well. Why hadn't they seen that this would happen? Why hadn't something been done? It was impossible; it couldn't be true. It was a nightmare. And yet there was no waking up.

They had been unable to foresee, to prevent this terrible thing that had happened, and it certainly could not be undone. They had cried. They felt so useless in the face of this senseless tragedy. But now, suddenly, there was something they could do, a way that they could be useful and do something for Hanna—and this was something that they were very, very good at.

These were farm women. They were taught from a very young age the value of hard work. Many of them had even worked as maids in wealthy households in the city before settling down to marriage and families. Every one of them knew that cleanliness was next to godliness, and it was time to put things right in Hanna's house. They'd packed the wagons full of the supplies they'd need that morning and were driven to the farm by their husbands and sons. The men helped haul things and worked outside while the women turned to the housework.

Furniture was quickly and silently moved out onto the lawn; rugs were rolled up and carried away. Brooms and buckets were brought in; cleaning solutions were prepared and divided up. Teams were formed, and the little army of women began to methodically sweep and scour. All evidence of the terrible wrong that occurred there was obliterated. It felt good to finally do something—to roll up their sleeves, to purge, and to cleanse. For the most part, it was sweat and muscle, but it wasn't long before they returned to tears. For here, they were surrounded by reminders of Hanna and her boys. Their clothes hung in the closets. Hanna's brush and comb lay on the dresser, and her shoes were carefully placed by the door. The life Hanna had poured into her family was evident in every nook and cranny.

Scene after scene caused a moment of sorrow, the realization that they wouldn't see Hanna or the boys again in this life.

Other items caused a shiver of dread to run up the spine of the observer—they were standing in the place that this horrible thing had occurred. Everywhere they turned, they were confronted with it. The broken jar on the basement floor elicited thoughts of Hanna's intent to feed her young ones, unaware of the danger they faced. A single child's shoe, so tiny, its little shoe latches undone—bringing to mind the time that Hanna had been fastening it while talking with a friend in the children's room at church. And so they worked and tried to keep their emotions in check. There was no time for tears; they'd all been shed already.

The dozens of jars carefully preserved and stacked on the shelves of the basement could not go to waste. Hanna would not have wanted them to spoil. The clothes that hung in the closets were taken out to be given to needy families; they wouldn't go unworn. The many decisions were not easily made, but it was important to be practical. It was important to do the right things and honor God even in this. And so the glass was swept away and the stained rugs carried out to the burn pile.

The men discussed the care of the animals, the distribution of the goods among the family, what would happen to the house and property itself. They talked through the farming situation and who would take over the planting and harvesting of what acres. They talked about the best ways to distribute the salvageable things, how to talk to their children about what had happened to their cousins, who would tend to the needs of Hanna's grieving parents, deliver food and care for them through the coming days. Life would go on. In times like these, there was nothing to do but be practical—and Hanna and her boys were in a better place.

> Heaven is comfort, but it's still not living.
> —Alice Sebold, *The Lovely Bones*

On Wednesday, May 16 of 1900, the visitation for Hanna, Ezra, Benjamin, and Baby Moser was held at the home of Samuel Moser. People began flocking there early in the day. The house and yard was crowded with mourners; many of whom were clearly still in shock.

In a way, it felt good for all the family, friends, neighbors, and church members to gather in one place. It was a comfort just to be together. But they were all so exhausted, so spent from the enormity of it all. No one had slept, and the frustrating search for the man who had likely killed them was still underway.

Finally, the wagons were loaded for the procession to the New Amish Cemetery in Morton. It extended for over two miles and was the largest that anyone could remember. The scene at the cemetery was one of the most pathetic imaginable. The four coffins were lowered into the grave side by side while the great crowd looked on in silent respect. Choking sobs of grief could be heard throughout the crowd. Just when it seemed they'd gained some composure, something else would stir a fresh ripple through the crowd: the sight of Hanna's mother or a child's tears. It was an exhausting day for everyone.

On Friday, May 18, the Tazewell county board of supervisors announced a $200 reward for the arrest and conviction of the person or persons responsible for the murder of Hanna Moser and her three young sons. Of course, everyone knew that her husband, Sam Moser, had disappeared the night of the murders and had not been seen since.

There was talk of putting the bloodhounds on Moser's track, but the house had been visited by scores of people, and the scent would have long before been lost. Excitement ran high, and it was certain that Moser wouldn't fare well if he were caught. An additional reward of $300 was offered by Herman Stoller, whose wife was a sister to Hanna. It was said that he feared for his own safety due to an old quarrel with Sam.

Little had been revealed by the Tazewell authorities about the investigation, but everyone had their theories. There were search parties out, and many thought he would soon be found, dead at his own hand. Some thought he'd gone to nearby Bloomington or boarded a train at Tremont. It seemed much more likely that he might have traveled on foot or on horseback over the country, where it would be more difficult to track him.

Train station attendants in Morton and Tremont could not remember having sold a ticket to anyone answering Moser's description on Sunday evening. A Big Four conductor, however, said that he had a passenger that night up to the C & A junction who might fit the description of the murderer. Some thought he might have fled to Utah, where there were large Mennonite settlements.

SAM MOSER STILL MISSING.
Pekin, Ills., May 18.—The Tazewell county board of supervisors offers a reward of $200 for the arrest and conviction of the person or persons who murdered Mrs. Sam Moser and her three young sons last Sunday afternoon near Tremont. Sam Moser, her husband, who disappeared the evening of the murder, has not been seen since. The authorities are trying to locate him.

A special edition of the Bloomington paper the following morning said that a frenzy from brooding over his grudge against the Amish church from which he had been expelled might have been the direct cause of Moser's inhuman act. The Amish (Apostolic Christians were often confused with the Amish, and the two terms were used interchangeably) were numerous in the area and supported a large church in Morton. For some infraction of church discipline, Moser was said to have been expelled from the church.

The Amish people, who were usually quiet and law-abiding, were especially staggered by the enormity of the crime carried out by one of their own. While it was common knowledge that he'd had problems and was estranged from the church, it was ordinarily supposed that Moser's family life was tranquil. By all accounts, he was a man who showed considerable affection for his wife and children.

Mrs. C. H. Ummel, who had gone to school with Hanna and now lived in Bloomington, was interviewed by a *Pantagraph* reporter. She said that Mrs. Moser was one of the most estimable women of her acquaintance. Concerning the usages of the Amish church, she said that she had, through long acquaintance with the Amish people, learned something of their customs, though she herself was not a member. She knew they were very rigorous in their treatment of "backsliders" (people who have been expelled from the church). A wife would not have been allowed to eat at the same table with a husband if he had been expelled. In the case of Moser, Mrs. Ummel says she knew nothing as to the details connected with the tragedy except what she had read in the papers.

A peculiar letter was received by the postmaster at New York City. It had been mailed on the Big Four Train which passed through Bloomington at 9:20 Sunday night on which Moser had evidently been a passenger.

> Tremont, Illinois
> May 13, 1900
>
> Inform the postmaster at Morton, Tazewell Co. that my wife and boys can be found dead at my place. Sam Moser
>
> They have gone to rest, and I will follow.

The New York postmaster immediately notified the postmaster at Morton of this request; and the sheriff, who was apprised of the communication, wired for the original letter, hoping that it would furnish some clue as to the whereabouts of Moser and at what point the letter was mailed. The letter was expected the next day, but authorities were of the opinion that their efforts would be without avail and that Moser would carry out his implied idea of self-destruction. It was thought that the communication strengthened the belief that his mind was disordered.

On Tuesday, the local paper reported that talk of lynching had almost entirely died out. The feeling against Moser in Morton and the surrounding vicinity was that he ought to hang for the horrible crime he committed, after having a fair trial. It was not that the people thought he was not guilty but that they wanted the courts to give him a fair chance to tell what drove him to commit the horrible crime he was charged with. Their curiosity was piqued.

Finally, on Saturday, there was news: the Tazewell County sheriff's office had received a telegram from Thomas Hilton, the chief of police in Salt Lake City, Utah. A man giving the name of Samuel Moser had been taken into police custody after attempting to commit suicide there early that morning.

The story of the capture of Moser, the cold-blooded murderer, spread like wildfire. Moser was reported to have left letters in Salt Lake City as he had at Tremont. They showed that he
was far from insane but had deliberately planned his crime. It was
expected that public sentiment would demand swift justice for
Moser.

According to his story, he had gone to a bridge across the
river Jordan and attempted to shoot himself. He fell from the
bridge, but the wound was slight and the water very shallow.
He made his way uptown in a half-dazed state and fell down on
Second South Street. He attracted the attention of a policeman
because of his bloody appearance.

The police searched his pockets for identification and
retrieved a note bearing his name and the address of the hotel.
An officer went to his room and recovered two stamped enve-
lopes. The first was a rambling indictment that his trouble was
the result of Amish people from the church of his home.

The second letter was more to the point: "I know I deserve
the rope."

Chapter 4
Research

Libraries are full of ghosts, books being the most haunted things of all.

—Maya Panika

2000

I'd made so many calls to archives and repositories searching for information about Sam's trial that by now it was like a prerecorded message: "Yes, I'm hoping you can help me. I am looking for information about a trial that took place at the Tazewell County Courthouse in Pekin in 1900. Yes, I know you don't have records that old. This would be in the archives. I was told to ask about..." Most people seemed slightly annoyed at first, but once I explained the reasons, the connection, the project—they got interested and were usually helpful.

But then one day, the response was different: "Oh yes. You called the other day."

"No..."

"Huh. That's the second request we've had for that same information this week."

What?!

"For case number——?"

"Yes."

I was blown away. Who else would be researching this? How did they know about it? I asked a few questions. She couldn't answer them. I asked if she could take my information and give it to the other person when they were given the records they'd requested. She thought that could be done. There were follow-up phone calls. There was waiting. In the meantime, I put in a few calls to Ben Hohulin, who had originally helped me with the case. I thought he would be so interested to hear that someone else was looking into the case. That there was a new mystery to think about. He didn't reply, which was unusual. It had been a while since I'd seen him. I tried to think how old he would be now.

The next week, when I called the courthouse to follow up on my request for information, I asked if the other researcher had been given my information.

"Oh, well, I'm not sure. You see, she's a lawyer. She's in and out of here often. But her grandfather just recently passed. I think the services are tomorrow. She probably won't be in until next week."

Was Ben Hohulin her grandfather? Was this why he hadn't answered my calls?

A few weeks later, my suspicions were confirmed when Lynn called. She was indeed Ben's granddaughter, and he had passed not too long before. She brought me up to speed on her grandmother, Ben's wife, and told me the story of Ben's illness and passing. He'd lived a good life. I told her about my visits with her grandparents and how Ben had wanted the story to be told. She was excited about this as well. She said that she was interested in the legal particulars of the case but was not a writer. I laughed. I wanted to write but had no understanding of the legal particulars of the case. We agreed we'd be a good team. During the discussion, we realized that we were both the same age that Hanna had been when she died. It all felt like some kind of divine appointment. It was fate.

We made plans to meet, but time and circumstances would get in the way. It seems there is a timing to these things, and it would be many years later before we met.

Meanwhile, I was reading a lot of newspapers. My research had begun with newspapers: the headlines I'd found in the library and the poster tube collection that Ben Hohulin had given me. But the newspaper articles that Ben had shared were cut from the papers; the laminated clippings were out of context and stood alone. I decided to go through the original newspapers so that I could put the story into the context of the days in which it happened. What else was going on at the time? What were the major news stories? What was life like then?

I'm sure I knew that life wasn't like *Little House on the Prairie* in 1900, but I was (like most people) under the impression that those were simpler times and that crime and lunacy had increased drastically since then. So these newspapers were a surprise. There were lots of stories of drug use, usually about housewives committing suicide due to laudanum abuse. There were many stories of lynchings and murders. Abuse, divorce, scandal—you name it.

I thought about yellow journalism. Was this that kind of sensationalistic storytelling or a true reflection of the time? One article I found, from August of 1897, featured a lecture given by Dr. J. W. Roberts, pastor of a Trinity church. He took newspapers and newspapermen severely to task in a scorching sermon on the "Exceeding Sinfulness of Sin." The article was called "Warm Roast for the Newspapers."

Dr. Roberts spoke of the causes of sin and crime. The low order of literature, for example, whether in trashy dime novels or in newspapers. He said that people who are partially insane, criminally inclined, or laboring under hallucination were easily affected by these stories of crime, and many might be caused to do rash things.

He went on to explain that reporters were after sensational stories rather than the truth. Many reports, he said, were so misleading that it would cause a person to almost believe that the reporter was malicious. Many young newspapermen, he said, were hardly out of their teens and demonstrated immature judgment.

It certainly seemed true in this case. Some early newspaper reports incorrectly gave Hanna's name as Mrs. Thomas Moser, said that there were four small children, and told that their throats were cut from ear to ear. These reports were published in out-of-town newspapers—Albert Lea, Minnesota, and Fairbury,

Illinois, were two that were found—and so were maybe passed by word of mouth, "telephone game" style. However, these are areas where family members of either Sam or Hanna were living. One expects information published in the newspaper to be correct (maybe that was less so back then). While we can assume the corrected information was given shortly thereafter, imagine hearing such gruesome details about your family members' murder and finding out it wasn't even so. Imagine being Thomas Moser when this comes out. Or his wife.

Other reporters got the details correct but added a bit of sensationalism, such as "first kissing each of them goodbye." Speculation abounded. A suggestion that jealousy may have been the cause of the crime and that his own brother, Noah, was the cause was scoffed by those who knew the families and circumstances. To a casual observer, looking in upon the case, it would have seemed that Noah's companionship with Mrs. Moser on the day of the murder might have had something to do with the tragedy.

When I ran out of newspapers, I spent months researching the families—finding their roots, tracing them forward and backward, and looking at the connections. I was fascinated with each person's history: where they'd come from, their unique role, how they would have seen the world. I wrote each of their biographies. I looked at what happened again through their eyes.

Hanna's father was Gottlieb Hohulin, an old and respected leader in the Amish Church and a teacher who had been instructing the children in the northeast part of Tazewell County. He grew up in the Grand Duchy of Baden, Germany, not far from the city of Freiburg. His father taught him the art of weaving linen which would be used to make shifts, tunics, towels, bedding, and ship's sails. It was intense, exhausting work; and when he was seventeen years old, Gottlieb was left to carry on after his father died. Though he tried to support his mother, it was all too obvious to the young man that his opportunities were dwindling as the industrial revolution swept across Europe. Machines were doing the work that many men had done in the past.

After his mother died a few years later, Gottlieb decided to immigrate to America, where he might become a landowner and make a success of himself as a farmer. He traveled to the city of Bremen and soon set sail for New York City. It took a little over a month to sail across the ocean, and he was very, very grateful when they finally spotted land in the distance. In Illinois, he worked as a laborer until after the outbreak of the Civil War.

Gottlieb married Ms. Augusta Wenger, who had also immigrated from his home province in Germany, arriving with her parents in 1859. They purchased 120 acres of land in Montgomery County, on the road to Eureka, Illinois. They had seven children: Julia, Joseph, John, Samuel, Timotheus, Elizabeth, and Hanna (the youngest, who would grow up to be the wife of Samuel Moser).

Sam, Tim, and John Hohulin founded the Hohulin Brothers Fence Company, which was credited as the first business to commercially manufacture chain-link fence fabric in the United States. Their website says "On April 27, 1897, they filled their first fence order—396 feet of 48-inch-high fence with one gate—that rang in at a grand total of $26.90." So Gottlieb was a weaver of fine jacquard fabrics, and his sons were weavers of chain-link fence. The business is still going strong over one hundred years later.

Sam's father, Benedict Moser, was nine years old when his father died in France in 1849. His oldest sister had recently married, but her husband had gone to America to start a new life for them. With their new brother-in-law away, the responsibilities of the man of the house fell to Benedict's older brother, Christian, who was then twenty years old. He was no stranger to hard work, having labored in the sand and clay pits near the Rhine River since he was twelve years old. The entire family pulled together and worked hard to help Benedict's mother, Elizabeth, and keep the family afloat.

Three years later, in 1852, the brother-in-law who had gone to America sent for his wife to come to their new home in Ohio. It was decided that Christian, now twenty-three years old, would accompany his older sister to America. He liked the stories of America and wanted a chance to seek his own fortune in the challenging, promising new world. The responsibility of the family in France then fell to Benedict, though he was only twelve years old.

When they arrived in America in 1853, the sister and her husband moved to their home in northwest Ohio while Chris worked on farms in Wayne County, Ohio, for families who had been known to them in Alsace. In only two years, hardworking Christian was able to send the money for his mother, three sisters, and Benedict to come to America.

They sailed to New Orleans, which had become an established route for Mennonites and Apostolic Christians at that time. It was less expensive overall to come by ship to New Orleans and go up the Mississippi and the Ohio by boat than to come through the eastern ports and travel on by land.

The mother, three daughters, and Benedict arrived in Ohio in 1856 at the Ohio River in Adams County, where Chris was waiting for them. He helped get them settled in northwest Ohio, near their older sister and her husband, near the present-day city of Wauseon.

With his family taken care of, Chris proceeded with his own plans. Believing that there was more opportunity in Illinois than Ohio, he verbally contracted to work in Illinois on a farm owned by Christian Kempf. He traveled to the Farniville/Slabtown area in central Illinois in June of 1856. On arrival, he found that Mr. Kempf had died only a few days earlier on July 15, 1856. The forty-eight-year-old man had fallen while helping to repair the roof of a neighbor's barn. His leg was shattered, and his injuries later resulted in fatal blood poisoning.

Mr. Kempf's wife, Magdalena, was left with nine children, from eighteen years to five months old. The grieving widow, who was clearly overwhelmed with running a farm and helping her children through such a difficult time, was of course greatly relieved when help arrived from Ohio.

Chris Moser worked regularly at the Kempf farm for the next three years. In that time, he earned enough money to purchase the first eighty acres of his future 160-acre farm, about a quarter mile northwest of the Kempf property. At first, Chris took a liking to seventeen-year-old Anna (Nance) Kempf, but she did not share in his interest. In 1858, she married John Schmutz, and Chris and Magdalena began courting. This courtship resulted in marriage on April 5, 1859, at which time Magdalena was forty-three and Christian thirty. The newlyweds moved to Chris Moser's new eighty-acre farm. The older Kempf children stayed and worked the Kempf farm.

Benedict Moser visited his brother and worked for him and other farms in the Farniville area as far as Morton, a few miles to the west. Returning to Ohio, he worked for the Steiner family, where he'd developed an attraction to their daughter, Verena. They were married in 1862 and moved to Morton near some of her relatives, where he wanted to live and farm near his brother.

The Civil War brought some prosperity to farmers. In 1865, Chris bought the Kempf farm from the older Kempf children. His brother, Benedict, returned to Farniville and ran the Kempf farm until he could save the money to purchase a farm closer to Morton. Three of Benedict's children were born there: Daniel, Aaron, and John Ben. Later, when they were old enough, the boys often hired out to Uncle Chris.

Twice, in 1869 and 1873, Chris bought forty-acre parcels adjoining his farm from the Illinois Central Railroad, increasing his new farm to 160 acres. By the time that Benedict and Christian's mother died in Ohio, eight of Benedict's children were born. The youngest of these, Lydianna, was born just two weeks before Elizabeth died on May 19, 1876. Two more would soon follow, for a total of ten children. By 1888, all four of Benedict and Christian's sisters were married, three of them living in Ohio and one in Indiana. Christian's wife, Magdalena, died in 1890. He waited about a year before he married again, this time to Clara Emma Habeck Doebler, a thirty-year-old widow with two small children (by now, Chris was sixty-two).

For forty years, the two brothers lived and farmed and raised their families within a few hours by wagon ride. They'd come to America to seek their fortunes and left their families behind in Ohio to make their way together in Illinois. All these years later, they were upstanding men in their communities.

Christian passed away about nine years later, on November 17, 1900, while Sam awaited trial. We can only imagine how Christian would have felt about his nephew's tragedy. I'm certain that Benedict and Christian would have had conversations about what happened that only two brothers, patriarchs of their families, that had made the journey from France to the new world together could have.

I was immersing myself in the story. One day, I set off on a mission to find the Moser house. I had the description of where the house was located from the newspaper articles—so many miles north and so many miles east of town. I had this image of standing under the quiet trees, gazing at the house, feeling the gravity of the location, looking down the road in the direction that Sam had gone. I drove around slowly, looking this way and that until I finally found it. It was definitely the house. It had been covered in shingles but still looked old and sad. I got out of the car and tried to take in the vibes—feel the feelings. But it was weird. The road was modern, the houses down the road new. And someone clearly lived in this house. There was a modern satellite dish affixed to the sad old house. Suddenly a German shepherd came flying around the side of the house; he looked like he was serious about his job of guarding the property. I jumped back in the car. The dog's owner called him back. She walked out to my car, curious. I rolled down the window and explained that some family had previously lived here. I was in the area and wanted to take a picture. She smiled and studied me for a second. She seemed to make up her mind and then asked, "I've heard that something bad happened here. Do you know about it?" I didn't want to tell her.

Later, I travelled to Salt Lake City, Utah, the place where Sam had gone. I searched for him in the world-famous archives but found little. My husband and I drove out to Tremonton, the tiny

Apostolic Christian settlement on the outskirts of the city, where not much remains of them but a quiet cemetery outside of town.

I researched the Mormon church. It's very, very different from the Apostolic Christian faith. But it's interesting that the trail that was blazed by the Mormons to Utah, one that resulted in a land of religious freedom out west, also appealed to the Apostolic Christians. At the time, these immigrants had traveled to a new land where they could worship freely. But they soon found that there were still pressures and conflicts that pushed them to go farther west.

Back in Illinois, I went to Genealogical Guilds, Historical Libraries, and the Apostolic Reading Room. I realized how amazing it was that I live so close to all the places that were connected to this story. I found a book about the founding of Pekin, where the trial took place. So many interesting stories, so many connections to make.

In 1824, Jonathan Tharp built a cabin and began farming in the area that would become Pekin, Illinois. He encouraged his family to follow him to the area, which offered good farm ground and friendly Indians. His father and a brother settled nearby. The father, Jacob Tharp, was about his business one day when he heard "the angel Gabriel's trumpet" echoing through the wilderness. Certain that the end of the world was upon them, he hastily gathered his family in prayer. The first steamboat had landed at the town site, blasting the whistle to announce its arrival.

County surveyor William Hodge did the first survey of the town in 1829 with a length of knotted string since he did not have a surveyor's chain. In 1829, the "town site" plat was taken to Springfield and placed on sale at public auction. The lots reportedly cost twenty-eight cents each.

The town grew from a typical frontier town. On August 21, 1849, Pekin was officially incorporated as a "city." Around this time, it was declared the seat of Tazewell County, after a long-running feud over this distinction with the nearby village of Tremont. A large Grecian-style courthouse was built on the corners of court and capitol streets. A two-story brick jail was also built at the cost of $20,000. This building also contained living quarters for the sheriff and his family. This was where Samuel was housed during the trial, but I hadn't realized that Sheriff Mount resided there as well.

TAZEWELL COUNTY JAIL, Pekin, Illinois

In the 1850s, many Germans immigrated to the Pekin area. It was noted in Pekin's sesquicentennial book that these "hardworking, thrifty newcomers" brought with them "the first indication of antislavery sentiment. However, Pekin remained a basically pro-slavery community with Stephen Douglas, not Abraham Lincoln, the local hero." They even had their own newspaper: the *Die Sonne* was the German-language newspaper in the area and was first published in 1878. So many Germans settled there; however, it became a problem. People who didn't speak German found it difficult to live there and moved on. The traditional, conservative practices that were brought with them from the Old World led to a stagnation not experienced in surrounding communities.

It also had a somewhat violent history for so small a town. In 1861, a man named John Ott axed to death a woman and her two small daughters near Delavan. A crowd estimated between five to ten thousand people jammed the streets to witness his execution. Three companies of troops were brought in and martial law declared before order was restored.

The second murder of the decade is still a mystery:

> *On October 19, 1865, the body of a man was found in the Illinois River at Pekin. The head had been severed from the body around which a quantity of iron was fastened. The corpse was not positively identified but was believed to be one George Jackson, a well-known resident of the county who had been mysteriously absent for some weeks. The mayor of Pekin offered a reward of $500 for the apprehension of the murderer, but no leads were uncovered until 1866, when Jackson's wife went to England.*

Nearly the first person she met upon her arrival in Liverpool was her supposedly murdered spouse. Who the dead man was had never been determined, nor was anyone ever arrested for the crime.

On July 30, 1869, a sheriff's posse was ambushed as it attempted to serve a warrant. The Berry Gang, described as a group of thieves and cutthroats, operated out of a headquarters about eight miles south of Pekin. They had long terrorized the entire county, committing crimes and intimidating people. The next day, the gang's leader, William Berry, boldly came to town. He'd assumed the people would be too afraid to confront him, but a line had been crossed. He found himself surrounded by a posse of armed citizens and was taken to the county jail. That night, several hundred men stormed the jail and forced open Berry's cell. They dragged him out, shot him three times, and hung him from a tree in the courthouse square. The other members of the gang were soon captured, tried, and sentenced to between fifteen years and life.[1]

By the 1870s, Pekin had become a center for more organized and politically endorsed crime operations. A national issue of the Grant administration, this hub of the "Whiskey Ring" was headquartered in St. Louis. A high tax was placed on whiskey after the Civil War, and these operations worked to bypass the tax by bootlegging liquor.

> *The power of the ring was said to be tremendous and something of a potency here as indicated by an incident in which a revenue man was arrested by local authorities and held in custody on a trumped-up charge while a boat-*

---

[1] James Bercher and Jim Conover, *Lynch Law* (Pekin, IL: Lynch Law Productions, 1992).

load of whiskey was cleared off a dock and hidden away. Officials were party to the secret alliances which made it possible for some whiskey makers to present false reports, with the effect of paying taxes on as little as one-third of their actual production. Many of the city cisterns built for fire protection were emptied of water and then refilled with highly flammable liquor instead. Fermented spirits were also cached in corn shocks, and kegs were sealed and sunk in the Illinois River. Hundreds of those kegs were recovered by federal agents during later dragging operations.

In February of 1887, there was another sensational trial held in Pekin, Illinois. Gottlieb and Catharine Santoehl were indicted for inhuman treatment of their ten-year-old son. The evidence showed conclusively that the parents had inflicted the most heartless punishment upon their helpless child for the slightest offense. The child's hands had been held on the hot stove until they were burned in a fearful manner. He had been beaten until his back was covered with sores. He was strapped to the floor at nighttime during the cold weather of January, with no covering. He was kept in that condition until his feet were frozen. They had been amputated about a month before the trial. He was so weak and emaciated that an improvised bed had to be prepared for his use while giving his testimony.

There was scarcely a dry eye in the crowd when the little fellow was carried into the courtroom that afternoon to testify against his parents. He told his story through an interpreter (the Santoehl family were German) in a straightforward and impressive manner. The child's testimony corroborated that of the other witnesses and made a very strong case against the parents. The parents appeared to be affected not in the least when the child was brought into court, and it was said that they were only anxious as to their own fate.

In 1896, a man named Albert Wallace of Delavan had shotgunned to death his sister and severely wounded her husband. He was hanged on Saturday, March 14, while several thousand people milled around the walls of the stockade which had been built to keep all but official "ticket holders" from witnessing the execution. His neck was not broken in the fall, and it was not until fourteen minutes later that he was pronounced dead of strangulation.

While the newspapers might have been sensationalistic, these crimes give us some context when it is said that Moser's was the worst in the history of Tazewell County. These were the recent memories of the people who resided in Tazewell County. The people who heard the news of the Moser murders remembered these stories.

Of course, when you put them all together, it gives a very different view of the county than what the people who lived there experienced. They went about their lives, for the most part untouched by these crimes. They worked, married, had children, went to church, read these things in the newspapers—and wondered what the world was coming to. As it was written in the *Pekin Sesquicentennial*:

> *And so the decade ended, characterized in part by saloon fights, gambling, and arrests for carrying concealed weapons but also by progress in education, religion, and government. Most store windows bore signs assuring potential customers "German spoken here,"*

yet most of Pekin's 8,420 residents were now native Pekinites, born in its buildings, educated in its schools and churches, and increasingly aware of the more social and sophisticated facets of community life. Indications were that Pekin was leaving behind it that "frontier, river town" image and preparing to meet the Twentieth Century head on.

In May, the news came from Tremont, a much smaller little village—nine miles east and a little south. Shocking news—a woman and her children murdered, the husband on the loose. The residents of Pekin had followed the story in their newspapers. Sheriff Mount had gone to retrieve the offender, traveling some 3,000 miles to bring him back. And there he would be tried—in Pekin, Illinois.

Chapter 5
The Arrest

Suicide is a form of murder—premeditated murder. It isn't something you do the first time you think of doing it. It takes getting used to. And you need the means, the opportunity, the motive. A successful suicide demands good organization and a cool head, both of which are usually incompatible with the suicidal state of mind.

—Susanna Kaysen, in
Girl, Interrupted

Saturday
May 20, 1900,
Salt Lake
City, Utah

CHIEF THOMAS R. HILTON.
Appointed Patrolman, Oct. 1, 1853; appointed Duty Sergeant, May 5, 1891;
appointed Chief April 5, 1891.

In a cell at the police station that night, doctors watched over Sam Moser. His wound was severe, but not dangerous, and it was thought that he would recover. He wept bitterly, though, over his failure to end his life. Chief Hilton gave strict instructions for an officer to watch him, fearing he might make another attempt. The officer thought he was not what you might expect a murderer to look like.

After being taken to the station, Moser admitted his identity. At first, the officers didn't believe him, but in his pocket they found a sheet of paper upon which was scrawled, "My name, Sam Moser. Investigate Harris house, 140 West Second Street, opposite post office."

They asked him how he'd gotten to Salt Lake City. He responded that he'd walked from his home in the country to Tremont and took the train for Bloomington, paying the fare on the train. In Bloomington, he bought a ticket for Kansas City. When he arrived there, he bought a ticket to Denver, then to Salt Lake, arriving on Thursday morning. He'd been exhausted and slept, then wandered the city with no particular destination. On Friday night, he'd bought a Chicago paper and seen the account of his crime. That's when he'd decided to end his life.

The officers divided up the letters that had been brought back from the room at Harris House and began to read.

I did not see any change or show for a change unless I agreed to the church order: therefore, I chose to die and take my family along. If only so much had been granted that I could have gone home with my family and had satisfaction and pleasure, I perhaps would have been contented, that as it was, my wife, as it appeared to me, was most of the time in sorrow, and in the latter days we had more or less trouble or disagreement, and our dear little boys began to notice it. A short time ago, we had trouble, and it appeared to me it hurt the dear little ones, but before I would be ruled by my wife, I chose to die with them. What is this life worth if there is no pleasure or enjoyment?

* * * * *

I know I deserve the rope, but as a good many people know me in Tazewell County, and I think most people could make out what caused me to bring such dark and mournful days to their especial friends. If you don't feel able to publish, send it to my father, B. Moser, Morton, IL.

* * * * *

I am a murderer of Illinois, from Morton, Tazewell County. Wire to my father, Ben Moser, Tazewell County, IL, that the body of their son, Sam, was found. I did not suppose that they wanted to see me anymore.

They read and reread the letters, passing them around and pointing out various passages as they speculated about their meaning. They expressed their shock in discovering that the man they'd thought was just drunk was actually the murderer from Illinois who had killed his entire family. Of course, it was all anyone was talking about.

The proprietor of the brewery near the river had heard the shot and fixed the time at around 3:00 a.m. Sergeant Burbidge visited the spot in the afternoon and searched for Moser's gun, but he couldn't find it in the four feet of water. It was said to be a .32 caliber, as was used in the murders.

The authorities of Tazewell County were at once notified of the finding of Moser, and Chief Hilton received in reply the following dispatch:

> Hold Samuel Moser till I can get
> there with proper papers.
>
> —John D. Mount, Sheriff

The next morning, the *Peoria Herald-Transcript* was provided with a verbatim copy of a letter written before Samuel Moser attempted suicide:

> I am 30 years of age and reside on a farm in Tazewell County, Illinois, three miles from Tremont. This trouble is all due to the Amish community I formerly lived with, of which my wife was also a member. Eight years ago, I was married, my wife also belonging to the community. The Amish community is a religious order, having their own church. They do not believe in any

worldly pleasures, such as music, going to shows, or anything of that kind. I grew away from their beliefs, but they kept control of my wife, and the church people came between us continually.

One time in the church, I took my baby, eight months old or so, on my lap and was looking at him. The minister rebuked me, saying I was becoming an idolater and thought too much of my child. That is part of the religion, not to care too much for the family. I was not happy in the community and, at last, two or three years ago, got my wife to leave, and we went away. But they wrote her and got her to go back. I remained away a little while longer but could not bear to be separated from my children and so I returned. Then they interfered between us, and peace was broken up in my home. I could not have my friends at my home anymore, and the little boys commenced to notice it. The oldest asked why it was my wife would eat her meals with the boys, and then I would go to the table. The boys asked why it was. It hurt them and hurt me. I tried everything, but matters did not mend. There was no chance for a change. My children noticed the trouble, and this made me very unhappy. There was no chance of any improvement, and I became desperate.

On Sunday, May 13, my wife went to church with the children, and I was left alone in the house. Between four and five o'clock in the afternoon, they returned, and my wife commenced making preparations for supper. The boys were out in the yard, and she went down cellar for something. I followed her down, and as she looked at me, I fired just one shot. She didn't know anything about it; she was dead. I shot her in the head. The eldest boy came in and went into the bedroom, or I took him there. I shot him only once; he died right there, never felt it at all. I called the second boy in and sent him for a bucket of water. When he came in and went into the pantry, I fired again. It didn't kill him at once, and I fired again. That killed him. Then I went back into the bedroom where the baby was lying, only six months old. I fired and hit him, but he moved. I did not want him to suffer and fired three times; then it was all over. Then I went down cellar and threw a carpet over my wife, put some dresses over the other bodies, locked up the house, and left. I did not want them to find the bodies all at once.

I am not sorry I killed my wife and children. I am glad they are at rest. I could not bear it any longer, living that way with those people interfering between man and wife and the little boys noticing it. I had to do it. I couldn't do anything else.

Asked whether he was insane when he committed the crime, Moser said that he was not, but the actions of the Amish people had driven him to despair. Moser stated, in conclusion, that his parents were Germans.

> If I had been better educated, I could have withstood this. But you see, I am an ignorant man, though American born, and my father is rich. That is the way of the Amish community though.

Sheriff John D. Mount was descended from a well-respected pioneer family. He had made a name and a living for himself, building the Delevan Electric Light Works, of which he was owner

and proprietor. For years, he was a special detective for the Chicago & Alton Railroad, and it was said that he had made many clever and important captures. He was formerly the city marshal of Delevan and was now happily married with three children: two girls and a boy. At the time of the murders, he was forty years old and had been the sheriff of Tazewell County for two years. He left Pekin as soon as he received information of the arrest.

Mount wired the Salt Lake City police that the requisition papers would be obtained, and he would start out immediately. He arrived in the capital city of Springfield, Illinois, that Saturday night with the necessary papers, including a warrant charging Moser with murder. Governor John Riley Tanner was not at the executive mansion when Mount arrived. Thankfully, J. Mack Tanner, the governor's brother and private secretary, was able to issue the necessary requisition papers.

Returning to Pekin on Sunday morning, Sheriff Mount spent the day with his family before the departure time of 8:45 p.m. He was relieved for the late departure so he could sleep through the night. The train rumbled into Kansas City on Monday morning and left an hour later over the Missouri Pacific. Tuesday morning, he arrived in Pueblo, Colorado, where he'd have a stop of two hours.

While waiting in Pueblo, Mount overheard talk of a recent crime. Asking details of a nearby passenger, he learned that the Sunday before, a Negro man named Calvin Kimblern had shot and killed two orphans in a nearby home: Ethel Straussen, aged thirteen, and Jessie M. Skaggs, aged eleven, whom he was accused of molesting. Kimblern murdered the two girls because they had told his wife that he had said he wished she would go away and never come back.

Kimblern also shot his wife, Hattie (who worked at the orphanage) twice: once in the stomach and once by the neck. She was taken to the Pueblo hospital, where she stated that her husband's actions were the result of insane jealousy. Calvin Kimblern had not yet been found. The city of Pueblo, like the one Mount had recently left behind in Illinois, was crazed with talk of finding the murderer and lynching him. As he listened to the men's promises of justice, the full realization of his own situation sunk in—that he'd be traveling for days with a man who was a similar target.

Mount reached Salt Lake City at nine thirty on Wednesday morning. There, he went directly to the statehouse, where his requisition papers were honored by the governor of Utah, Heber Manning Wells. He found that the state house and city hall were combined—a magnificent building, fully as fine as the statehouse back in Illinois. He'd thought the Wild West would be a bit more backward.

Moser sat in the main room of the police station when the sheriff from Illinois arrived. He was a small man, scarcely over five feet in height and did not appear to be over 140 pounds in weight. He was dressed in the coarse blue-black suit that Amish men wore. His shirt was badly soiled, his shoes well-worn. His hair and eyes were dark, his expression blank—he was clearly exhausted. He had the rough, calloused hands of a farmer. There was a growth of stubble on his lips and chin, not having been shaved for a week or ten days. A cotton bandage was wrapped around his head to protect his wound.

Sheriff Mount introduced himself to Sam, and the two men had a short talk. Moser related practically to the sheriff what had already appeared in the papers. His thick German accent made him somewhat hard to understand. When Mount explained that he'd be taking him back to Pekin, Moser replied that he'd only been to Pekin once, and that was when he'd brought in a load of hay.

Sheriff Mount found that he did not need the requisition papers that he'd traveled so far to obtain, for Samuel would have come along without them. He explained to Samuel what the papers were for, but a blank look came into his eyes. He had no wish to return to Illinois; his only thought had been to get as far away from there as possible.

Mount was shown around the city afterward for a few hours by Judge A. B. Sawyer, who was a former well-known attorney from Tazewell County, Illinois. He reported that he was looking fine, and they had a most enjoyable time together for a few hours. In the evening, Mount toured the city with the chief of police of Salt Lake City, Thomas A. Hilton. The two lawmen visited the magnificent Mormon tabernacle (which had been built between 1864 and 1867) and the much more recently completed Mormon Temple, which had just been dedicated in 1893.

Mount returned about seven o'clock the next morning (Thursday) to collect the prisoner, and they began their journey home over the Missouri Pacific. The Salt Lake City papers reported that Moser had become strangely quiet, answering questions only by a nod of his head. The sheriff reiterated his belief that there was no fear of a lynching.

He was probably somewhat less confident, however, when the news was broken that the Pueblo Colorado fugitive had been caught and murdered in the street by a mob of 1,500 people.

The suspect had fled to Denver. On Tuesday afternoon, he was apprehended and returned to Pueblo late that night. It was said that on the journey from Denver, Kimblern was fully aware of the fate that awaited him in Pueblo, but he retained his composure and smoked or slept much of the time.

Upon the arrival of the Rio Grande train at approximately 11:50 p.m., a mob of determined citizens surrounded the train. Not the slightest attempt to protect the prisoner was made by the half-dozen officers that accompanied him. In fact, they had drawn the charges from their revolvers lest by any chance blood should be shed in a feint at resisting the mob.

As the train pulled into the Eighth Street depot, Kimblern was pushed to his feet out of the front end of the smoking car and into the very hands of the mob. Heavy steel manacles bound his wrists, and he was helpless. A noose was cast around his neck, and Kimblern was dragged to the corner of Eighth and Sante Fe Avenue, a distance of about three blocks. It was said that he made but the slightest attempt at resistance.

Apparently in the melee which attended his capture from the train, somebody—either moved by mercy or impelled by a desire to add a personal atrocity to the tragedy—struck the Negro a blow on the side of the head with a sledgehammer, inflicting a wound which must have caused instant unconsciousness.

He was dragged face downward over the railroad tracks, the noose tightened around his neck, and he was undoubtedly dead before he was hanged to a telegraph pole two blocks from the depot.

Twice the rope broke after the body had been hauled up, but the third attempt at hanging was successful.

After the body had been allowed to dangle in the air a few minutes, the rope was cut, and the corpse was dragged half a block farther, the crowd clamoring for a fire to burn the body. Mayor West, in the center of the throws, exhorted them to disperse, but his words were unheeded by many.

Long after the more respectable element in the crowd had gone home or stood upon the outskirts, boys and young men danced about the body, thrusting sense-less indignities upon it and insisting that the man was not dead. They stripped him to the waist, and a man who claimed to be a doctor said that his heart was still beating. The mob tore the clothes from him, tied a cloth around his naked loins; then they hooked the manacles into one of the spikes on the side of a pole where the body was again hanged up. The rough treatment had almost torn one side of Kimblern's face from his skull. The noose had cut deeply into the neck, and blood splashed his clothing.

Calvin Kimblern was pronounced dead at 1:33 a.m. Wednesday, May 23, 1900—not even twenty-four hours after Sheriff John Mount's arrival in Pueblo, Colorado. It was exactly what the lawman feared for his own prisoner.

LYNCHING AT PUEBLO.

Colored Murderer Taken From
the Train by a Mob.

STRUNG UP TO A TELEGRAPH POLE

Officers Make No Effort to Protect Their
Prisoner—Many Well Dressed Women
In the Crowd Which Witnessed the
Hanging—Savage Work of the Mob.

Sheriff Mount reached Omaha, Nebraska, about 4:45 p.m. on Friday. With Sam chained to him, he could rest a bit without fear that he would escape. Not that he was very worried—Sam slept about two-thirds of the time. After about a three-hour stop in Omaha, they continued on their way.

When the Burlington drew up in the union passenger station at Peoria the next morning, the platform was crowded with people hoping to witness the murderer from Utah being transferred from one train to another. Mr. Mount and his prisoner stepped from the train. They were met by a *Herald-Transcript* reporter and hastily entered the Peoria and Pekin union passenger train, which pulled out for Pekin a few minutes later.

Here's a strange mixture of religion and fanaticism, love and murder...

```
A religion that denies one
the right to love his fam-
ily is not a religion in the
proper sense, and it ought
not be tolerated in a country
of intelligent people like
ours. The sect should be pro-
hibited by law, the constitu-
tional guarantee of religious
freedom notwithstanding. The
framers of the constitution
never meant to grant reli-
gious freedom to sects that
practice polygamy and make
conditions of murder possi-
ble, as in the case of Moser.
Such sects need to be utterly
destroyed from the face of
the earth and should not be
```

allowed to practice tenets
under the protection of the
constitution which secures
religious liberty and freedom
to worship God in any manner
they please. Such religions
were not contemplated by the
fathers of the Republic and
framers of the fundamental
law of the land. Moser ought
to suffer the penalty of his
crime, but his sect is primar-
ily to blame, and it should be
investigated by United States
authorities.

Letter to the Editor
February 18, 1901

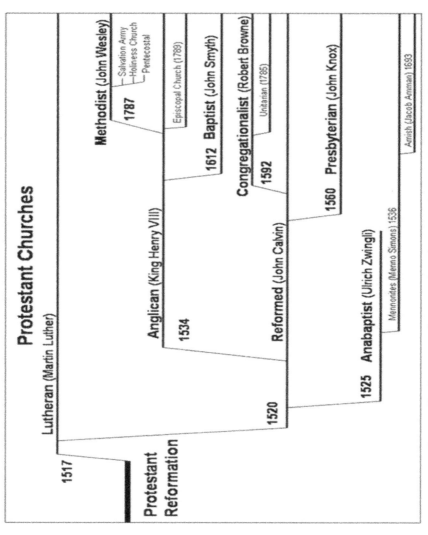

Protestant Churches

Lutheran (Martin Luther)
1517

Protestant Reformation

Methodist (John Wesley)
1787
— Salvation Army
— Holiness Church
— Pentecostal

Episcopal Church (1789)

Baptist (John Smyth)
1612

Congregationalist (Robert Browne)
1592

Unitarian (1785)

Presbyterian (John Knox)
1560

Anglican (King Henry VIII)
1534

Reformed (John Calvin)
1520

Anabaptist (Ulrich Zwingli)
1525

Mennonites (Menno Simons) 1536

Amish (Jacob Amman) 1693

Evangelical Baptist / Apostolic Christian (Samuel Froehlich)
Early 1830s

71

Chapter 6
Apostolic Christians

Society can overlook murder, adultery
or swindling; it can never forgive
the preaching of a new gospel.

—Edmund Burke

1850—1901

To begin with, they were incorrectly called Amish. The members of the Apostolic Christian Church were often confused with their fellow Anabaptists, both Amish and Mennonite. They are similar in many ways—seeking to preserve the religious and cultural traditions of their ancestors. They are mostly German or German Swiss. They dress plainly, live simply, and distrust modern advances.[2]

Menno Simon formed the group known as the Mennonites in 1525. They believed that people should be baptized into a discipleship with Christ as adults, which brought persecution from both the Roman Catholic and Protestant state churches. They rejected paid clergy, tithes, the holding of civil office, use of the sword, the employment of armies, and the swearing of oaths. Their goal was to serve God in the way of the apostles of the New Testament. A split within a group of Swiss and Alsatian Anabaptists in 1693, led by Jakob Ammann, brought about the Amish church.

---

[2]   Steidinger, Amy L. "A Paradox of Modern Christian Thought, Enlightenment and the Apostolic Christian Church of America." M.A. Thesis, Illinois State University, 2009.

The Apostolic Christian Church[3] was established in 1850 by Samuel Froehlich, who was a student of theology in Zurich and at the University of Basel. Prior to this time, people were generally very superstitious and fearful. They clung to talisman, relics, rituals, and protections that would ward off evil and keep their households from harm. The Enlightenment taught people to view the subject of faith through their ability to reason. Rather than trust in the priest to act as an intermediary to grant them forgiveness or prescribe a remedy for their sins, they began to approach God on their own terms—through their own learning and understanding.

As a student, Froehlich was trained in theology, which was strongly influenced by rationalism, the doctrine of reason. He studied the Bible as he would any other book of literature. He applied the principles of scientific method and was taught to study everything through the lens of rational thought. But Froehlich was failing in his personal quest for meaning and understanding. He felt that his faith was no longer in something that was bigger than his ability to understand it. He was going through the motions without feeling a genuine sense of connection with God. Ironically, Froehlich's "enlightenment" would come when he had thrown off the oppression of Reason.

He experienced a dramatic conversion which led him to reject the teachings of the state-church. He admired the Anabaptists, who were radical reformers at that time. Some of the reformed and Mennonite believers followed Froehlich and became known as the *Neu-Täufer* or, later, the Evangelical Baptist Church. He taught adult baptism of believers, separation of church and state, scripture alone as the sole rule of faith and practical living, holiness in life, and nonviolence.

---

[3] Originally called the Evangelical Baptist Church, it was formally organized as the ACCA in 1917.

There were many different sects at work in Europe during this time, and people differentiated between themselves and other belief systems mainly by the leaders that they followed. Thus, the early Evangelical Baptists referred to themselves as "die Froehlich." In their minds and hearts, they were literally fighting to recreate the original New Testament Church to its rightful place, an uncorrupted state. They were involved in a monumental class struggle against the political forces of the state and aristocracy, as well as the spiritual forces of Satan himself which drove them.

In Europe, these people had been persecuted. While Protestant reformers worked to change the church from within, many Anabaptists believed that the church was so corrupt as to be unsalvageable. In order to be the pure and spotless bride of Christ, the church would have to be free of state influence. Anabaptists completely rejected the institutions of the state. While the reformers had many issues with the Catholic Church, including the sale of indulgences, celibacy, purgatory, simony, and general corruption, the focus of Anabaptist reform (as their name implies) was their aversion to infant baptism. Anabaptists pointed to the New Testament church and their baptism of born-again believers as they made a choice to join themselves with the church.

By rejecting the idea of infant baptism, Anabaptists were denying the very salvation of those who practiced Catholicism and deceased loved ones, who were viewed as being sealed by their baptisms. The idea that "the way it had always been done" was wrong; that the learned men of the cloth weren't reading their Bibles correctly and that these simple commoners would show them the correct way was shocking and offensive. In addition to their stance on baptism, Anabaptists refused to bear arms or go to war and did not believe in the swearing of oaths. These beliefs also brought them into the spotlight of suspicion and added to their conflicts with the state and their fellow citizens.

Anabaptist faiths were literally formed out of their objections to the state church and thus questioned the legitimacy of the state. The king based his right to the throne on a divine calling from God, so people who had a different idea of God were a threat to him politically.

They not only brought his authority into question, they were sure to be treasonous, placing God's law in higher esteem than that of the king. The king vowed at his coronation to pursue heretics (those doing the devil's work) to the extent of his ability.

The result was that one's citizenship—one's life, faith, marriage, burial—was not recognized if one was not conformed to the church. If one chose to go outside the lines of what was acceptable practice of the religious community, no price was too high to pay to obtain confession and forgiveness as the very soul was at stake. They were beaten and imprisoned, their property was confiscated (which usually meant loss of livelihood), and their marriages were not recognized as legal (which made people who'd been married for years with many children suddenly "fornicators"). Like the accusations against witches in years past, the persecutions suffered by heretics put friends, neighbors, and fellow church members in terrible situations: they could not offer assistance as it was very dangerous to be sympathetic to one who had been accused of heresy.

At the same time that persecutions and struggle were pushing the believers away from their homelands, they were also being pulled in a new direction where many of the brethren were finding religious freedom and opportunity on the other side of the ocean. At the request of a group of Amish-Mennonites who had heard about his teaching, Froehlich sent a young convert, Benedict Weyeneth, to establish the church in America. This group helped to establish churches in Lewis County, New York (1847), and Sardis, Ohio (1848). The movement spread westward, where the small congregations gained most of their membership from the local Amish and Mennonites. Thus, they became known as the New Amish. Weyeneth himself settled in the small town of Roanoke, Illinois, and soon there were thriving churches in the surrounding communities of Tremont, Morton, Peoria, Fairbury, and Gridley.

In his book *Crosswinds: From Switzerland to Crown Hill*, James Lehman tells the story of Jeanne "Anna" Steiner, who was born in Alsace, France, and immigrated with her family to Wayne County, Ohio. In 1860, Anna and her half-sister Elizabeth Steiner became members of the newly emerging Apostolic Church. Anna was the wife of the Swiss Mennonite bishop, John Steiner, and the two sisters were daughters of the previous bishop, Daniel Steiner. Elizabeth's husband, Ulrich, who was also the brother of Bishop John, became a member of the Apostolic Christian Church, as did another brother, Peter, and his wife.

Such a betrayal would be very difficult in a small farming community that was so completely immersed in issues of religion and tradition. Suddenly families that had always worked and worshipped together were completely split apart. With their parents attending different churches, John and Anna's fourteen children (ages two to twenty-five) had to choose sides. Everyone had an opinion on the eternal consequences of going to one or the other.

Perry Klopfenstein relates in his book on the Apostolic Christian Church, *Marching to Zion*, that

> sometimes (Anna) would walk as far as five or six miles to church. Often she would carry a young child, with other children following behind her. Sometimes when she would return home from church, it would be dark, the door locked, and she would have to spend the night outside.

The realities of what these new converts went through—shunned by the congregation and their families, unable even to be buried in death alongside husbands and parents—are a moving testimony to how closely held their newfound faith must have been. Anna's daughter Lydia is Samuel Moser's mother.

Amish and Mennonite church members who were dissatisfied with their churches or disagreed about doctrinal issues were often drawn to the Apostolic Church, which seemed more open and less legalistic about traditions. Ironically, they often brought their traditions with them and gradually changed the AC congregations to become much more traditional. Thus, the congregations in America wore much more Amish-looking clothing than those that were taught by Froehlich in Europe.

People tend not to stray far from what they have always known. They left churches that enforced rules and demanded conformity. But often they simply changed from one set of rules and authorities to another. Cultural diversity among immigrants complicated things further. They knew how things had been where they had come from and equated those practices with holiness and right living. They were offended by others whose ways were different. The difference in habits and customs then led to disunity within the church.

This conflict and strain finally came to a head over the unlikely issue of the wearing of mustaches. In the Apostolic Church, members greeted one another with the holy kiss. But the members from Hungary wore mustaches, which made the others very uncomfortable. They were said to be unclean, but it was actually a much more deeply rooted issue.

Mustaches carried a strong military connotation from the Old World—highly offensive to this peaceful people. For these (mostly German) people who were conscientious objectors and pacifists, the mustaches represented the pride and militarism of the French, whom they'd been at war with for years. Their reactions were deeply rooted and heartfelt. Mustaches were not allowed.

Arriving in May of 1892, the Hungarian brethren had heard a rumor that those who came to America were compelled to shave off their mustaches. One of them, Wendel Kalman, explained that they "did not know that this had become a man-made commandment or law" and "presumed that it were merely of fashion or custom in which the brothers participated with brotherly love."

He and others were excommunicated and shunned as a result of their refusal to shave their mustaches. Elders told Kalman that their refusal to submit to the customs and order of America could not be allowed. Although they viewed the request to shave their mustaches as very strange, Kalman and others did shave at first, but did not agree with the rules that were forced upon them. He explained in a letter:

> When I met my wife, she did not recognize me, until I spoke to her; then she recognized my voice and began to weep. It was not on account of the mustache but because I had so readily accepted these man-made rules. Sister

AMY STEIDINGER

> Irion and I laughed at her as we did
> not consider the matter a serious one.
> However, my wife was deeply worried
> and said that if she had known of this,
> she would not have come to America.
> Namely, that one were compelled to
> win the love of brothers and sisters
> with such trivialities.

This was especially difficult for them because they were going against their own convictions, in deference to the convictions of others. Kalman goes on to describe another incident demonstrating similar treatment of his wife:

> She wore a scarf on her head as was her
> wont in the old country. Then an elderly
> brother with the name of Zimmerman
> told her that if she only knew how much
> more love the sisters would give her if
> she dressed as they did, she would surely
> do so. Then we went downtown together,
> and she bought a very plain hat. The
> Sunday after, when she went to church,
> the sisters surrounded her with great
> love, to her surprise, and she remem-
> bered the warning the old brother had
> given her. When we returned home, she
> said to me, "Now I can see that here
> love is merely attached to costumes
> and dresses."

The story told by Wendel Kalman is corroborated by an article printed in a Central Illinois newspaper during the Moser trial in February of 1901, called "Five Funny Mustaches." According to the reporter, a group of ministers visiting from the Old Country were met at the train station by the elders of the Morton and

80

Gridley churches. Upon finding that they had mustaches, the European brothers were turned away, and the other members of the church instructed not to feed them, house them, or welcome them in any way. Some of the locals were torn; they knew what it was to travel so far. How could they leave them with nowhere to go? Didn't the Bible tell them to feed the hungry? Weren't these men their brothers in Christ? Before the incident was over, about twenty members who refused to shun the brethren were excommunicated.

The Apostolic Christians who were members of these early American churches had given up everything they'd known to immigrate to a new land where they could be free of the persecutions of the state. Yet in a short time, they were replicating them. They were trying to keep the church from being polluted by the worldliness that surrounded it. It was simply how they knew to behave in these situations.

They had been uprooted from all that was familiar to them. Dropped down in the middle of this strange place, among the "English," whose ways were entirely different from their own, and thus lacked spiritual meaning. The only way for these religious believers to protect themselves from becoming like the world around them—a fallen world that was going to hell—was to cling to their traditions. Living in a land that lacked the social controls that had once shaped their own morals, they feared that chaos would be the result.

As they began to build churches and Christian communities, they felt more secure within the boundaries of structure, discipline, and direction to which they were accustomed. The ethnic church was a safe haven for the immigrants—where they could go for protection, guidance, and encouragement. They shared of themselves and felt included in something familiar and comforting. The church was the center of the family's social life, providing men a place to make business connections and women a support group for help and sharing. Through these church activities, the younger generation became acquainted with other local young people from whom they would choose their future spouses.

Traditional understanding viewed external control as essential within a society: of the sovereign, of religion, through laws and through discipline. If these social controls were allowed to break down, anarchy and chaos would result. Mankind was seen as inherently evil, and social problems such as poverty, mental illness, and depravity were seen as the consequences of moral failure. Individualism, secularism, industrialization, and the reform movement were seen as threats to social harmony. Unity of belief must be maintained at all costs.

Relationship with God and the church was measured by outward appearance, like-mindedness, and willingness to obey authority. They had recreated the churches which had demanded conformity from them in Europe here in the new world.

Discipline, therefore, was very rigid. An article pertaining to church discipline reads:

> *We believe and confess that if anyone has so far fallen off, either by a wicked life or perverted doctrine, he is separated from God, and consequently justly separated from and corrected or punished by the church. Such a person must be shunned, according to Christ and his apostles, and avoided without partiality by all members of his church, especially by those whom it is known, whether in eating or drinking or similar temporal matters, and they shall have no dealings with him, to the end that they may be contaminated by*

intercourse with him, nor made partakers of his sin; but that the sinner may be made ashamed, corrected, and again led to repentance.

Though one can certainly understand this need for community, not everyone understood the need the immigrants had to retain their cultural identity. Many older settlers in the area who had worked hard to learn the language and blend in were frustrated that these new immigrants stuck to the Old World ways and kept to themselves. There began to be questions and rumors about these strange people who seemed to think they were the only ones going to heaven. The Germans were looked on with suspicion and distrust.

This was the time at which the Moser tragedy unfolded. These were the people that found themselves thrust into the spotlight.

Deadly Devotion

You need not call the devil.
He'll come without calling.
—Amish Proverb

In 2013, a new television series debuted on Investigation Discovery that promised to tell the "true stories of everyday people who live within America's unique subcultures and secret societies." The first episode aired on June 4 and told the story of Amishman Ed Gingerich.

Within the Amish community of Brownhill in Pennsylvania, Ed was considered a disobedient rebel. He did not want to follow the traditions of his family faith or attend church. He was fascinated with modern tools and technology, which were rejected as distractions of the devil. He also spent time with friends who were not of the church—"Englishmen," as they were called by the Amish.

It turned out that Ed was suffering from paranoid schizophrenia. Though he received enough medical attention to be diagnosed and be prescribed medication, the Amish rejected modern medication, and Ed returned to the more traditionally accepted herbal treatments.

On March 18, 1993, Ed brutally murdered his wife, Katie. A jury found him guilty but mentally ill, and he was sentenced to only five years in prison. When he was released, Ed was shunned by the Brownhill community. He later took his own life.

His lawyer stated on the show that Ed was the "first Amishman charged with murder in the United States." Sam Moser, however, was charged with the murders of his wife and children eighty-three years before this.

A year before the murders, there had been a series of seven articles published in the *Bloomington Pantagraph*. Many were curious about the growing numbers of "Amish" in the area: by that time, there were more than one hundred families who were members of the Apostolic Christian Church near Morton, Eureka, and Roanoke, and Tremont. They interacted very little with those of other faiths. They kept to themselves, even speaking a different language from those around them. They were an isolated people—independent, secretive, and mostly unknown. A reporter was sent to get information about them, which would then appear in print.

The reporter said that if you ask a member of the Apostolic Christian Church what his creed teaches, he will tell you invariably that it tells you to live as "the Bible teaches." Simplicity and humility were the rule. They worked hard, as unto the Lord. They owned large farms, were good citizens, and worked together within their community, helping one another as brothers in sisters in Christ. They were pleasant to strangers generally, although they associated intimately only with persons of their own belief. They were educated through the elementary grades and mostly taught by their own people.

When there were differences among them, they were settled by the elders; the people did not go to the law with their problems. They took no part in politics, they did not belong to secret societies, and they did not vote. They did not go to doctors but rather employed simple home remedies from the old country. They did not use tobacco. The men drank beer, but not unto drunkenness. Reading newspapers was not strictly forbidden but considered frivolous and risky. They were opposed to war under any circumstances.

They lived well, but not extravagantly. They dressed comfortably and in accordance with the season, but with no regard to the prevailing fashion. The women pulled their hair back into a simple bun and wore sunbonnets or a plain black hat with some-times a ribbon bound around it. The dresses were generally black but always plain, without trimmings of any kind. A similar article on the group from Cissna Park, Illinois, went on to say: "Not even a very little ribbon or a chicken feather is allowed. Fashion maga-zines are looked upon as tempting lures sent out by the Evil One, and any sister who dares to sew a ruffle on her skirt is disciplined and made the subject of special prayer."

The men were nearly all clean-shaven. They were permit-ted to wear beards, but not mustaches. They never wore neck-ties and only recently had taken to carrying watches. They drove good horses to good vehicles and, until somewhat lately, had made use of heavy wagons for all occasions. Now they could be seen in handsome carriages at church or at funerals. They never attended religious services of any sort except that of their own denomination. Neither would they attend a funeral of any but their own people, although they were kindly and would assist a sick neighbor if called on to do so.

In the AC Church, the bishops, elders, and deacons were usually chosen by casting lots. Their pastors neither received nor accepted stipulated salaries or any kind of remuneration for preaching or attending to the functions of their religious offices. No preparations were necessary for the ministry, and while all members of the sect had fair educations, illiterate ministers were not uncommon.

Their church service was simple and conducted in the German tongue. There were no musical instruments. Sunday ser-vice at the church began early and lasted all day. The food was cooked and served at the meeting house, and strangers were always welcome. Their churches were fitted up with a large assembly room, cloak department, and a roomy kitchen, where dinner was prepared for all present each Sunday. Rows of stalls were built around the grounds, and the teams quartered there.

When a member of the Apostolic Christian Church met another member (of the same sex), they greeted one another with a holy kiss. In the church, all the men sat on one side and the women on the other. At the close of the services, the men kissed one another, and the women did likewise among themselves. They were described by the reporter as an honest class of people. It was said that they did not vote, but he clarified that of late years they had gone to the voting places and cast their ballots. In some instances, they had run for road commissioner or a small office. He explained that they wanted to be responsible citizens, but did not want their children to be cheap politicians.

If a member wanted to marry and had set his heart on a girl in the congregation, he would go to the preacher and tell him about it. The preacher, in turn, conveyed the news to the lady in question and reported the answer. If she consented, the engagement was announced in church. If anybody had anything to say concerning the approaching wedding, they were at liberty to do so. After three or four Sundays, the marriage would take place, and that settled it. Once married, they could never get a divorce. If the husband committed an act of folly, the wife could not obtain a divorce but had the option of going to her folks and living with them. If the husband was thrown out of church, he was not in any way separated from his wife. They lived together and ate at the same table. The husband could attend church with his wife, but when the congregation ate at noon, he was not allowed to eat at the same table with the rest of the members but was given food at a separate table. He could come back into the church again, providing he had reformed; and if he had offended any member, he must go and ask his pardon.

The Amish / AC were a curiosity to their neighbors because of their odd clothes and habits, but they were also wondered about for a more practical reason. Their neighbors were jealous and a little bit suspicious of their huge success as farmers. It was noted that they paid as high as $150 an acre for land and had grown rich while neighbors on much cheaper lands had narrowly escaped bankruptcy.

A banker, Colonel A. J. Davis, who had worked with the Amish, explained that the reason the Amish succeeded where others failed was that they practiced the virtues of industry and frugality. Large families were the rule, and work commenced for the little ones as soon as they were able to do anything, no matter how slight. It was nothing uncommon for an Amish family to consist of ten or twelve children. When the entire family worked under direction, something was bound to be accomplished. "All work and then keep everlastingly after it." He went on:

> Economy is a virtue taught from the cradle by examples and precept. No money is ever spent for amusements, for fine clothes, for travel, or for pleasure of any kind. No "Amish" ever smokes or chews tobacco. None ever attend any circus, show, concert, baseball or football game, horse race, theater, or even a home talent show, or anything of the kind. When all earn money and spend comparatively none, there must be an increase in the savings.

> The creed of this church also prohibits its members from wearing jewelry, having pictures on the walls of their homes, or having any kind of a musical instrument on their premises. They are a thrifty people, and many of them are wealthy. Wherever a church is established, within the course of a few years, the land within a radius of from five to ten miles is all bought up by these people. They frequently pay much more than the real value of the land simply to be able to reside close to their place of worship.

They are always ready to work. Up early in the morning, they work all day and keep this up from year's end to year's end. When plowing time comes, they are ready to plow and do not have to wait till something else is out of the way. When it is time to harrow, they harrow; and when the time for sowing comes, why, they sow. Their work, never under any circumstances, gets ahead of them, but they always keep ahead of their work.

Then they never have any wasteland. Every inch is cultivated. They believe thoroughly in tilling and practice what they believe. Nothing is ever wasted by any of the Amish. All the manure is carefully saved and used on the land. Nothing is thrown away that can be possibly made use of. Weeds are kept down by labor, incessant and continuous. Once in a while, an "Amishman" will be found who is a little neglectful about farming matters, but such a one is disciplined by the others, and he soon falls into the prevalent habit of doing all things well.

They keep many cows and sell a great deal of milk to the local creamery. They always use the most improved machinery and are progressive farmers. The women are not a bit behind the men when it comes to making and saving money. The great majority of these women sell enough butter, eggs, poultry, fruit, and vegetables to supply the family table. The money the men make is thus saved to buy more land or to stock up on cattle or to pay for machinery. This work of the women in supplying the greater part of the family table is not common to but a few but is a general habit.

The men believe in going in debt for land at least. Generally, though, those around here are out of debt, possibly because there is no more land for them to buy just now. They are good borrowers, but not very good depositors. That is, they always pay when they borrow, but they generally have a place for their money when they get it and so do not keep large deposits in the bank. Their deposits, though, are larger now than formerly.

Amish/AC men and women come to Pekin to do business. They rarely stop at the Tazewell. They obtain food by buying crackers and cheese in the groceries. But they pay their bills, they have no poor, no almshouses, no prisons, no tramps, no fallen women, no starving children. Big red barns rise on their land and well-built white houses. Hedges surround their fields, and they get more out of the soil and treat it better than their American rivals. The homes are comfortable but devoid of all ornament. Their horses and cattle are of the finest. All that they own is good and substantial. Very little drunkenness is manifested, and quarreling is almost unknown. When suffering cannot be removed, it is borne in silence.

Their blind devotion was the one great fault that the people found with them. But others said that they followed the simple teachings of the Bible, and in this respect, they were right. The newspaper account concluded that this was one of their striking peculiarities. They declared themselves not capable to judge but left others to do that.

The public was eager to learn more about the "peculiar creed" of the new Amish denomination that had driven Sam to kill his family. The headlines read "Religious Fanaticism" and "Church Had Expelled Him." As they read more about the church, however, people began to feel that the church seemed to consider itself "holier than thou." There was a reason they kept their distance—they felt they'd be tainted by the sinners around them. They were the only ones going to heaven. They felt no one was as good as they were. Their English neighbors began to look for the chinks in their armor. If someone talked to an ex-member of the church, someone who'd been kicked out or hadn't made it in, that person became an "insider," and their stories (true or not) spread like wildfire. Suddenly everyone delighted in stories that brought the church firmly back to earth—showed that they were not so high and mighty and were, in fact, just like everyone else.

Expelled from Church

This is a tale of marital woe in which a sister-in-law breaks in upon a happy family circle. Sometime ago, we stated that there was a sensation in the quiet little village of Tremont, which would soon come to focus. We learned the following facts from a well-known trademark of this town, who spoke with perfect freedom about the case. The party concerned, according to the citizen, is Sam Schmutz. He is a well-known farmer at Tremont and is reputed to be wealthy. He lived with his wife in a beautiful home, and their domestic relations were one long dream. A content family grew up about them, and peace and happiness where theirs.

Suddenly a cloud appeared upon the domestic horizon, which grew larger and larger until it overspread the home, which was once bright and full of sunshine. Mr. Schmutz's sister-in-law resided with them, and we are told that he fell desperately in love with her and continued his attentions for a long time. It is said that his affections were recip- rocated. Whether his wife noticed this or not, we have not been told, but it seems that this good woman was over- devoted and suspected no evil. Her husband and the sister-in-law became very intimate, and it was soon learned that she was about to become a mother.

It was then that the Amish church took up the case. They wanted no such sinners in their congregation, and Schmutz was called before them. When Schmutz was asked why he violated his marriage vows, he replied that he loved the girl much better than his wife. Even then, and though he was shunned with all turning against him, his wife did not leave him. She would not sue for divorce.

The paper noted that her love for him was of the kind that is rare on earth and will perhaps make a better man of him.

It was now obvious to everyone that the upcoming trial was, in many ways, to become a trial of the Apostolic Christian Church.

The church definitely felt that way as each day more space in the newspapers was dedicated to them. It was unimaginable that they could be so misunderstood. Their ways had always been of peace. But Sam Moser's murder of his entire family had somehow become a reflection on their faith.

Christians are taught to turn the other cheek, and these very private believers in no way wanted conflict. But this had gone on for way too long. From May (when tragedy had struck their church family!) to the following February, their names had been dragged through the mud. People were leaving to settle out west, tired of the accusations and grief. Their church was being attacked, maligned, and crucified all because of the actions of a man they had tried to distance themselves from years before the murders. Someone had to defend the name of the good church. Someone had to turn this tide. Someone needed to speak with the papers.

Chapter 7
Jail

One need not be a chamber to be haunted,
one need not to be a house. The brain
has corridors surpassing material place.

—Emily Dickinson

1900–1901
Pekin, IL

Sheriff Mount finally arrived with the prisoner at the Tazewell County jail in Pekin at seven thirty on Saturday morning. As the train pulled up at the junction, Deputy Sheriff Ball was walking up and down the platform. State's Attorney Cunningham and another *Herald-Transcript* reporter were also waiting. The group quickly entered a closed carriage and were hurriedly driven up Court Street to the front door of the jail. Officer Clark opened the door, the party quickly alighted, and before the people who were passing up and down the street came to a realization of what was happening, the party were in the sheriff's residence. The door of the jail was opened, the party entered, and the door locked. News of the arrival of the sheriff and prisoner soon spread, and crowds gathered at the office of the sheriff in the courthouse to learn the details.

The first cell on the main floor of the jail was hastily arranged, Moser led in, the door closed and locked. He was pale and emaciated, with a bandage tied around his head. There was an air of helplessness about him. He stood leaning against the wall, dejected and helpless. He took no interest in what was going on around him.

When the reporter from the *Herald-Transcript* attempted to interview him, Moser talked with difficulty and apparent effort. He wasn't exactly crying, but tears leaked from his eyes and ran down his face. He looked tired and weak, about to drop from exhaustion. It was decided that he should not be questioned further. He crawled onto the iron bunk and was asleep almost instantly.

Mount checked in with Deputy Sheriff Ball, who was in charge of affairs during his absence. He briefly summarized the trip and reported that there had been no trouble. Ball said that he'd seen Benedict Moser, the father of the murderer, when he was in Pekin a day or two before and had a talk with him. The man had come to Pekin to see whether he had a right to take care of the stock and crops which had been put in. It was stated that Sam Moser had no property with the exception of his household goods, a few horses, cows, and hogs. He was assured he had the right, for the farm belonged to him. At that time, Moser stated that he was not going to assist his son. The crime had been committed, and he was going to allow the law to take its course.

The two men's discussion was interrupted by the arrival of O. A. Smith, an attorney in Pekin, who requested a private interview with the prisoner. Sheriff Mount refused to allow this, and Mr. Smith became very indignant. He stated that he had been sent to see the prisoner just as soon as he arrived. He refused to name the person who had sent him and was noncommittal as to whether he had been engaged in the case. In view of the fact that Benedict Moser had stated shortly before that he was not going to engage counsel, the sheriff refused to allow Mr. Smith or anyone else to see him. He insisted that the prisoner would be allowed to rest.

After Sheriff Mount had breakfast and rested a little, he detailed his trip from start to finish for the reporters who had waited patiently. "He made no statement to me on the train and seemed inclined to sleep through the entire trip. He did say that she opposed everything he wanted, and he knew if she was dead, she would be in safe hands."

"No, sir, I do not think him mentally unbalanced. He is very ignorant. He seemed to feel bad because the baby moved every time he shot it. His picture would look well in the rogue's gallery. It is about the style of a face you find there. He is thirty-two years of age, and his wife was thirty-seven. He related a few incidents to show the cause of the trouble. He realizes that the chances are that he will be hanged, but he doesn't seem to care in the least. It was a very tiresome trip because I had to watch him continually, and I am glad that it is over. There was no excitement. He hadn't eaten anything for a week, but on the trip home, his appetite began coming back. He is thoroughly imbued with the idea that when a person is dead, he is at rest."

"One thing very noticeable was his dread of women and children. Whenever he saw one, he crouched in his seat as if afraid and begged me to take him into the smoking car where there were no women. He could not bear to have them eye him, so we made the greater portion of the trip in smokers."

"About the only thing else I think of is that Southern Kansas is going to have a very heavy crop of wheat. They are erecting a large beet sugar factory in the southern portion. Nebraska was the only state that struck my eye however." Wherever the sheriff went, he was followed by a crowd, all eager to have him relate his story. He repeated it time and again, and his office was thronged the entire day with eager listeners.

Sheriff Mount stated that he did not anticipate trouble of any kind. He thought that had the people of Moser's home section got hold of him at the time the crime was committed, they might have strung him up. Things had quieted down somewhat, though, and the general sentiment among the people of Tazewell County was that the law be allowed to take its course. He had brought the prisoner back safely and intended to see that he was held until the case came up for trial. He said that Moser looked fifteen years older than he had before he committed the crime.

The sheriff said Moser shot himself with the same revolver with which he had killed his family. The wound was in the right temple, but Moser had evidently held the gun in such a slanting position that the bullet merely grazed along the skull under the skin and came out of the forehead. It would soon heal up. The gun fell into the river with Moser and was never found.

While in Salt Lake, Sheriff Mount saw A. B. Sawyer, who had been a well-known lawyer in the Pekin-Tazewell County area and moved to Utah a few years before. It was reported that he was doing splendidly in the West.

Some of the sheriff's friends were inclined to cajole him and ask him how he would like the job of hanging Moser, seeking to test Mount's nerve. To all such, the sheriff replied simply, "If the law orders a hanging, I am here to carry out the law."

When Sam woke later that morning, he seemed more ready to talk. When Sheriff Mount and the *Herald-Transcript* reporters entered the jail, he had a question: "Do my parents know I'm here?" He was told what the officers knew so far.

A reporter asked Sam, "Will you make a defense?" He didn't seem to understand the question. "Will you hire a lawyer and make a defense?"

"I have no money for a lawyer. The people can do with me what they think is right."

"Do you have any regret for the killing of your wife and children?"

"I believe they are better off where they are. Why should I fight for this poor life of mine? No. I ain't sorry for the children. They are at rest."

"Have you no regret at all?"

"No, only that I am here. I did all I could to kill myself, and I don't see how it is I am here. It must be God's hand that he didn't want me to die yet. I am not sorry for my wife. She is at rest. They are all out of trouble."

"How long had you meditated killing them?"

"It had been going on for a long time, until all of a sudden it overcame me."

"When did you write the letter you sent to the postmaster at New York? Was it before or after you shot the family?"

"I am not sure, but I believe I addressed the envelope in the kitchen before shooting them and wrote the letter afterward."

"What do you think should be done with you?"

"Let the law do what it thinks is right. I didn't realize it until now that it is done. I expected to be dead too."

"Did you and your wife have any quarrel after she and the children came home from church?"

"No, we only spoke four or five words."

"Did she say anything or make any resistance when you shot her?"

"She did not know anything about it. I went down to the cellar and shot her. She fell and never moved."

"When did you get the gun ready?"

"After they came home from church."

"Was there anything back of the church trouble to cause you to kill them?"

"Life was no good the way we lived. We quarreled, and I could not go anywhere with her. When we did go to her folks or my folks, I could not eat at the same table with them, and the children noticed this. I ate with them at home. I got tired of living that way."

"Was your wife always kind to you?"

"Not always. Sometimes she talked rough and sassy like before the children, and this made them cry. I wouldn't have things that way."

On the subject of Moser's trouble with the Amish church, the question was asked, "How long has this trouble been going on?"

"Since my brother moved near that schoolhouse," was Moser's reply.

"What started it?"

"Oh, it all started about the little boy."

"How was that?"

"It was in the church at Gridley five years ago. One Sunday I hold my baby on my lap. My wife not sit with me. The women sit on the other side of church. My baby get tired—he was only one year old then. It was Israel, my oldest boy. When he get tired, I take him on my lap. Then the preacher told me not to do it."

"What was the preacher's name?"

"Witzig."

"How did he tell you not to hold your boy?"

"He call my name out in church. Then I not put the baby down because I didn't think it wrong to hold him, because he was tired sitting on hard seat. Then Witzig call out my name second time, and I see other men look sharp at me. But I not put my baby down."

"Then what did they do?"

"After church, Witzig came and told me that I done wrong, and I not acknowledge. I only hold my baby on my lap. If I done something wrong—if I committed adultery or such thing—then I would acknowledge. But I not acknowledge I was wrong for what I done, only hold my baby."

"How long did they give you to acknowledge your wrong before they put you out of the church?"

"They didn't set any time. But then all the trouble begin."

Moser then related in his broken and disconnected way some of the troubles to which he said he was subjected during the next few years. These began, he said, by his own relatives shunning and avoiding him in every way possible. If he met them on the road and stopped to talk with them, they would answer him as shortly as possible and pass on. If he went to visit at his father's, his own brothers and sisters and parents refused to receive him. He was compelled to remain outside the house while the family ate at the table. If any of his relatives called at his home, it was only for a moment, in which time they would avoid speaking to Moser, if possible. If his wife started off to visit at a neighbor's, she would take the children along, but her husband could not go. This caused the little ones to cry and ask why papa could not come.

As time went on, Moser said, the rigor of the banishment against him became more severe. Finally, he felt it in his own home. His wife carried it further and further, until it reached all their domestic relations, he said. "My wife said last few weeks, if I not like to stay here, I can go. This, I could not stand, and I thought best we all die and be at rest," sobbed Moser.

The children were always crying and asking their mother what was the matter with the father, and he thought if his wife were dead, he wanted them to be "at rest" also, for he did not want the children to be in the hands of the Omish people.

"Did you tell anybody of your troubles and ask advice from any of your friends?" was asked of Moser.

"Yes. Doc Crawford and Foster."

"What did they tell you?"

"They say get divorce."

"Why didn't you do that?"

"I rather die."

Then Moser was asked if his wife never showed a disposition to counteract the actions of his relatives in their treatment of him.

"No," he replied, with more feeling than he had shown previously. "She stick to the church. All stick to the church."

Further along, the question was asked, "Will your father or brothers help you out in this trouble?"

Again Moser answered, "They no go to law. They stick to the church. Oh, it would not be so bad," said Moser, "if I could have satisfaction to go home, if I could only have some company. But I could not go home. I could not see anybody who come to my house. It was always the same—keep away, and I see no change."

Several times during the conversation, Moser asserted that his determination had been to kill himself. Asked why he started off on a long journey after the crime, Moser said he at first was impelled by the idea to get as far away as possible and then commit suicide where nobody would know him. Then after arrival in Salt Lake, he changed his mind and decided to write a couple of letters telling who he was and what his past had been. These letters he wrote and then set out to kill himself.

"I wanted to die," said Moser. "But now things have happened this way, and I am here. It begins to work the other way."

With this expression, Moser broke into renewed sobbing. His meaning was probably that since he had failed to take his own life, remorse for the killing of his family began to be felt. Moser was again getting weak and was speaking with difficulty. At times he wept bitterly. He finally told them there was nothing further he cared to say. After he had rested more and had time to think, he might make an additional statement.

The reporters discussed their impressions as they left the building. There was no indication of insanity in his demeanor. He had brooded over the matter until he had decided to end it all. He didn't seem to be overly intelligent, but this may be due to his dejected condition. He'd given them a lot to write about.

At seven o'clock on Monday morning, Moser was taken from the jail to the courthouse and given a hearing. It was early, and no one outside of the officials and a reporter were present. Sam didn't have a lawyer, so Sheriff Mount walked beside him. When they arrived in the courtroom, Sam was surprised that the justice of the peace was someone he knew from the Morton church. He was even more surprised when Justice Rapp spoke to him in German. It seemed to somewhat put him at ease, and he began to talk. He said his trouble had worried him for years, and it finally reached such a stage that he thought he was doing right in killing the family. But then the tide turned. When questioned further, Sam wept like a child.

The state warrants were read. Moser was charged with killing four people. Sam pleaded guilty and waived examination. He was told that the state's attorney, George W. Cunningham, would probably schedule his arraignment some day later that week. He would then be bound over without bond to the grand jury, when he would be indicted. His trial would probably not take place until September. He was led from the courtroom and returned to his cell. People who saw him expressed sympathy for Sam. It seemed that the enormity of his crime was beginning to dawn on him. He was on the verge of collapse.

Late that morning, Sam's father called on Sheriff Mount and asked to see his son. In the company of Judge Rider, he was taken to his son's cell in the county jail. As soon as father and son saw each other, both shed tears. For fully ten minutes, neither spoke a word. Finally, the father broke out, "Oh, Sam, my son, why did you do it? Why did you do it?" Moser could not reply, and the tears continued to flow in a steady stream.

After some time, father and son engaged in an earnest conversation. They discussed Sam's personal property and what should be done about the crops which were planted on his farm. It was agreed that Sam's property should be turned over to his father, who would pay the expenses of the burial of Sam's wife and children. He had done nothing about retaining an attorney for the defense of his son as the church forbade him to do so.

The letters that Moser had written to a Peoria paper and the postmaster had already been printed in the newspapers. But now there was another—written to the Salt Lake chief of police:

> I wish to say to the people of this world
> if there is any truth in the Bible, so

by my judgement you are in your last hours, it appears to me that man's doing is appearingly only for that mighty dollar. I do not say this to alarm Salt Lakers in no way as this city I like, and if I thought I would be safe and never come known that I commit the crime, I would have tried to pull through, but I think there are enough bad people for the sun to shine onto.

If I could have got around penalty of death and could have gotten friends and satisfaction, I should have been content with my day's work and meals with a good appetite as long as it reached.

Before I would agree to the rule or ruin creed of Amish people of my home, I choose to die. I had been under this circumstance five years, with no show of a change unless agreeing to this order.

If my wife could have content herself outside of community of these people and would have respected me as a husband by depriving some of those people, idea this crime had been saved, but their relatives kept her from doing so and forced their religion. However so, that she should esteem it more than me. It is a hard matter to express all their doctrine and rule. They keep their children ignorant of things of this world by not letting them have music and enjoyment as many wished to have. They raised them ignorantly, partly, and after they become old, many are not fit for law and rule of this world. I beg to say to the people of this world to destroy and clean the face of the earth of all such ministers, interferers between man and wife.

While Sam was being brought back from Utah, the news-papermen had worked hard to keep up with the public demand for news of the crime. Sam's brother Dan was interviewed by a Peoria journalist on Thursday, May 24. He was described as quiet, unassuming, pleasant, and not inclined to talk of his brother's deeds. When asked what steps would be taken to defend the case, Mr. Moser said that he didn't know. After a few moments, though, he began to soften. He said that while he in no sense condoned or tried to mitigate the enormity of the awful crime, he was nevertheless naturally inclined to regard it in some respects in the same light as that betrayed by his unhappy brother's Salt Lake confession.

Personally, Dan and Sam Moser had seen little of each other during the last two or three years. They had lived apart and not been closely associated. Dan denied that his brother was of a harsh or morose disposition. He said that he was a man of few words but pleasant and kindly and completely devoted to his family—a man who meant what he said.

Speaking of the trouble with the Amish community at Gridley, Mr. Moser declared that Sam did not adhere to the Amish faith, would not accept the rules of the church. He left the state and got a good job in Minnesota. His wife followed him there. Later, Mrs. Moser came back on a visit, and the doctor and minister persuaded her that it would be better for her health to remain in Illinois. This forced the husband to return, and the interference of the minister appeared to unsettle and embitter him.

As to the line of action to be taken in his brother's defense, Mr. Moser had naturally but little to say. He stated, however, that the papers report his father as saying that he would do nothing to defend his son. He failed to understand this. If he himself had a son, he would not abandon him in trouble. In the church matter, he could understand better, perhaps than outsiders, the difficulties under which one who is a member of an Amish community labors when not in good favor with the authorities of the church. He had suffered from the same trouble himself and could well understand the awful strain his brother must have been under for some time. Matters could be made exceedingly disagreeable for one who abandons the faith or who does not comply strictly with the rules of the community.

Dan concluded that his brother's side of the story would look different when presented by a good lawyer. Again clarifying that he didn't defend or justify the killing in any way, he said that he could easily understand his brother's troubles. He believed that Sam worshipped his boys and undoubtedly thought that they would be better off as they now were than to be left alone in the world, for there was no doubt in his mind that the father intended to kill himself.

Sam passed the long, hot summer days behind bars in his jail cell. In June, his son Benjamin would have turned five years old. Word came from nearby Bloomington that a devastating fire had ripped through the downtown area. In only eight hours, 45 buildings and 4 1/2 city blocks had been destroyed. Newspapers reported that the first Zeppelin flight took place and that the Boxer rebellion ended in China. The same day that a tidal wave hit Galveston, Texas, killing six thousand people, the newspaper announced that the Tazewell County circuit court would convene the next week. One of the largest stories in the nation's history next to one of the largest stories in Central Illinois's history:

> **The most important case to be heard is that of Samuel Moser, accused of the murder of his wife and three children last May. His father, who is wealthy, has been forbidden by his church, the Amish, to aid him in the defense, and the court will appoint an attorney to defend him. It is the intention of the defense to show that the teachings of this peculiar religion brought about his mental condition and caused him to commit murder. It will be one of the most interesting murder cases ever tried in Tazewell County.**

On September 13, 1900, Samuel Moser was indicted for the murder of his wife, and Moser was taken before the Tazewell Circuit Court in Pekin. He was arraigned on four counts of murder. Moser, through his attorney, pleaded not guilty. The attorney for Moser asked for a continuance, which was agreed to by the prosecuting attorney, and the case went over to the November term of the circuit court.

It marked what would have been the first birthday of Sam's youngest son, who had died without a name. The New York subway opened later that month, and William McKinley was elected president, with Theodore Roosevelt as his vice president. The next week, Sam was back in court. The newspapers reported on "Samuel Moser's Strange Case," saying that "Tenets of the Amish Church Had Assumed Prominence."

In his motion for continuance, Attorney T. N. Green stated that postponement was requested because three of the principal witnesses had absented themselves from the state in order, if possible, to avoid testifying in the case. One of these was Reverend Rudolph Witzig, the minister who reprimanded Moser during church services.

It was explained that the rules of the Amish Church forbade the members to participate in lawsuits. All their disputes were settled by the minister of their congregation. An edict had gone forth to the effect that the members of the Amish Church were to offer no resistance whatsoever to Moser. This was supposed to be the cause for the departure of Reverend Mr. Witzig and two other of the principal witnesses.

In the statement to the court, it was indicated that the plea of insanity would be made the main point of defense in the trial of Moser. It was stated that Moser's brother had, for eight months, been confined in an asylum and that it had been intimated by many that the accused was unbalanced previous to the commission of the crime.

Benedict Moser, father of the accused, was worth in the neighborhood of $100,000 (three million in 2017), but he would not give a cent toward employing counsel for his son, having been notified by the church that he would suffer expulsion if he aided the defendant in any way. He stated that he would "trust to the law of the land" to do what was right by his son.

On Wednesday, November 7, 1900, Jesse Black Jr. learned that he had lost his election bid for Congress in the fourteenth district by only 331 votes. The year before, he had represented the district in Springfield. At only twenty-seven years old, he had done remarkably well and was unanimously nominated to run on the Democratic ticket. It had been a long, frustrating campaign. Finally, it was over, and Black would be available to work with state's attorney Cunningham on the Moser trial, which would soon be underway.

The case was called in the circuit court of Tazewell County. An affidavit was presented for a continuance, which his counsel supplemented with a petition. Upon the strength of these documents, the case was continued until the February term of court. This affidavit and petition were intended to show that Moser was a martyr in that he had been the victim of a systematic course of persecution shared in by members of his own family and which ultimately drove him to madness and to murder. The affidavit alleged that Rudolph Witzig turned him out of church because he was attempting to pacify his baby during service. It was also claimed that the Reverend Rudolph Witzig had now fled the country in order not to be a witness at the coming trial and was believed to be in Germany.

The *Bloomington Pantagraph* followed up by publishing an article called "Their View of Moser: How the Amish People Regard the Man Who Is Now in Jail on Charge of Murdering His Family." But the Amish people, it seemed, were done "turning the other cheek." There were two sides to the story, and the Amish were ready to talk. On November 19, 1900, the *Peoria Star* ran an article titled "Martyr or Murderer: Diabolical Character of Samuel Moser as Presented by His Amish Brethren":

> Is Samuel Moser a martyr or a mendacious liar, as well as an unconscionable, deliberate, and cold-blooded murderer? This is a question in which the Amish people of this city and section are deeply interested, and their side of it is far different from that which has been so far advanced for public consideration by Moser and his attorney.
>
> According to the prisoner and his counsel, he was driven to murder his wife and three children by the perse-

cution of the people of his church—a persecution manifested in a hundred different ways.

According to the Amish people, Moser has been possessed of the devil from his youth up. He was always sullen, obstinate, dogged, mean, treacherous, and murderous. On one occasion, he attempted to murder his brother-in-law, but the latter being a man of superior strength, soundly thrashed him, and then Moser lay in wait for him with an axe. Only the circumstance of the brother-in-law taking another road home prevented Moser from becoming a murderer at that time.

There is much to be said for the Amish people. For frugality, thrift, industry, correct living, and close adherence to the simple faith of the fathers, there is no other class of people like them. They trust one another implicitly, will not take a note, a receipt, or go to law over any difficulty. In fact, they are virtually free from business troubles. They prize truth, honesty, and all the common and nobler virtues, and what they see can be relied upon.

John Schneider, the Fulton street locksmith, is one of the most prominent representatives of this people in this section, and he is eminently qualified to speak for them. He throws an entirely different light upon the character of Samuel Moser from that which has been hitherto advanced, and at this time when Moser has attempted to calumniate his people in order to save his neck, it is or more than ordinary interest.

To the specifications of the affidavit, Mr. Schneider enters a denial in detail. Moser declared that the Rev. Rudolph Witzig turned him out of church because he was trying to pacify his baby during service. He states that Moser was never turned out of church for anything, was never denied any of its holy offices, but that he stubbornly and doggedly refused to go to church even when repeatedly solicited to do so by the several members thereof and his own wife and family. In the service referred to, the baby was in a merry mood, and Moser was dancing it up and down with the evident intention of disturbing the congregation. Nothing was said to him at the time, but after the service, the preacher, in the mildest terms that did not even reach the rigor of a reproach, requested him not to play with the baby during the divine service again as it distracted the attention of other members of the congregation. Here again, Moser's morbid character asserted itself, and he at once conceived a bitter dislike to the preacher, a dislike which has become intensified the more the man has brooded over it.

Mr. Schneider continued that the claim that Rudolph Witzig had left the country was a deliberate falsehood. The reporter for the *Star* confirmed this as "the reverend gentleman" was in Peoria on Saturday evening and was seen by the *Star* representative, who conversed with him. Mr. Witzig has not flown, nor has he any thought of fleeing, but can be found on his farm near Gridley at any time. This morning, he went to Pekin to give the state's attorney positive proof that he was within reach.

Moser had stated that his brother Daniel had been turned out of church because he wore a felt hat, that he had gone to Iowa and had there become insane. Mr. Schneider stated that Daniel Moser was never turned out of the church for any reason, and as for felt hats, all the Amish people wear them. It is true that he went to Iowa and, while there, went insane. He was confined in an asylum for eight months, but it was not religion that drove him crazy. Probably the most merciful construction of the character of the murderer, Samuel Moser, is that there is insanity in the family and that he also is touched with it.

To the statements that Moser was not allowed to eat at the same table with his wife and family and that he was persecuted at home and away from it in a hundred different ways, the denial is entered as to each specific statement.

Moser says he took his wife and family out West to escape persecution, but the fact is that when he got there, his conduct was such to his family that his wife began to droop, and that her decline and misery were so apparent that the neighbors called upon Moser and demanded that he take his wife back to Illinois, or she would soon be a corpse. When he married Miss Hohulin she was a buxom girl, with dark hair, and was an utter stranger to sorrow. During the few years she lived with Moser, her hair because quite gray, and long before her cruel death, her joyousness had forever fled. The man cast a shadow over all with whom he came in contact. He was morose, taciturn, coldly reserved, generally disagreeable, and given to playing the most annoying and devilish tricks upon his wife and family.

For instance, when his wife desired to go to church or to visit her folks, he invariably hitched up the wildest and most vicious horses he had in the hope that there would be a runaway and disaster, resulting in injury to his wife and little ones. He was given to long periods of dark brooding, during which he gnawed his own heart. When that was gone, he meditated murder. One morning, the wife and three children were shot down in his own house—under the roof that should have protected them from violence and by the hand that should have defended them. This is the man who now poses as a martyr.

The *Peoria Star* published a similar article, denouncing Sam as a cold-blooded murderer. It was the most scathing article which had yet appeared against Moser and accidentally reached his cell. Sheriff Mount furnished Moser with all the reading matter he desired in the shape of books and newspapers. He made it a point, however, to look over the entire paper and cut out all the articles which pertained to the coming trial. On this particular day, the sheriff was in a hurry and did not see the article on the Peoria side. The next morning, he gave Moser the paper, who read every word of it.

Then he fled and, when pursued, attempted his own life, or pretended to; but as the bully is ever a rank coward, his hand failed him, and he merely inflicted a trifling wound. He was brought back to the county in which he had perpetrated a most horrible crime in its annals, and now the cringing wretch sought to save his worthless neck by lying to the court in a perjured affidavit and defaming without warrant as pure a people as live on God's green earth. The fact is that Moser is a murderer at heart, and if he had not slain his wife and children, he would have killed someone else. He so shaped his destiny as to make the crime as horrible as possible, and now from the depths of his craven heart, he makes his cowardly plea. That is all there is to the Moser wail.

After he read those words, Sam tore the paper into a hundred shreds. He began to pace up and down the length of his cell, his face turning purple as he sucked in air, then loudly blew it out. He ripped off his coat and the shirt he was wearing and threw them out of his cell. The sheriff tried to apologize and explain that he hadn't meant for him to see such articles, but Sam's agitated state made it difficult to pacify him. This was the first time since his imprisonment that Moser lost control of himself. He finished by lying down on his cot and crying like a child.

In the morning, his brother called and gave him fruit. He took the apples and peaches and gave them all away to his fellow prisoners. Sheriff Mount said that during the last week, Moser went to sleep early in the evening and about midnight would awake, unable to sleep anymore. He ate mostly eggs, bread, and potatoes and drank nothing but milk and water. He was very grateful if anyone did him a favor and was very kind to his cellmates. He said little to them, however, and refused to speak about his case.

The holiday season passed, and still Sam sat in his cell. The newspapers announced the turning of the century:

January 01, 1901

New Century Is Heralded

Thousands of people thronged the city tonight and celebrated the dawn of the new century. Watch meetings were held in the churches. In the business district, crowds of men and boys marched up and down the streets—blowing horns and cheering while every steam whistle in the city was turned loose. It was the noisiest greeting ever extended a new year in Chicago. The great watch meeting of the night was under the auspices of the Red Cross society held in the Coliseum, which was packed to the doors. William Penn Nixon presided, and an oration on the new century was delivered by Gen. John C. Black. Greetings from rulers of the different countries addressed to the Red Cross society were read by Nixon and heartily cheered by the immense audience. At 11:58, the audience rose and began to sing "Ol' Hundred"; and as the song was finished, the members of the Illinois naval militia fired a salute of twenty-one guns to the dawn of the new century.

For many people, though, the turn of the century was no cause for celebration. It was much more likely the beginning of the end. The book of Revelation had predicted the coming judgment and anyone could see that it was coming quickly. The world was changing much too fast, and people had grave concerns about where it all would lead. Only a short time before, it seemed, farm families were gathering over picnic lunches on the church lawns on lazy Sunday afternoons. Everyone knew their neighbors and pitched in together when help was needed gathering in the crops. Now young people often as not went off to the cities, leaving their morals behind and the farms shorthanded. The simple, easygoing lives of the farm were vanishing as the cities grew and became modernized. Horses and buggies were being replaced by motorized coaches and trains. Telephones were in wide use, cities were being electrified, and moving pictures were a curiosity that could only bring the temptations of the world even closer.

Three weeks into the start of the new year, during a crippling blizzard on January 22, 1901, the newspapers announced the death of Queen Victoria in England. Her reign, from 1837 to 1901, was known for its highly moralistic, straitlaced language and behavior. Her death at age eighty-one signaled the end of the historical period hallmarked by refined sensibilities identified as the Victorian Era. Her passing symbolized the old world that was vanishing before everyone's eyes.

All one had to do was pick up a newspaper to see that the modern world was destroying itself. Sin was everywhere one looked. The Moser murders were proof positive that the world had gone mad. For someone to kill a mother and three small children—what greater evil could be imagined?

The trial was drawing closer. Moser sat in his cell in Pekin. He could only hope that the predictions that the world would end with the turning of the century might come true. The pillow over his head did little to stifle the noise.

MOSER IN HIS CELL.

The artists who would draw Sam's portrait often put their own spin on him. In this, the first pen drawing of him in jail that would be published in the newspapers, he appears to be African American.

Chapter 8
The Jury

Gentlemen, a court is no better than
each man of you sitting before me
here on this jury. A court is only as
sound as its jury, and a jury is only
as sound as the men who make it up.

—Atticus Finch, To
Kill a Mockingbird

1901
Pekin, Illinois

On Monday, February 11, 1901, the horse case of Davis & Stoltz, which was being tried in the circuit court, was not quite ended from the previous week. It was announced that after the instructions were read, that jury would retire, and the Moser case would be called at about two o'clock.

The papers reran the stories of the killings to remind readers of the facts and also to educate their readers on the legalities of the case. Moser would have to face four separate indictments. He was charged with the murder of his wife, but if the jury were to return a verdict of not guilty, then he would be tried for the murder of his oldest child. Should a jury say that he was innocent of that crime, he would then be tried for killing his other child, and so on. Should his attorney succeed in freeing him, it was thought that he would have accomplished the impossible.

The newspapers promised their readers that they would cover the Moser case in detail—as much as space would allow during the trial. Many representatives and sketch artists for Chicago and other newspapers crowded the courthouse. Sheriff Mount had arranged two rows of tables with signs reading, "This table is for reporters only." One Chicago reporter attempted to interview Moser during the recess of the court but met with no success whatsoever.

Limited space in the courthouse and responsibilities else-where meant that many people would rely on the reporters to paint a picture of what was happening in the courtroom for them: "Sam was brought into court looking in the best of health. He did not seem to realize the importance of the trial, and if he did, his features did not betray him. He was clean-shaven and attired in a round sack coat of bluish texture. He wore a pair of brown trousers. He sat quietly in the chair and looked neither to the right or the left. The courtroom was crowded, and when he walked up the steps and into the courtroom, all eyes were turned toward him." What began as descriptions of the room and the people soon moved to speculation about motives and reactions. Reporters were usually either believers or rock-throwers, their opinions then swaying vast numbers of readers.

The entire first day was taken up in the examination of jurors. In nearly every case, the men who were questioned had read in detail about the case and formed a decision as to the punishment Moser deserved. As soon as the question was put to them and it was claimed that they had read about the case and formed an opinion, they were dismissed.

One reporter stated, "It may take a week to secure a jury. Every man, woman, and child in the county capable of reading has devoured every line written about the case, discussed it from every standpoint, and very likely formed a positive opinion. The first four venire men examined declared without equivocation that they had formed opinions, and the counsel on both sides feel that the same statement will come from several score more before the necessary twelve arbiter of Moser's fate are secured."

It was very evident from the questions asked by the attorneys that the defense would be that of insanity. Mr. Green planned to show that this client at the time of the alleged commission of the deed was insane, and under the laws of the state of Illinois, any-one committing a crime while permanently or temporarily insane

122

would not be held responsible for such act. The prosecution, on the other hand, would try to convince the jury that the crime was committed with due deliberation and that he was not deranged.

Moser seemed to be taking more of an interest, but he never spoke to his attorney and completely ignored the spectators. When he was led through the crowd, he looked neither to the right nor left but straight ahead of him. While coming down the courthouse steps at noon, a Chicago newspaper reporter took a snapshot picture of him. He was then heard to ask the sheriff, "Did that fellow take my picture?"

Whenever any of the attorneys in the case questioned a juror and referred to his murdering his wife and three children, he would quickly raise his eyes, look about him, change color, and then let his head fall forward upon his hand. He'd then look steadily at the floor, apparently lost in deep meditation.

It seemed that every issue of the Moser case had been discussed. But the army of newspaperman from all over the country who were in Tazewell County for the trial had so far left one stone unturned—insanity in the Moser family. Now they wrote that Sam had a brother, Dan, who, on various occasions, had been in the city. It was rumored that he would be one of the star witnesses of the defense.

Moser's brother had also been expelled from the Amish church for violating some of the observances. He fled to Iowa and was taken insane and treated in an asylum. He was dismissed after several months' confinement. Coming back to Illinois, he decided to clear his good name and had several times written out a statement telling of his religious prosecution and denouncing the Amish church. Now it seemed that statement would be made public.

It was also said that another relative was insane, but the name of this person had not been revealed. Attorney Green hinted at a great many surprises, and there was much speculation about what the prosecution would do should it be shown that there was insanity in the Moser family.

At ten o'clock the next morning, Samuel's parents and youngest brother arrived. There was quite a stir in the courtroom as their coming into court was somewhat unexpected. This was the first time that any of Moser's relatives had been near him since the commencement of the trial. Every eye was turned toward Samuel as they came forward, trying to gauge his response to their presence. He stood to greet them, but when they went on without coming to talk to him, he sat back down. Some thought he looked disappointed, but others thought that Sam seemed more relaxed knowing that his family was there. It was rumored that Benedict Moser had at last relented and would help his son financially. The elder Moser was said to be worth $150,000 (four million in 2017) while the son's fortune was estimated at $600 ($17,000 in 2017).

As Sam's father walked by, a star reporter jumped up and asked him questions:

"Is it true that you will not assist your son or have not in any way assisted your son and his trial?"

"I do not care to answer that."

"Did you come to Pekin to attend the trial?"

"Not exactly. My wife and I came here to learn when we are to testify."

"Was anyone in your family insane?"

"Yes. My son Dan was in an insane asylum in Iowa."

"Will you be present throughout the trial of your son?"

"No."

"Have you any statement to make?"

"I have none. Please do not ask me any more questions."

Mr. Moser said that he would tell his story at the trial and left the sheriff's office to seek his wife. The reporter speculated that Mr. Moser had evidently received word to keep a stiff upper lip and was following instructions.

As Sam's brother Reuben came down the hall, the reporter asked him questions also.

"Are you a farmer?"

"Yes."

"Do you belong to the Amish church?"

"No."

"Do you think that your brother was insane at the time he killed his family?"

"I do. Sam never acted on impulse. I think he was crazy."

"Will your father help Sam?"

"I don't know."

"Does your mother want to help her son?"

"She does. Only the church won't permit her to do it."

"Would you ever join the Amish church?"

"Never."

"Are you going to attend the trial?"

"I am."

"Is it true that your father will secretly meet his son?"

"I do not know."

The Moser family returned to Morton soon after being informed that the jury was not yet secured. They were expected to return Friday morning.

The first four jurors were accepted by the state in the morning: Bert Taylor, John Thompson, Henry Bartz (from near Green Valley), and Charles Arnold (from Fondulac Township). Court adjourned until one thirty, but that afternoon, the defense only accepted John Thompson.

The attorneys accepted Stuart Wilson next. He was a farmer from Little Mackinaw. Then two more were accepted: Clark Griffin and Edward Forbes. Though Mr. Forbes was a man of mature years and the father of a large family, he claimed that he had never had a Bible in the house, had never read a book, and had very seldom read a newspaper.

That brought the number to four, who were finally accepted on both sides on the first day: John Thompson, Edward Forbes, Clark Griffith, and Stuart Wilson—all farmers by occupation living in Malone Township. Each side would be entitled to twenty peremptory challenges. The prosecution had exhausted one and the defense two.

The attorneys had examined forty persons on the special venire. When the panel was exhausted, twenty-five more were ordered to arrive the next morning.

The headline that evening read, "Awful Fanatic Discipline: Murderer Moser's Counsel Says He Is Going to Expose the Horrors of the Amish Church."

Attorney Green would have a waiting world understand that such facts will be developed as will completely overshadow the discord following the investigation of the church of Brigham Young—not necessarily from the standpoint of connubial plurality but from that of fanatic discipline.

That it could be possible for one man in a community of a thousand or more to be so completely ostracized, to be so cut off from all communication as to be unable to secure for himself a daily sustenance with the money that he had saved and earned by years of toil, might seem impossible in this enlightened age and in the heart of the great state of Illinois; but such it is claimed by the Moser defense will be proven to be the fact. So restrictive are the rules of the sect that a non-member is denied purchases in a community store. A reporter attempted to buy a paper at an Amish newsstand,

---

and because he was not a believer in their peculiar doctrines, he was denied the privilege of a purchase. An orthodox member, however, condescended to make the trade, acting as the middleman and transferring the money from purchaser to dealer and the paper from dealer to purchaser. Such restrictions as this, it would be claimed and govern the entire conduct of the church and the elders who represent it.

This matter of the exclusion of nonbelievers, it is thought, will, before the trial has proceeded far, be subordinated from a standpoint of human interest to that of the great power wielded by the elders. Their word is law. Their will be the will of God, so the Amish discipline says, and whosoever decries this or questions that sins in the eyes of God and is expelled from the church. That evidence to this effect will be offered in a measure there is no doubt, but how far it will go depends on the measure of investigation adopted by the state.

Moser continues to lose in mental and physical strength. Loss of sleep and continual brooding have begun to tell on him, and complete collapse before the trial is not unlooked for. The jury battle is growing in intensity. The dismissal of Stuart Wilson after his acceptance by both sides shows how closely the venire men are being watched by Attorneys Cunningham and Green, representing the state and defense respectively. Three days after Wilson was chosen, it was shown beyond a doubt that he had declared he would like to see Moser hang. This fact was not brought out until last evening, and he was promptly released from the jury box.

Moser's intense hatred for his former church this morning reached such proportions that he now finds it necessary to turn to the Bible to secure words sufficient to satisfy his efforts to heap contempt on the Amish religion. He seems to find more satisfaction in voicing his opinion of the church in the fourth verse and eleventh chapter of Revelations, which reads, "And they worshipped the dragon who gave power unto the beast, and they worshipped the beast saying, who is like unto the beast? Who is able to make war with him?"

The page on which this verse appears is thumb-worn and badly soiled, indicating almost continual perusal. The corner of the page even is turned down. To Moser's troubled mind, the dragon is the elder and the beast the church, his cellmates say.

Wednesday morning, two more jurors were selected: Abe Thornton of Malone Township and William Kampf of Armington. Both of them were farmers. In the afternoon, another special venire of fifty was exhausted without the acceptance of a single juror.

"Have you ever heard of this Moser case before coming into the jury box?"

"Yes, sir."

"Read about it?"

"Yes, sir."

"From what you read, did you form an opinion touching the guilt or innocence of the accused?"

"Yes, sir."

"Is that opinion of such a nature as would require evidence to remove same?"

"Yes, sir."

"Challenge the gentleman for cause."

This went on, juror after juror. Here and there, a man clarified that he could neither read nor write, but this did not prevent his having heard of the case. One juror seemed to greatly desire a position on the jury. He said that he had absolutely no use for newspapers. He did not read the contemptible things and did not believe a word in them.

During the examination of William Wilcox, a juror, this question was put to him by one of the prosecuting attorneys: "Do you believe in capital punishment in a proper case?" The juror replied emphatically that he did not. Upon this answer, Moser quickly looked up into the face of the juror, as if to say, *Is it possible there is one man who would not hang me?* The juror, who was excused for cause, walked from the jury box, followed by the eyes of the prisoner. This was an unusual demonstration on the part of Moser, who usually seemed oblivious to his surroundings.

The attorneys on both sides exercised the greatest of care in the selection of jurymen, which made the work all the more tedious and slow. The examination of the jurymen was very rigid, and the attorneys often crossed swords in their objections to questions which were asked the jurors. Attorney Black asked the jurors if they understood the hearing was directed against Moser on the charge of murder instead of the Amish church. Of course, the question was ruled incompetent; but in many instances, jurors answered before an objection would be interposed.

Other questions were also put by the state, which plainly demonstrated they were prepared to refute the charges of the defense that the Amish church was to be held accountable for the murderous acts of Samuel Moser.

In questioning one of the jurors, Samuel's attorney asked, "If Samuel Moser was put on the stand, would you consider his testimony fairly and impartially?" This caused a stir in the courtroom, as it was the first suggestion that Sam might take the stand.

Finally, the special venires were exhausted. So far, only six of the twelve jurors had been obtained in three days. Judge Puterbaugh ordered another venire of twenty-five jurors returnable at nine o'clock the next morning, and the court adjourned at 4:20 p.m. At the last moment, he ordered another venire for one o'clock the following afternoon for good measure.

That night, Deputies Flood and Sutton scoured the woods in Mackinaw, Deer Creek, Spring Lake, Sand Prairie, and Dillon Townships, riding in search of fifty men whom they thought had not heard of the case. The farmers of Tazewell County were, as a whole, an intelligent class of people, and nearly all of them took the newspaper. When they saw the deputies approaching their homes, people would call out, "You needn't come here! We know all about the case and have an opinion." One deputy said that he didn't see how a jury in the case would be obtained at the present rate.

Deputy Sutton finally returned to the jailhouse with a story for Sheriff Mount. He had entered a farmyard and was about to knock on the door when a large dog took after him. Sutton tried to escape the ferocious animal and made tracks through the yard. In doing so, he fell into an open cistern with one foot. The animal was close to him, and Sutton felt like falling into the cistern to escape the dog. In desperation, he looked about for a weapon and saw a large bucket. He grabbed this and struck the dog. The dog fell into the cistern, and Sutton made his escape. Mount and the deputies had a good laugh over this and some other stories that came from the deputy's adventures.

In the middle of the night, Sheriff Mount walked through the jail to the prisoners' cells. He was surprised to find Moser awake and dressing. When asked about it, Sam gave no reason. He sat up for a couple hours, undressed, and went back to sleep. Mount and a deputy spoke about the strain that the hearing seemed to be putting on him. Sheriff Mount said that during the last week, Moser went to sleep early in the evening and, about midnight, would awake and sleep no more. The report in the *Chicago Times-Herald* that Moser drank liquor was a false statement as he never touched a drop.

The headline of the newspaper Thursday morning was "Murderer or Martyr?"

> Bearing all the earmarks of a cold, unimpassioned, unfeeling brute, close observation of the man around whom there is supposed to cling the tragedy born of religious fanaticism and persecution, obviously dispels the illusion that mere inability to display his devotion to his own flesh and blood as prescribed by the strict rules of the Amish church, to which he belonged, was not the motive for the crime of which he now stands accused, and of which he does not deny his guilt.

One-half had been chosen of the twelve peers who were to determine whether he should stretch hemp or be allowed to go free on the grounds of temporary insanity as a result of the rigid discipline of the New Amish religion. Three days' time had been occupied, one hundred talisman had been examined, and the work of securing a jury was only half completed.

Interest had been steadily increasing, and the courtroom was crowded to its utmost capacity from the time court opened until its adjournment. Though there had been nothing of a sensational nature in the proceedings to this time, the people lingered there hour after hour and endeavored to catch every word that was spoken. It was questionable if the courtroom was three times as large as it was at present if one-half the people could be accommodated. Under these circumstances, what would it be when the taking of evidence commenced?

Many Amish have been attracted to Pekin as a result of the trial. Some of them have been subpoenaed as witnesses, and the others were there as auditors of the trial; for if Attorney Green had his way, he would introduce evidence showing that the crime was committed as a result of temporary insanity, resulting from the rigid church discipline. A large number of visitors had been attracted from all parts of Peoria and Tazewell Counties, and the case would go down as one of the most intensely interesting and carefully fought in the history of the country. Important developments were expected at any moment, and each phase of the trial was carefully watched.

Those who were summoned began arriving in Pekin by breakfast time, and with the exception of one, all reported at the opening of court. George W. Hittle had missed his train. He arrived just after the adjournment of court and just in time to prevent the sheriff from sending someone after him.

Suddenly, the tide changed. The previously packed courtroom was nearly empty. If it wasn't for the jurors sitting about the room, the rear of the court chamber would have been deserted. What people wanted was sensationalism, and word had spread that the examination for jury qualifications would go on for a while. At two thirty that afternoon, they were out of potential jurors again, with only one having been accepted: Roy Miller of Hittle Township. Court was adjourned until Friday morning at nine o'clock, when another venire of fifty jurors would be present.

Court opened on Friday at nine o'clock, and another long, tiresome day commenced. The jurors silently filed into the courtroom and took their seats in the jury box with an audible sigh. The attorneys began the examination of jurors, knowing it would be a long, tedious day. It now looked as if the entire week was to be consumed in procuring a jury. For the trial, something over one hundred witnesses had been subpoenaed, but it was thought not over one-half of them would be examined.

It appeared that some of the newspaper men were getting desperate for material. It was reported that Lewis Ostrander, a wealthy St. Louis gentleman, had decided to place his money at Moser's disposal to escape the gallows. Apparently, the story was made up by some newspaper reporters. Ostrander was a traveling man from St. Louis. For the sake of a few dollars and a little notoriety, he'd consented to go along with the story.

Another story said that Attorney Green had been searching for the Reverend Witzig, the Amish preacher from Mrs. Moser's church. Some months prior, it had been stated that he'd left the country, which turned out to be untrue. Now Attorney Green was alleging that Witzig had been subpoenaed on behalf of the defense and had not responded. He speculated that the state had him hidden somewhere in Peoria so that he could be found at the proper moment by the prosecution should they desire to use him as a witness. After the story ran in the newspaper, Sheriff Mount received a phone message from Mr. Snyder in Peoria, who stated that Reverend Witzig was at his home in Gridley and would come whenever he was wanted to testify at the trial. Mr. Snyder was a friend of the preacher, who had communicated with the papers on his behalf a few times.

On Friday afternoon, Attorney Green objected to Stuart Wilson serving as a juror. He had been informed that Wilson had previously expressed an opinion in the case but was not honest in his answers to the court about it. After some argument, the judge and the attorneys in the case filed solemnly into one of the jury rooms, where they put Mr. Wilson through a course of questioning. When they came out, Attorney Green smiled; Wilson looked sheepish and immediately left the courthouse.

Saturday morning, Edward Keefe was chosen to fill the vacancy in the jury. Another special venire of seventy, returnable Monday morning, was ordered. The first week of the trial had been devoid of sensationalism, having been devoted entirely to the dull monotony of the selection of a jury, and the task was only half completed. There was little likelihood that the five men necessary to complete the jury would be chosen before Tuesday or Wednesday.

The seven jurors spent their first Sunday as wards of Tazewell county in a quiet manner. The gentlemen, who were well cared for by bailiffs Herman Becker and Charles Riley, were quartered in a suite of four rooms in the third floor, the west end of the Tazewell hotel. They were given the best that Mine Host St. Cerny had in his culinary department, and these luxuries were enjoyed by the men in the private dining room. Early morning finds these gentlemen astir. Sunday their presence not being required in court, the greater portion of the morning was spent in walking about the city and short strolls to the outskirts of town. During the afternoon, the men amused themselves in various ways in their rooms. As a diversion for the evening, they attended services at the First Reformed church, where they enjoyed a fine song service.

The jurymen that were selected enjoyed their day of rest. They arose early in the morning and took a stroll of several blocks; after which they returned to their hotel to eat breakfast. An ad in the paper next to a story from the trial advertises that one could have the finest breakfast in town: hot cakes, sausage, potatoes, bread, butter, and coffee for fifteen cents. They walked about town the greater part of the forenoon, taking in the various points of interest. The afternoon was spent in their respective rooms. A typical restaurant supper at the time was roast pork, mashed potatoes, vegetables, bread, butter, and coffee for ten cents. A slice of homemade, fresh-every day, best-in-the-city pie was five cents a cut. Also advertised: three fried oysters, bread, and butter for fifteen cents and turtle soup, ten cents. After supper the entire jury, accompanied by the deputies in charge, solemnly filed into the American Reformed church, took a front row and heard the services. Quite a transformation had taken place in the personal appearance of the jurymen. When the gentlemen were accepted, they were fresh from the country. Now one would hardly take them for farmers. They all wore their Sunday suits, boiled shirts, standing collars, and newly purchased neckwear.

The special venire issued the Saturday before appeared in court on Monday morning. Twenty-five of the gentlemen subpoenaed were citizens of the city of Pekin. It was hoped that the attorneys would have better success with them than they have been having with preceding jurymen.

A large assignment of additional chairs were placed in the courtroom, and these arrangements failed to provide a sufficient amount of seating room. Sheriff Mount found it difficult to keep the aisles open, and he now realized what a task he would have before him when the case actually started. There would soon be assembled a larger crowd than had ever before been congregated within the justice hall.

Shortly after 10:00 a.m., the eighth juror was accepted to try the case. His name was Jacob Huguet. He was only about twenty-five years old, a married man from Washington, Illinois. For several years, he was employed in the grocery store of a Mr. Ropp. He was a clerk who attended strictly to business and therefore had little time for street gossip; hence, his competency to sit as a juror. He underwent the most rigid examination and, at its close, was accepted by both sides. Attorney Green asked him whether he believed in the right for a man to love his children, but the question was overruled, and he was not permitted to answer.

Another potential juror from Washington township was very opposed to inflicting the capital punishment. Needless to add, he was not accepted by the state. From Fondulac Township appeared a man who greatly worried the attorney for the defense in the effort to get answers to the several general questions touching upon his qualifications. At last, the attorney became so disgusted that he challenged the gentleman under the preemptory rule.

The courtroom was crowded that afternoon. Among the spectators were a number of ladies, one of whom carried in her young infant, who was sleeping in her arms. The lawyers were examining one of the jurors when suddenly the plaintive cry of a babe swelled above the noise of the courtroom. Like a frightened animal, Moser, startled, looked up and around him in search of the location of the child's shriek. The newspapers speculated: Did the cry remind him of the wild cry of his own babe as he poured shot after shot into its helpless body? For a time, it looked as though Moser was upon the verge of collapse, but in a moment or two, he got himself together and assumed the same old stolid look he had worn all the time.

One of the jurors accepted during the day by the state was John Hoffman, who was assessor for Pekin Township. While he was acceptable to the prosecution, the defense found ample reasons that justified them in challenging him for cause.

It was about five o'clock when the monotonous and tiresome task of several hours of questioning was awarded by the selection of two more jurors. One of them was Henry E. Traub, a resident of Pekin for fifty years or more. By trade, he was a harness and awning maker and was the head of a family of several children. The other man, called his "companion in misery" by the papers, was Thomas Boyd, a man of fifty years of age and a prosperous farmer in Fondulac Township.

This increased the number to ten and gave the attorneys hope that a jury might actually be secured soon. It was as if an invisible line had been crossed. With the hope of a full box, Judge Puterbaugh and the attorneys decided to hold a night session and at six o'clock; court was adjourned to seven thirty, when the examinations were continued. William Samuels, a teamster of Minier and a family man, was the eleventh juror.

There were twenty-seven left on the last venire of seventy-five when both sides announced the acceptance of the final juror. The twelfth man, James L. Southwood, was a barber from Pekin and a single man. Attorney Green had just finished the examination of the twentieth juror tendered him by the prosecution, leaned back in his chair for a moment (the courtroom was as silent as the grave), and then said, "We will take the gentleman." It was 10:15 p.m.

A sigh of relief came from everyone in the room. Then murmuring was heard, which became louder and louder each moment until it was suppressed by order of the court. The long search and struggle for acceptable jurymen was concluded.

The county had been scoured in every direction, and hundreds of its good citizens had been brought to Pekin to undergo a searching examination. But finally the last man was agreed upon. The responsibility was a grave one, to say whether a human being would live or die. Some would say that it is one of the most harrowing duties an American citizen is called upon to perform. To say that the great, strong arm of the law shall be raised to crush the life out of one poor, little, insignificant atom of humanity is a responsibility that but few men would care to assume. The jury chosen was called upon to face this duty.

The community at large demanded that justice be done. Justice, however, should be tempered with mercy. For while there is an abhorrence of this crime in the minds of everybody, yet there is much sympathy for the unfortunate environment in which this poor criminal is placed.

The jurors were sworn in and court was adjourned until nine o'clock the next morning. It was announced that Jesse Black Jr.

would make the opening statement for the state the next morning and would be followed by T. N. Green for the defense. The latter promised some sensational statements in his talk to the jury.

Name	Age	From	Occupation	Married	Kids
Edward Forbes	26	Malone Twp	Farmer for 3 years	Yes	?
John Thompson	30	Raisd in Malone Twp	Farmer	Yes	2
Abe Thornton	40	Malone Twp	Farmer for many years	Yes	4
William Kampf	54	Born and raised in Hittle Twp			
Roy Miller	21	Born and raised in Hittle Twp	Farmer	Yes	1
Edward P. Keefe	36	Raised in Mason Co Moved to Spring Lake 4 years ago	Farmer	Yes	3
Jacob Huguet	25	Washington	Clerk	Yes	
Henry E. Traub		Pekin	Harnessmaker	Yes	
Thomas Boyd	50	Fondulac Twp Washington	Farmer	Yes	?
Wm G Samuels		Minier or Washington	Teamster	Yes	?
James L. Southwoord		Pekin or Washington	Barber	No	
Clark Griffin	34	Malone Twp	Farmer		3

Chapter 9
Opening Remarks

Everything in moderation,
even the truth.

—Marty Rubin

Tuesday
February 19,
1901

The crowd that clamored for admittance to the circuit court-room at Pekin on the first morning of the trial was so great that the sheriff was compelled to lock the doors and allow only those to pass in and out who had an actual role in the process. The largest crowd in the history of the county was packed into the courtroom at both the morning and afternoon sessions. The work of selecting a jury had progressed for more than a week. It was concluded late Monday night, and the next morning, the trial proper began. A few minutes before the trial was about to start, the prisoner was brought in and sat in his usual place against an iron pillar, a short distance to the rear of his attorney. He was obviously more uneasy now that the trial was advancing to the next step. Sheriff Mount had provided additional desk room for reporters. Every available space was utilized for spectators, and inside the railing was arranged space for members of the bar. At nine o'clock, Judge Puterbaugh took his place on the bench.

At ten minutes past nine o'clock, Attorney Jesse Black Jr., the eloquent young attorney who was assisting state attorney Cunningham appeared before the jury. He commended the jury, saying that they had been selected from many of the citizens of the county to try the issues set forth in the indictment. He realized it was not a pleasant duty, nor one of their choice. It was a duty forced upon them, and in their present condition, each and every juror was now an officer of the state.

"The charges contained in the indictment," explained Mr. Black, "are the charges upon which this man is to be tried and upon which you are to pass in judgment. The law was explained to you during the examination touching your qualification to sit as a jury. However unpleasant it may be, however much you may dislike to find him guilty, it is your duty to so find and fix his punishment."

Mr. Black explained that it was not a burden upon the state to prove that the defendant entertained malice. The commission of the crime was, in the sight of the law, evidence that the deed was done with hatred and malice poisoning his mind. The jury was cautioned to keep ever present the fact that the defendant at the bar was the person who was before them for trial and under the statements as contained in the indictment.

He then opened his case for the prosecution by reading the several charges in the indictment returned by the grand jury in detail. He described the way Sam Moser had laid out his plans for the quadruple murder of his family, recalling the letter he wrote and mailed at Tremont about the killing, sending it to the postmaster at New York to be mailed to the postmaster at Morton to be given to his people.

Mr. Black walked the jurors through the killing of Moser's family in detail. At times, he became quite dramatic in his speech. There was a deathly silence in the courtroom, and it seemed that every eye in the courtroom was riveted toward Samuel Moser. He sat leaning back in his chair, with his head bent forward, resting his chin upon his right hand. Clasped in this hand was a handkerchief, and as the story of the crime was recited from the lengthy legal document, he grasped the kerchief convulsively.

"The defendant, Samuel Moser, was the father of three children and the husband of Hanna Moser. One day, a brother of Samuel Moser called and invited the family to attend church. The mother and children went, but the father did not. He had brooded over the family troubles for some time and concluded to kill his family and end his troubles. This is not the first time that Samuel Moser had entertained such a resolution. He had made the decision while in Minnesota, where he bought the revolver in order to kill his family.

"When the family had gone to church that day, Moser sat down and began to brood over his troubles and decided that 'since he wouldn't be ruled by his wife,' he would see that they die. He sat in the south room of the house until the family came home. The wife and children came into the house, and Hanna Moser began preparing the meal. She put the food on the stove to cook and then went into the cellar to obtain something. Sam Moser saw her go into the cellar, followed her, and as she stooped over, he came up to her and fired the revolver in the back of her head and killed the woman that he had sworn to love and cherish.

"Not satisfied, he went upstairs and sent the oldest boy out for a bucket of water. He called the other boy into the south bedroom and shot him dead. Then the boy who had gone out for a bucket of water came in, and Moser shot him. The boy made a circle and fell to the floor dead. Then Moser went to the bed where the little nine-month-old baby slept and shot the little one three times until it was dead."

Sam could take no more. Tears began to course down his cheeks. He reached for his handkerchief, placed it to his eyes, and burst out crying like a child. Attorney Black rushed ahead, hoping to avert any possible sympathy: "Then this man, whom the defense claims to be insane, pasted papers to the window and pulled down the curtains and fled to Tremont, leaving behind him what had once been his family. The prosecution will show by Moser's own confession that he hid in box cars so that no one could see him and left at dark on the night train. He took every precaution to cover up his identity, thinking that he could get away from everybody who might know him and thus escape the death penalty."

Mr. Black then told of Moser's escape to Salt Lake City: "When he reached that city, he purchased a Chicago paper on the street, which told of his crime and his escape. But his guilty conscience hounded him so unmercifully that he, like all cowards, attempted to take his own life. After reading the papers, he wrote letters of his crime and then went to the River Jordan to commit suicide. But so black a scoundrel is he that the holy water of that

River Jordan refused to receive that polluted body." He then told the jury of Moser's attempt to take his own life, his confession, and his return to Pekin.

Black explained that the usual plea of insanity would be brought up in this case by the defendant's attorneys. "Insanity is a good defense, if offered in a good case," said Mr. Black. "But the law presumes every man to be sane until proven otherwise, and Samuel Moser is to be considered a sane man until sufficient evidence is given to cause a doubt as to his condition." In concluding his statement, Mr. Black read the statutes governing the crime of murder and its punishment and again impressed upon the jurors their duties as officers of the state. The attorney said that this case was one of the most cold-blooded, red-handed, and reeking murders ever brought before the people of the state of Illinois— and one that should not go unpunished.

Mr. Black concluded by reminding the jurymen of their duty. His address was logical and sensible, stating the case as it was and what the prosecution intended to do. Mr. Black sat down. It was 10:20 a.m.

Attorney T. N. Green, the attorney for the defense, then stood to plead the case of his client. "I never realized my utter weakness as I realize it today as I stand before you in my effort to protect that lonely man as he sits before you. No man ever sat in this courtroom, No man ever came into this courtroom so absolutely unprotected." Such were the words with which the attorney opened his statement to the jury on behalf of the life of Samuel Moser. And the words and manner in which they were spoken had a telling effect upon both jurors and spectators—they clearly pitied him.

The jury was cautioned to weigh carefully the introduction of lengthy statements alleged to have been made by the defendant as he was incapable of doing so. Not even he, Mr. Moser's attorney, could get the defendant to say anything beyond short sentences, and they were answers to questions. This was certainly true to the jurors' experience in the courtroom. So far as any discourse between Moser and his attorney was concerned, one might as well be in Pekin and the other in Chicago. They had not spoken a half dozen words since the commencement of the trial. Each morning, Moser took a position by one of the iron posts, where he remained the entire day, looking neither to the one side nor the other and speaking to no one around him.

Green went through the entire case from the very commencement. Beginning before the crime had been committed, he told of the killing and of Sam Moser going to Utah. He spoke with feeling and earnestness, saying that he was thoroughly convinced that Moser was the victim of religious persecution.

"There was murder done in the little home of Sam Moser nearly a year ago, and the prisoner now confronting a jury in the Tazewell County courthouse was the man who pressed the trigger of a revolver that sent his little ones—the little ones that he loved above all—into another world, along with the wife for whom he had labored and worked hard all his years. But it was not Sam Moser who committed the crime. It was the New Amish Church. It was Benedict Moser, the wealthy father of the defendant, who destroyed the cord of reason and turned the man—who, a few years ago, had been a loving, kind husband and father—into a demon."

The responsibility of the brutal acts that occurred at the home of the defendant were thus accredited to the Amish church. Witnesses from Woodford, McLean, and Tazewell Counties would swear as to the amiable disposition of the defendant and the love and affection he displayed for his family before he had been cast out of the church and treated as a pariah. Clearly, he had been driven insane by the people who had persecuted him.

"Out of heaven, swift and sure, will come a punishment on the heads of the new Amish church. Their lands will be swept away. Their homes will crumble before the just vengeance of God. They will know sorrow and suffering, and in the end, they will shout for mercy. This fate is in store for the New Amish Church. These things will happen. For there is a wise and just God ruling all, and in time, all wrongs that have been heaped on the head of Sam Moser will be righted."

In his highly emotional address, the practices of the Amish church were severely denounced. His voice was one moment ringing at its highest pitch, the next murmuring a sad story in pathetic tones. Reporters said that the powerful flight of oratory caused men and women alike to weep aloud in a scene seldom witnessed in a courtroom. While tears coursed down the cheeks of the jurymen, the official court reporter forgot his duties. The score of newspapermen leaned forward, lost in the flight of words that rang through the old-fashioned courtroom.

"There is only one God for the new Amish church," declared Attorney Green, "and that is the almighty dollar." The Amish knew nothing about the Constitution of the United States and avoided the duties that fall to all citizens. He stated emphatically that he did not want any more of the Amish church people in the community, and they could go back to where they came from.

The Amish preacher in the eyes of the Amish was nothing more than a God and that the church was to blame for the condition of Samuel Moser. Mr. Green called the Amish old, unfit, and tramps, and he said that we would raise our hogs better than the Amish would raise their children. He continued that Moser was hounded by the preacher and was derided and suffered to such an extent that it drove him insane and caused him to commit the terrible crime while in that state of mind. Not only was the defendant's mind impaired by treatment at the hands of the new Amish church, he stated that Moser would take the stand

and that the defense would show a hereditary taint of insanity in the prisoner's blood, his mind being affected and insane.

Mr. Green then spoke of the father of Samuel Moser, who, instead of being a comforter to his son, appeared as one of the prosecuting witnesses. He said it would be a sin for Samuel Moser to regard Benedict Moser as his father. He asked the jurors where their fathers would naturally be upon a trial for such a serious offense. The attorney claimed that it was the fear of his family being entirely estranged from him that eventually brought about the ruin of Samuel Moser's mind. If the mother of Moser was permitted by the church to take the stand, Mr. Green proposed to show by her that Moser inherited a diseased mind, there being three members of the family on his mother's side who were demented. "The very acts of Moser," alleged Mr. Green, "as described by Mr. Black after the shooting had been done, were those of an unsound mind."

"My heart, my soul is in this case. I know that the New Amish Church is the most infamous sect in all this world, and as a man who prays to his God, I want the world to know that this poor, insane man is a victim, like scores of others, of a creed born of the devil. See this man, alone, forsaken. Not a soul on earth will extend a hand to him but myself. And why do I do it? Because I know the new Amish church. I know the people that make up this narrow, bigoted, devilish organization. I went to Sam Moser because I know that he had been driven insane by the new Amish church. To hang that man would be wrong, and I have taken up his fight."

Mr. Green informed the jury they were vested with unlimited power, and they alone could say whether the man who sat facing them was to be deprived of his life or given his liberty. Following Black's logical and sensible talk, Attorney Green's terrible denunciation of the heads of the Amish church must have been quite a shock. The papers would later say that "his attitude and address was such that it will never be forgotten."

He also quoted the law and reminded the jurymen of their duty, asking the jurymen to be fair in their considerations on behalf of Sam Moser. In what was called "a masterful speech" for the defense, Attorney Green had spoken for an hour and twenty minutes. He finished his address at 11:45 a.m., and at its conclusion, Judge Puterbaugh adjourned court until 1:00 p.m.

SAM MOSER

Chapter 10
The Prosecution

The monstrous act by definition
demands a monster.

—Rick Yancey

Tuesday
February 19,
1901

At one o'clock, the courtroom was crowded. But in the ten minutes before the hearing was resumed, the courtroom suddenly filled to its utmost capacity. Moser had put on a white shirt and collar and tried to look cheerful, but as the case continued, his mental anguish was plainly visible.

The witnesses for the state were then called forward and sworn. State Attorney Cunningham wanted all the witnesses excluded with the exception of reporters. Attorney Green said he had no objection to all the witnesses remaining as he did not see how the testimony of one could affect that of another. These witnesses were establishing the basic facts of the case: the finding of the bodies, the description of the house, and the bullet wounds found in each corpse. The court decided to allow the witnesses to remain in the courtroom.

Dr. H. V. Bailey, a physician and surgeon, was the first witness to take the stand. He testified that at the time of the commission of the alleged crime, he was coroner of Tazewell County, having held that position for eight years. The sheriff had informed him that there had been a murder in the vicinity of Morton. He immediately left for the place, accompanied by the state's attorney, deputy sheriff, and Edward Rollins, for the purpose of holding an inquest. The east door was entered, and he found the bodies of three little children in the south room. They were lying side by side, or nearly so. An old dress skirt had been carelessly thrown over them.

All the bodies had mortal wounds to the head, but not all the wounds inflicted were mortal ones. The baby had wounds to the head and the body. They went into the cellar and saw the body of the dead woman lying upon her back. Grasped in her right hand was a broken case knife. About her feet was strewn remnants of a broken bowl. He examined the body and discovered a bullet wound in the skull large enough to admit the insertion of an ordinary lead pencil. He thought the bullet had been fired from a .32 caliber revolver. There were no powder stains upon the body. A dress skirt was thrown over her. The cellar windows were covered up with newspaper from the inside. There was blood on the floor of the kitchen, where he found the cartridge box. No weapons were found. The cistern was dragged, and all the buildings searched in the thought that the body of the one who had done the deed would be found.

Upon cross-examination, Attorney Green learned that the inquest was held at Tremont. Dr. Bailey said that he was sure that Benedict Moser, the father of the defendant, was in attendance there. Phil Hoffman was sworn at the Moser home, to the best of his recollection. His impression was that he examined one or two witnesses at the Hoffman house. The evidence was reduced to writing and affirmed to. The verdicts and names of the witnesses were copied in his record and the originals and the evidence filed with the clerk. He said that he had seen part of the records in the grand jury room since, but he could not tell whether any of the evidence was there.

Clarence Ball, Deputy Sheriff of

Clarence H. Ball, deputy sheriff, was then placed upon the stand. He explained that he had gone to the homestead of Samuel Moser in the company of Dr. H. V. Bailey, George W Cunningham, and Edward Rollins on the fifteenth day of May 1900. When he first arrived at the house, it was tightly closed. The windows were covered from the inside with newspapers. He was the first one to enter the house, where just inside the door, the bodies of the three little children were found. They were covered with a dress skirt or carpet. Later, he went into the cellar and discovered the body of a woman lying on the cellar floor, covered up with a carpet. There was a wound to the head. She had a broken case knife in her hand, and there was a broken bowl beside her. The cellar window was covered up from the inside. There was a streak of blood across the kitchen floor. He walked outside and noticed that the cattle and horses had been turned out into the pasture. When cross-examined by Attorney Green, Mr. Ball stated that Mr. Hoffman and Benedict Moser were at the inquest, along with twenty or thirty others.

Mark Cottingham testified that he lived at Tremont, was the editor of the *Tremont News*, and was not acquainted with the defendant, who lived about three and a half miles northeast of Tremont. He went with several other gentlemen to the Moser place on May 15 at about 10:00 a.m. They found the home closed up. The doors were all locked and the curtains pulled down inside. There was no one around the house. He tried the doors and found them all locked. The windows were all closed except one, which was down about four inches from the top. He could not see in the house at all as the drawn curtains prevented him from being able to see inside. One of the party having a key which unlocked the door, they were finally able to enter. He and the undertaker Winzeler entered the house together. They found the bodies as described by ex-coroner Bailey and Deputy Sheriff Ball. He gave a description of the interior of the house and contents of the rooms.

Under cross-examination, Mr. Cottingham answered that it had been about a year since he had been in the Moser house before the murders. Several others were there before he arrived with the other men on that day. He also testified that they found pants that they assumed belonged to Sam Moser that had blood spots on them. During the cross-examination of Mr. Cottingham, an alarm of fire sounded. It was only a few seconds after that that the crowded condition of the room was relieved, and those who were anxiously awaiting an opportunity to enter wasted no time in taking advantage of the vacancy.

John Winzeler of Tremont testified that he had been the undertaker for eight years. He was not acquainted with the defendant. When he was called to the residence of Samuel Moser on May 15, there were only a few men already there: Mr. Cottingham and Mr. Davis. They gained entrance to the south room through a door, but he remained in the room for only two or three seconds. He then went out and closed the door. He found a ladder, which he placed against the porch on the north side of the house. He climbed up and looked into an upper window but saw nothing of any particular importance. He saw a window, which was lowered from the top. The window was covered with a curtain, which was tacked. He put his hand to the opening and tore the curtain loose but could see nothing within. He came down and examined the windows of the first-story windows.

Finally, he entered the house through a door, which had been opened by some member of the party and found the bodies of the three children and the woman, and saw bloodstains trailing across the floor. When the coroner arrived, he entered again with the coroner and made an examination of the house. He knew that the woman was Sam Moser's wife, Hanna. After the coroner had viewed the remains, Winzeler took charge of the bodies for burial. He found the bullet wounds on each of the bodies: one in the head of the oldest boy, two wounds in the head of the second boy, and one wound in the head and one in the heart of the baby. When asked on cross-examination, he answered that he didn't know where he was on May 12, he didn't know the condition of the house or cellar on May 13, and that he did not notice Benedict Moser there on the fifteenth.

Frank J. Davis testified that he was a banker and resided at Tremont. He was at the house three and a half miles northeast of Tremont on May 15. He and three others (Cottingham, etc.) arrived at the house about 10:00 a.m. They impaneled a coroner's jury and viewed bodies as they lay in the house. He saw dark-red spots of blood leading to the northeast corner of the pantry door to the door on south of room. He was not personally acquainted with the deceased. On cross-examination, Davis stated that testimony of witnesses before coroner's jury was reduced to writing. Benedict Moser and Henry Hoffman were witnesses before the coroner's jury.

George Hinman testified that he was a farmer in the neighborhood of Moser's residence, approximately one and a quarter mile northeast of Tremont and about one and a half miles from the farm occupied by Samuel Moser. He said that the Sunday evening that the crime was supposed to have been committed, he was coming down the road on his way home from Tremont at about 7:00 p.m., when he saw someone walking toward him. As they drew nearer, he recognized Samuel Moser. He was dressed in what was termed Sunday clothes, walking on the road from the north and going west, which would take him to Tremont. They had never been introduced but had a speaking acquaintance. As they passed each other on the road, Hinman spoke to him. Moser, with his head bowed down, passed by without speaking. Hinman related that he thought this action strange at the time but did not know the reason until two days later.

At the conclusion of this examination, court adjourned until Wednesday morning at nine o'clock. As people filed out of the courthouse, the sheriff was asked, "Where did you have all of these people?"

Now that the case was getting more interesting, the courtroom was crowded to such an extent that the doors were locked, and many had to remain outside. People were fascinated to get a look at the Amish, who were attending the trial in large numbers. There were also many women attending the court, which was unusual for the time. The sheriff and his deputies made every effort to seat them. They were given places inside the railing so that they could see and hear the trial. The ladies reportedly felt very sorry for Moser, who sat with his face buried in his hands. They gazed intently at the man charged with the murder of his family, sympathy for him plainly visible in their faces.

The first Amish churchmen that were put on the stand was Sam's neighbor Henry Hoffman. His house was only about three hundred feet from Moser's on the road from Tremont. He had known the defendant from his boyhood. Mr. Hoffman went with

Noah Moser to Samuel Moser's house about eight o'clock the morning of May 15. He walked around the house and tried to look into the windows but did not see anything. When the other men arrived, they tried the windows in an effort to get in but found all the shutters fastened. A ladder was placed against the upper windows, but nothing unusual could be seen within. Next, they pried open a window on the cellar but were unable to discern anything in the darkened underground room. They opened the trap door to the cellar. Putting a box to the foot of the steps, Noah stood upon it and looked through the transom of the cellar door. With the light from the window opened opposite, they were able to distinguish the body of the murdered woman lying on the cellar floor and covered with the quilt. Mr. Hoffman then went for additional help to investigate. Returning a couple of hours later, he found a number of people there—among them the corner and other officials.

His evidence was given in the most painstaking detail, with great effort being made to answer the questions with the strictest regard for the letter of the truths. Upon cross-examination, Mr. Hoffman confirmed that he was Amish and had been a citizen of the United States for the last eight years. There was a question as to whether or not he had taken this step only in obedience to the law requiring real estate owners to be citizens. This was objected to by the state and the objection sustained.

Attorney Green then asked if there had been ill feeling between Mr. Hoffman and Sam Moser. This was objected to and sustained. He then asked if Mr. Hoffman had been forbidden to eat at the same table with Sam. Attorneys Cunningham and Black objected to this also. Mr. Green further brought out that the witness did not assist Moser in his farmwork, as was customary between farmers. While Mr. Hoffman didn't have to answer most of these questions, Mr. Green succeeded in getting before the jury that Moser had been regarded as an Ishmael by the Amish.

They would have nothing to do with him because of his violation of church regulations.

Thomas Harris took the stand and was examined late that morning. He lived in Tremont and was at Moser's residence on May 15 with several other men. Noah Moser was not there at the time. Ernest Abbott and John Wilson opened the door and looked and then shut the door. Mr. Harris was of the opinion that no one entered the house until the arrival of coroner. The cellar windows were covered with newspapers that were tacked on with carpet tacks. The curtains were drawn inside the house also. He saw the bodies of the three boys lying on the floor. He described in detail the appearance of the bodies and the furniture of the rooms.

After a five-minute recess, the postmaster of Morton, Illinois, William H. Voelpel, took the stand. He said that he had resided at Morton for thirty-three years. He had known Sam Moser for many years and received a letter from him on May 15, 1900. It had been mailed at Tremont, sent to the New York postmaster, then to him at Morton.

The letter was shown to Mr. Voelpel and identified by him as the one referred to, but its introduction as evidence was objected to on the grounds that it had not been connected with Moser, nor was a sufficient foundation laid for its introduction. The letter, which had not yet been admitted, is as follows (exhibit A):

> Tremont, Illinois
> May 13, 1900
>
> Inform the postmaster at Morton, Tazewell County, that my wife and boys can be found at my place—Sam Moser—they are gone to rest, and I will follow.

Edward W. Palmer testified that he was thirty-five years of age and employed as a police officer in Salt Lake City, Utah, for three years. He saw the defendant, Sam Moser, in the central part of the city on Saturday morning, May 19 at 5:00 a.m. He was leaning against a telegraph pole from a wound in the head. His clothes were wet. Moser asked him if he was an officer and asked him to take care of him. The officer accompanied him to his room at Harris House. The night watchman there went up to Moser's room with them and asked him what his trouble was. Palmer asked Moser if he tried to kill himself. Moser answered that he had. Asked why he tried to kill himself, he said he wanted to die away from his people. He then indicated an article in the *Chicago Times Herald* under the date of May 16, 1900, which contained an account of Moser killing his family.

Moser pointed to some letters lying on the center table and told the officer to read them. The policeman tore them open and, for the first time, found that the prisoner was Moser. He could scarcely believe it—the letters addressed to different parties all detailed the crime and stated that the New Amish Church was responsible for all this trouble. At that point, Mr. Cunningham handed Palmer three letters and asked if they were the ones he read in Moser's room. Mr. Palmer identified these letters, and they were offered into evidence.

The letters were read by Attorney Cunningham. They were written by Sam Moser and confessed that he was the murderer of the family. He did not want them to live as he had lived and would rather see them dead. One of them stated:

> I am a murderer of Illinois from Tazewell County. Wire to my father B. Moser Tazewell County, Illinois, that the body of their son is found. I do not suppose they want to see me anymore.

Another letter written by Moser to the chief of police is as follows:

I wish to say to the people of this world, if there is any truth in the Bible, so by my judgment you are in your last hours, it appears to me that all men's doing is apparently only for the mighty dollar. I do not say this to alarm Salt Lakers in no way, as this city I like, and if I thought I would be safe and it would never become known that I committed the crime, I would've tried to pull through, but I think there are enough bad people for the sun to shine unto.

If I could've got around the penalty of death and could have gotten friends and satisfaction, I should've been content with my days' work and meals with a good appetite.

As long as it reached before I could agree to the rule of our Amish people in my home, I choose to die. I have been under the circumstances five years, with no show of a change, unless agreeing to this order.

If my wife could've contented herself outside of the community of these people and have respected me as a husband by depriving some of those people, I have an idea this crime could've been saved. But these relatives kept her from doing so and forced their religion.

However so that she should esteem it more than me. It is a hard matter to express all their doctrine and rule. They keep their children ignorant of things of this world but not letting them have music or enjoyment as many wished to have. They raise them ignorantly, partly, and after they become older, they are not fit for law and rule of this world. I beg to say to the people of this world to destroy and clean the face of the earth of all such Amish ministers who inter-fere between man and wife.

During the reading of the letters, Moser hung his head and covered his face with his hands.

Mr. Palmer said that they were in his room about fifteen minutes before he took Moser into police custody. He described the clothes that Moser had on when he arrested him as a light-weight suit, white shirt and soft hat. When he searched him, he found .32 caliber shells in this pocket, a pair of spectacles, three or four dollars, and a letter in his coat pocket. Moser was then taken to the city hall about two miles away. Very little conversa-tion was had with him.

On cross-examination, Mr. Green endeavored to bring out the fact that Moser had the appearance of a person mentally dis-ordered, and after the most strenuous objections on the part of the state council, the witness was permitted to describe Moser's appearance and the impression made upon him. He said that Moser acted peculiar, odd, different from other folks, that he did not converse intelligently but replied to questions in monosylla-bles and sat staring without speaking. In short, he appeared to be irrational. He was dripping wet when he accosted the officer, and his head was bleeding from a glancing revolver wound to the temple. He told the officer that he did not wish to die in the community where the Amish church was. He told of going to the Jordan River to kill himself and of his futile attempt at suicide, but the story was hardly credited by Palmer, who seemed to have believed the man to be demented.

Court was adjourned until 1:30 p.m.

When court convened for the afternoon session, Mr. Palmer was cross-examined. He said that on the morning of May 19, Moser was found with blood flowing from a wound on his head. Moser looked worn out and did not carry on any conversation, except in monosyllables. He talked about Witzig. He testified that at times, Moser had seemed irrational and not right in his talk— he had never seen a drunken man act like him. Moser told him that he went to Utah to kill himself because he did not care to die in the Amish community.

Sheriff John D. Mount, Who May Hang Moser.

John D. Mount, sheriff of Tazewell County, was the next witness. He testified that he first saw the defendant in Salt Lake City at the office of the chief of police on May 23. He had very little conversation with him. Mr. Green objected, and the objection was overruled. Mr. Mount said that he asked Mr. Moser if he knew him, and the defendant replied that he did not. He asked if Moser wanted to go back to Pekin, to which he said, "I will go if you want me to." He went on with the details of Moser's arrest and his return to Pekin. Mr. Green asked the sheriff if he advised the defendant that he was not required to talk or to tell him anything at all. Mr.

Mount thought he told Moser that whatever statements he made would not have to go into court.

He told of how they rode in the smoking compartment during the day and the sleeper at night because Moser wished to be out of sight of the women and children. He asked the sheriff if there were any hard feelings against him. The sheriff told him that if the people could get hold of him, they would hang him. He told Moser that he would take care of him. On cross-examination, he testified that Moser had told him more than once that the New Amish Church was responsible for his crime, that he was banished from the church by Reverend Witzig—his offense being the taking of his crying child on his lap during church services.

On the second day, Moser spoke with some freedom to the sheriff, who asked him why he had done this. He said he could not live with his wife any longer and could not live without her. Moser said the trouble all came out of the church and that he went West to get rid of them. His wife left him and came back. His wife thought more of the church than she did of him. He had made up his mind to kill himself at home, then thought it would be better to get as far away as he could and get away from all. He went to Salt Lake City, Utah. He recognized the spectacles that he found in satchel. Sam had purchased the spectacles in Kansas City. Moser informed him of the road that he had taken on this trip West: Tremont to Bloomington to Kansas City, Colorado Springs, and then Salt Lake City. He told Sheriff Mount that he was sorry for the trouble of it.

Under cross-examination, Mount said that Moser had related to him that all his trouble was due to the Amish church. Reverend Witzig was to blame. He was put out of the church because he held his child on his lap. The preacher told him that he was making an idol of it. Sam was told that the devil was in him. Rudolph Witzig wanted Sam to apologize to him, but he would not. His own mother would not shake hands with him. His own father would not eat with him. Amish people who came there would not eat at the table with him. The Amish would not assist or help him. Neighbors would not help him because he was a sinner.

Attorney Green asked a witness if he knew Benedict Moser, the father of Sam. The witness made a negative reply. Mr. Green arose and said, "I mean that man over there in the corner." To the surprise of everyone, Benedict Moser arose from the corner in which he was sitting so that everyone could see him.

Mr. Green asked if Moser had spoken of his brother Daniel, who Moser said was driven to insanity by the Amish church. Sheriff Mount replied that Sam had told him that Daniel had been confined in an asylum for eight months. He had been thrown out of the church because he wore a soft hat with a crease in the center. Moser also told him that he had tried to commit suicide far away from home at Salt Lake City because he didn't want to be buried near the Amish. Questioned as to the apparent mental condition of the defendant, Mr. Mount testified that he seemed to be in distress and have a heavy weight on his brain. He was acting in a peculiar manner and did not talk unless questioned.

Jacob Rapp was next called to the stand. He testified that he had resided in Pekin for forty years and was the police magistrate. He knew Samuel Moser and spoke to him in German when he was brought before him as a justice of the peace. He bound him over to the grand jury without bail. He was asked to testify to a conversation with Moser he'd had at the time of the preliminary hearing. Because this conversation was held while Rapp was acting as police magistrate, it was deemed inappropriate, and Rapp was excused.

Timothy O. Hohulin said that he was the brother of Hanna Moser. He stated that he was thirty-one years old and resided in Deerfield. He was a member of the New Amish Church. He testified that he went to the house after the murders and saw his sister and nephews dead there. Later, he took the initiative to complete the funeral arrangements.

Up to this time, the testimony of the witnesses had been very favorable to the theory of the defense. Under the skillful cross-examination of Mr. Green, the state witnesses had contributed much testimony calculated to impress the jury. Mr. Green alluded to the defendant as "the poor boy," whose ignorance of the law and simplicity of mind had been taken advantage of by officers and reporters to gain from him the story of the crime. His father, although wealthy, refused to send any assistance. His mother would not shake hands with her boy and had told his children that they must not be like their father but like their mother. In all the community where he had been born and raised, there was not a friendly voice—this had made an impression on jurors and spectators.

With the appearance on the stand of Edward Rollins, city editor of the *Pekin Times*, the tide turned. Mr. Rollins, who had been connected with the Pekin paper for six years, had a long interview with Moser on the twenty-sixth day of May—the day that Sheriff Mount returned from Utah with Moser. He saw him at the jail, and after a little preliminary conversation, the prisoner began to tell of having trouble in the church up at Gridley. The important fact was that Moser told him he left the church five years ago because he could not agree with the preacher and that he had made up his mind that if his wife would not leave the church and go to a new home with him, he would kill the entire family and himself.

He did not think he had been treated right. He told about going to Minnesota and his efforts to get his wife to join him there. He said he waited for her until he got angry. He came back here to bring her. He had concluded if she would not come, he would kill her and the family and himself. She was lonely in that barren country and begged him to return to Illinois, believing they would have no more trouble, and he finally concluded to do so. The wife continued to go to church, but he did not want anything to do with those people. He did not like them. His brother Noah Moser took her and the children to church each Sunday. He got to thinking it over on that Sunday and saw that his wife did not want to quit the church, and he decided to kill the whole family. After their return from church, he and his wife, as Moser expressed it, "did not talk much." She changed her clothes and the children's and began to get supper.

The jury learned forward in their chairs in close attention. Stripped of sentiment, the bare recital of the brutal murder of the children went on. By the time he had concluded, the change of feeling was evident. Mr. Rollins, after relating Moser's story of his flight from Tremont to Bloomington and from Bloomington to Kansas City and from Kansas City to Colorado Springs and from there to Salt Lake City, stated that he asked Moser if he would make a defense, and the first time he replied that he did not know, that he supposed people thought he deserved the rope and that was what he would get. "I asked him again before I left," said Mr. Rollins, "if he would make a defense, and he said he would like to, that if the people knew about it, they would not hang him." He was the strongest witness the state had thus far presented.

On cross-examination, Mr. Rollins said he understood Moser, that the conversation with Reverend Witzig relative to the child had taken place during the noon hour at service. They could not agree, and Moser went out. He said he was not permitted to eat with them nor they at his house.

Howard M. Fuller was the city editor of the *Peoria Transcript-Herald*. He testified that he had met Sheriff Mount and Sam Moser at the B & W Depot on May 26 of 1900. He then interviewed Moser when he was locked in the Tazewell County jail. He stated that there was no one there to advise Moser of the nature of his visit nor that he was required to talk. Mr. Fuller said he could not state what the defendant's mental condition was. He manifested no fear but said he was so weak and worn out that he wished to rest for a couple of hours, which he did. In the interview that followed, Moser told Mr. Fuller that his brother came to his house that Sunday morning and took his wife and children to church and that he remained at home; that upon their return, she commenced to prepare the evening meal and that he followed her to the cellar and there shot her. Asked if she made any resistance, he said she knew nothing about it. He detailed the murder of the children to Mr. Fuller and described his flight and subsequent attempted suicide. Said he was sorry that he had not killed himself. Asked if he would retain a lawyer, he said he had no money, adding, "Let the law take its course."

Under cross-examination, the witness stated that Moser did not speak of any family trouble before the murders, except the separation caused by the church. With the conclusion of this testimony, the court adjourned until Thursday.

SAM MOSER.

When court opened on Thursday, February 21, every available space was filled and a couple of hundred people turned away. The interest in the developments of the Moser trial continued unabated, with the courtroom being filled to an uncomfortable degree at each session. Hundreds of farmers came to the city hoping to hear the trial but were greatly disappointed in not being admitted. One man drove ten miles to attend and then could not gain entrance.

A newspaper feature mentioned:

> The courthouse of this county is entirely too small. It was never more evident than at present. This county is one of the richest in the state—and deserves a better courthouse than the present one. The Moser case will cost this county several thousand dollars, and for this reason, we will have to be satisfied with the present structure for many years to come.

Most of the witnesses spoke in low tones, requiring some encouragement to make themselves distinct to counsel sitting only a few feet away. Much of what passed between counsel and court was lost on those in the back of the room. But this did not prevent a crush for standing room, the stairway leading up to the door of the courtroom being thronged all the time with people eagerly waiting on an opportunity to crowd in. At one point, the noise in the hall became so annoying that the sheriff was requested to clear the stairway, which was done. Many ladies attended, particularly in the afternoon, sitting patiently through the somewhat tedious proceedings, waiting for the sensations that did not develop.

Sam sat in his usual position by the iron post, behind his attorneys, but they did not converse in the courtroom. Moser seemed to be aware that all eyes were on him and tried to compose himself. He often failed utterly to disguise the suffering that he was enduring. The opinion was expressed on all sides that he would break down before the close of the trial. He was said to look very downhearted and had not been shaved in a week.

Edward Rollins of the *Pekin Times*, whose testimony the previous day had told so strongly against the prisoner, was recalled at the opening of court this morning for the defense. He was asked if it was not true that his testimony of the day before had been prepared and printed in his paper before he went on the stand, the paper containing the report of his evidence being for sale on the streets before he had testified. The question was objected to as improper cross-examination and the objection sustained. Mr. Rollins was dismissed.

Thomas H. Jarvis, passenger conductor on the Big Four railroad, was next called to the stand. He said he was a conductor on passenger trains between Peoria and Indianapolis. On Sunday night, May 13, his train arrived at Tremont at 8:13 p.m. It was then dark. He remembered seeing Moser on the train and that Moser paid cash fare from Tremont to the C & A junction at Bloomington. Moser inquired of the conductor when he could get a train for Kansas City. He seemed nervous and spoke to the conductor twice about the train, which he was told he could catch at the C & A junction at 10:05 p.m. The witness did not know how Moser boarded the train at Tremont but knew it was at the platform. Moser got off the train at Bloomington.

When cross-examined by Mr. Green, the witness could not remember that any other passenger paid cash fare. He could not tell how Moser was dressed, but on redirect, he said that his attention was attracted by Moser's apparent nervousness.

A ripple of excitement stirred the courtroom when Benedict Moser, the father of the defendant, took the stand, though his son did not so much as look up. After bringing out the relationship, the letter to the postmaster of New York, purported to have been written by the defendant and mailed at Tremont, was shown to the witness. He was asked if it was his son's handwriting. With some hesitation, he stated that it appeared to be. After the usual objection by opposing counsel, the letter, labeled exhibit A, was admitted as evidence. The envelope was not insufficiently identified and was excluded.

When he was turned over to Mr. Green for the defense, the latter subjected him to a severe cross-examination, but all the questions were objected to and the objections sustained by the court. Mr. Moser said that he had lived around Morton for forty years. Then Mr. Green rose to his feet and in full tones asked, "Are you the father of the defendant in this case?"

The answer came: "I am."

"Have you not ill feeling and animus against him?"

This was objected to and sustained.

Mr. Green continued, "Is it not true that by reason of the fact that you belong to the New Amish Church and by reason of the fact that you believe he is a sinner, have you not got ill feeling against him to such an extent that you refuse to lend him aid and assistance that a father would naturally lend a son?"

The question was objected to, and the objection sustained.

"Is it not true, as a matter of fact, Mr. Moser, that you are testifying in this case against your own son by reason of ill feeling and that you have refused to come to my office and talk to me after making an engagement to do so?"

State objected and was sustained.

"Are you a member of the New Amish Church?"

State objected to this as was not proper cross-examination and was sustained.

"And you never became a citizen of this country, did you, until after the law was enacted, prohibiting an alien from holding land here?"

State objected to and was sustained.

"Is it not further true that you will not permit a child to attend a school where the American flag is flying over the building?"

State objected and was sustained.

"Is it not further true that by reason of your being a member of the New Amish Church, you won't go to the aid or assistance of your country when it is at war?

"Is it not a fact that because you belong to that church, you are not permitted to put your hand on your own son?"

State objected.

"Is it not true that you do not dare to sit down and break bread with your son at your own house? You would not assist him in any work or hauling, even in thrashing time. The Amish church forbade you to so help him, didn't they?"

State objected and was sustained.

"Is it not further true that, for five years, you have treated him as an outcast and refused to go to his house and eat a meal there?"

State objected and was sustained.

"Is it not true that your feeling is so strong that you cannot accept anything from his hand? That he could not be buried in the New Amish Churchyard by reason of the fact that you think he is possessed of devils?"

State objected to and was sustained.

"Are you or are you not the Benedict Moser whose name appears on the indictment of your own son?"

Objection sustained.

"That is all," said Mr. Green.

Though Mr. Moser answered none of the questions, they had the desired effect on the jury. Benedict Moser left the courtroom immediately upon leaving the witness chair. Throughout the testimony of his father and that of his brother Noah, Sam did not look at them. Tears constantly filled his eyes.

Noah Moser then took the stand. He stated that he was living about four miles northeast of Tremont. He went to his brother's place on Sunday, May 13, at about eight o'clock in the morning for the purpose of taking the family to church. Sam was in the kitchen, sitting in a rocking chair in the center of the room. Noah drove Mrs. Moser, the three children, his wife and their two children, and the hired girl to church in Morton. They returned about four o'clock. When he returned, Sam was sitting in a chair in the south bedroom. Noah did not leave his wagon but "unloaded" Mrs. Moser and the children at the gate.

Two days later, on Tuesday morning, he went to get some straw. As he was leaving, Mr. and Mrs. Hohulin came. He asked them if they knew where Sam and his wife had gone. They did not know. Noah knocked at the door and tried to look in the window, but could not as the curtains were down. He opened the southeast window of the kitchen and looked in. He did not enter the room but climbed up into the windowsill and looked in and saw a red streak on the floor. He then stepped back into the yard and took Mr. and Mrs. Hohulin to Mr. Henry Hoffman's. After returning to the house with Hoffman, they pried open the cellar window, and both looked in, but could not see anything as it was dark.

Mr. Green asked why he did not take Sam Moser to church and continued persistently, "The reason you did not take Sam Moser to church was that he could not sit down and eat with the rest of the members of that congregation, was it not? Is it not true that you treated him as an outcast? Is it not true that, by reason of your religious beliefs, by reason of being a member of the New Amish Church, you are precluded from having dealing with your own brother? Is not that kind and character of feeling generated in your mind by reason of the doctrine and discipline of the church? Is it not true that you are not even permitted to sell your brother even a sheaf of oats by reason of the doctrine and discipline of your church, that he cannot buy a pint of milk off you by reason of the doctrine and discipline of the church, by reason of the fact that in the eye of the church, he has devils in him? Is it not further true that the same feeling that is engendered in your mind against your own brother is in the mind of your father and your mother, and none of you dared to have any dealings with him, but it was your duty to shun him, and you did shun him and avoid him in obedience to the mandates of the church?

"Is it not true that by the teachings and doctrines of the church, you are not permitted to take the stand in his behalf? Does not your church tell you that it would be a sin in the sight of God if you should take that witness stand to testify for your brother Sam? Is it not true that by reason of the persecution of this church that he was driven crazy? Is it not further true that by reason of the persecution by that church of your brother Daniel that he was driven insane, that by reason of the doctrines of that church your brother John was driven insane and jumped into a well? Do you not feel ill will against him because he had an organ and had his children taught to play? Is a parent precluded from loving his children? Is a parent precluded from having his children taught music?"

In this manner, Mr. Green contrived to get before the jury the facts he wished to impress on their minds, although they were bitterly opposed by the counsel for the state. Every question relating to the Amish church, as well as those intending to show the mental disorder of the defendant, was objected to. The objection was sustained and exception taken by Mr. Green, who then proceeded with his next question as calmly as if he had been answered in full to his satisfaction.

Mrs. Julia Stoller then took the stand. She was the sister of Hanna Hohulin Moser. She stated her sister's age and the names and ages of the children. She said that she'd last seen her at the Amish church on Sunday, May 13. The next time the witness saw her and the boys, they were dead at their home. She was asked to describe what she saw when she reached the house on the afternoon of May 15, and she did so with broken voice and tearful eyes. Sam was touched by her emotion, and he sat quivering in his chair, his eyes covered with his hands while tears rolled down his cheeks.

On cross-examination, it was stated that Moser loved his children and played with them. Moser had, on one occasion, ordered Mr. Stoller out of the house. She soon gave way to tears again. Not wanting to risk further sympathy from the jury, Attorney Green dismissed her without further cross-examination.

But for the prosecution, this was a powerful moment. The jury's sympathy was exactly what they wanted. And so, at 10:30 a.m., Mr. Cunningham announced, "The people rest their case." The sudden conclusion was clearly a surprise to Mr. Green.

Witnesses for the defense were called, but Attorney Green stated that he had informed them not to appear until Friday morning as he thought this day would be taken up by the prosecution. He wished to have court adjourned until then. Judge Puterbaugh said that the case should not be delayed as a few of the witnesses were here and adjourned court until one o'clock that afternoon.

Sam had to be assisted to the jail by two deputies. He was growing weaker and weaker. The trial was taking its toll.

Chapter 11
A Juror Takes Sick

Sickness and trouble and worry and
love, these things will mess with
you at every level of life.

—Domhnall Gleeson

Friday
February 22,
1901

Friday morning was the eleventh day of the Moser murder trial, and the courthouse was once again full to capacity. Reporters noted that Sam didn't look quite as depressed as usual, perhaps because of all the witnesses to his good reputation the day before. Before the jury was brought in, though, the court bailiff announced that one of the jurors was too ill to take his place in the box. The juror from Hittle Township, Roy Miller, who was only twenty-one years old, had been very sick all night. In fact, he hadn't been feeling well the day before. He didn't want to cause a problem, so he hadn't mentioned it to anyone.

Dr. Warren, the city physician, was called in to check on the juror. After conducting an examination, he stated that Mr. Miller's condition was very serious, perhaps life threatening. He appeared to be very frail, with a heavy cold. The doctor thought that it might be caused by the poorly ventilated and overcrowded condition of the courtroom. His chair in the jury box was in the back row, directly in front of one of the windows that was lowered from the top. The tentative diagnosis was a serious case of the grip with symptoms of pneumonia. It was ordered that the windows be tightly caulked to avoid any further trouble as a result of draughts blowing in on the jurors.

The next morning, Miller was no better, and it was thought that he might have to be out on Monday as well. After a consultation with the lawyers, Judge Puterbaugh adjourned court until one thirty in the afternoon, at which time Miller might be able to resume his place on the jury. This was a disappointment to the large crowd of people, many from all over Tazewell and Peoria Counties, who wanted to hear some of the evidence and see what was going on at the trial.

As Sam sat waiting for the afternoon session, his brother Dan arrived. He shook hands with him earnestly, causing a smile from Sam—the first that had been visible through the trial. Reporters described Dan as a good-looking man, though considerably heavier than his brother. One paper described him as a "sour grape who was expelled from the Amish church for a good reason and comes here to testify against them." Dan sat down beside his brother, and they chatted for a few minutes. As Dan walked back to his seat, it was noted that he stopped to shake hands with a number of Amish in the room.

At one thirty that afternoon, the judge related to the attorneys that the attending physician had informed him that Roy Miller's condition was very grave. The doctor reported his patient's condition unimproved and stated that his life would be endangered if he attempted to take his place in the jury box. He would be unable to continue the trial even the next day. Judge Puterbaugh adjourned court until Monday morning at nine o'clock. All the witnesses were excused until then, and Sam was returned to his cell in the county jail.

At that point, the discussions began in earnest about what would have to be done as a result of the sick juror. In criminal practice at that time, if a juror were to become incapacitated during the progress of the trial, it was necessary to discharge the entire jury and commence again from the beginning. The law was not wholly definite in such cases, and the decision would be left largely to the judgment of the court.

It was hoped that by Monday morning, Miller would have recovered sufficiently to appear, both for his personal well-being and for that of the trial. The already heavy burden of expense to the county was increasing with every day's delay, which was being discussed all over town and in the newspapers.

It was decided that the trial would have to be suspended until Miller had recovered. This would give Attorney Green ample time to get all of his witnesses there. Rudolph Witzig, the Amish preacher of whom so much had been said, was there the previous afternoon and was ready to testify. The Amish were attending court in large numbers and would not be afraid to take the stand since they felt strongly that they were "in the right." Moser took a much-needed rest and was reported to be spending his time reading the Bible. Later that night, it was reported that Miller was doing better and would be ready by Monday.

Roy Miller's wife arrived Saturday morning to help make him comfortable while he recuperated. He was confined to his room in the Tazewell hotel as it was discovered that he had the measles. He ran a very high temperature Saturday night but was better on Sunday. The eleven other jurors were waiting. They were all reportedly in good health and spending their spare time writing letters to their families. The speculation was that if Miller was much better on Monday, they would adjourn for two or three days more and try to finish up as there were not many witnesses remaining. Otherwise, the case would likely fall through to be commenced anew at the next term of court.

State's attorney Cunningham and Jesse Black Jr., who was assisting him, were seen that afternoon by a *Herald-Transcript* representative and stated that they would insist at the coming in of court that the trial go on. They realized fully that it would likely be two weeks before Miller was again able to appear in the jury box, but they would insist on waiting that length of time.

Miller was described as the most expensive sick man that Tazewell County has had on its hands. Each juryman received $2 a day, and their boards cost $1.25 a day. There were three deputies who received the same pay, and then there were the costs of the doctor and the medicine. The case up to this time had cost the county of Tazewell $3,500–$5,000, with the case not half concluded. An abandonment of the trial would probably result in even more expense before another jury was secured. If the case was continued until such time as Mr. Miller was again able to enter the jury box, the expense would amount to only about $40 per day. It was not believed there would be any further trouble as a result of draughts blowing in on the jurors. The other eleven jurymen previously had the measles, and there was no great danger that they would contract the disease. They kept a safe distance from Miller's room and didn't take any risks.

Sam's lawyer, on the other hand, was all in favor of abandoning the case. It was held by Mr. Green that as the length of Miller's illness was uncertain and the visits of his relatives would constitute an irregularity, the jury should be discharged, and the case thrown over to the next term or court, a new jury to be impaneled at that time. He had a conference with the judge and said that he didn't think the juror would be able to sit the case again for sixty days. The disposition of the matter rested solely in the province of the court, and what Judge Puterbaugh would do was unknown. He gave no intimation of what to expect, to Mr. Green's frustration. Others who had questioned him on the subject met with no better success.

One theory was put forth, that if the judge discharged the juror, the state would insist on the remaining eleven being held. They would hold that these were competent to try the cause and would demand their acceptance for the second trial. The selection of a twelfth juror would follow, and the case would have to be commenced again, so far as the opening statements and the evidence were concerned.

J. W. Miller, the father of Roy Miller, was there Sunday to visit his sick son. Attorney Green objected to anyone seeing the sick man until after the trial, so a court bailiff was with them all the time. Miller later told reporters that his son was a married man and lived with him on the farm. He had been a well man and was never seriously ill until the present time, although suffering from catarrh (a disorder of inflammation of the mucous membranes). Mr. Miller said that two weeks before, his son had attended church at Armington. A number of young men who

had had the measles were present, and it was then that he contracted the disease, which did not manifest itself until last week.
The sick man was resting much better that morning and ate a
good meal.

The jurymen remained in the courtroom the greater part of
the day and, from all accounts, had a good time. They amused
themselves Sunday listening to songs and speeches from a
Graphophone, the property of Sheriff Mount. During the trial,
they took long walks every morning and evening, receiving daily
exercise. Reporters noted that some of them had no overcoats
but that they all seemed glad for the fresh air nonetheless. With
all the extra time they now had on their hands, they walked
to the distilleries and the sugarhouse and inspected the places.
Some of "the boys" had never been away from home and now
showed signs of being homesick. They received touching letters
from their families. They stayed at the Hotel Tazewell throughout the trial.

For some of them, it might have been the most fun and
excitement of their lives—eleven men hanging out at a hotel,
enjoying some notoriety, and not having to work or tend their
regular lives for a few weeks. While half the county clamored for
a glimpse of this infamous trial, these men had front-row seats.
For others, it was probably a nightmare of being out of their comfort zone, trapped listening to boring testimony, and not being
able to be home with their families. No doubt many prayers went
up for the decision that came Monday morning.

Meanwhile, the newspapers were going crazy. It seemed
everyone had an opinion, and everyone from the newspaper

editors, to the columnists, to the subscribers were making them known in print.

THE AMISH PEOPLE: HITHERTO UNPUBLISHED FACTS IN REGARD TO THEIR RELIGION— CAUSE OF MOSER'S EXPULSION

Up to the present time, the *Star* has refrained from taking either side in the Moser case, but all the time, we have made constant effort to learn some of the practices, and at last we have been successful and have learned facts concerning the Amish which have not been published. After a careful investigation, we believe that Samuel Moser is a cold-blooded murderer, and after the people know all the facts, they will agree with us. The Amish church, according to the investigation we have made, is not at fault, and the Amish are as pure and deserving a people as live in this country. Attorney Green is doing all within his power to save Moser, and he is doing it because he conscientiously believes that Sam Moser is the victim of religious persecution. Mr. Green has no doubt received letters from Amish people who have in the past been expelled from the church for good cause, and they now see an opportunity to play even. Having received letters of this character, Moser's attorney really believes that the Amish are a worthless sect, as he has stated. No man, unless he believed what he was saying, could have made such an effective speech as did Attorney Green in the beginning of the case. It was logical, forceful, and the flow of oratory carried everyone away. But for all that, Mr. Green is in the wrong concerning the teachings of the Amish church. The correspondent, in the course of the last few days, has interviewed several Amish, and one in particular who was expelled from the church told an interesting story. He said that since the time he was expelled from the church, he has worked among the Amish, and they have never shunned him. His wife is at present a member of the New Amish Church, and he lives with her just the same as if nothing had happened. One would naturally expect a man who was thrown out of the church to denounce its members, but this member said that the Amish expel no one without a just cause and that they are as pure and good a people as live on earth.

If the facts which we have gained are true—and we have every reason to believe that they are—a great injustice has been done these people, and they ought to be put right before the citizens of this country who are reading the accounts of the trial. So far, nothing has been brought out against them in the evidence, but Attorney Green was ingenious enough to ask questions such as, "Isn't it true Sam Moser was said to have devils in him, and he was thrown out of the church because he took his child up on his lap?" All these questions were objected to on the part of the prosecution and the objections sustained, but the impression was left with the jury that the facts as stated by Attorney Green were true, and it had the same effect upon those who listened. In this manner, certain supposed practices were revealed, but who can say that they are true?

If all the people in this country would be as good as the Amish, we would need no laws, and this nation would be as near perfect as it is possible for a country to be on earth. The Amish in their church are a good deal like the Quakers. They believe in equality. Among them one man is the equal of the other. They are against going into court but have all their cases brought up at the church when the members are present, and the complaints are considered in the respective order. It is not the preacher who decides the matter but the church as a whole. The preacher has no more power than a member of the congregation and only acts as a preaching officer. The one principle that underlies everything is simplicity. There is no declaration or elaboration of any kind in the church or the home. They do not want to be worldly and, for this reason, do not use a hearse in which to place their dead but convey the remains to the cemetery in a plain spring wagon. The rules and the regulations of the church are the same as that of any other church organization, only that the preacher is not paid at all and works like the rest of the congregation. Frequently, the church has as many as five preachers at the same time. After a member has belonged to the church for many years, he becomes an elder; and if the Spirit moves him and he has a desire to pray, he announces it and is proclaimed a preacher. The money in the Amish church is not raised by subscription. Whenever repairs are to be made or money expended, a meeting is called and the same laid before the congregation, and each member arises and gives his share toward the amount desired.

If any member should get in debt, he brings the matter before the church, and he will receive assistance, but he must make effort to pay it off; and if he does not, he is expelled from the church. The Amish want no deadbeats among their number.

Nowhere in this country can be found a more virtuous people. What is their crime? Why should the Amish church be put up for trial? The Amish worship God as they see fit, and the constitution gives them that right. Who can look into their kindly faces and say that they are guilty of any deception? Ambition has not mocked their useful toil, but they have been content to live simple lives among themselves, loving their families and worshipping their God. They have been prosperous and law-abiding citizens and, like the Puritans, left their native land and came here to seek a home. In the words of the poet, they are "far from the maddening crowds' ignoble strife, their sober wishes never learned to stray; Along the cool sequestered vale of life, they kept the noiseless tenure of their way."

There is a black sheep in every flock, and Samuel Moser is the one in the Amish flock. The reason that he was thrown out of the Amish church is different from the one which has been reported. It is generally thought that because Moser took his child upon his knee that the Amish said that he had devils in him, and for this reason, he was expelled. According to our investigation, Moser was a very stubborn and hotheaded man and had committed acts contrary to the rules of the church and was warned. One day, while attending church, he picked up his little child and threw it into the air, catching the little girl and playing with her before all the congregation. He was told not to do that, which aroused his ire, and he said what he should not have said and was expelled. He was asked to return to the church, and some of his relatives got down on their knees and implored him to reform before it was too late. But he was like so many who think they know it all and will not give their ear to the voice of reason.

And this is the man who is now asking for mercy. Did he show any mercy when he murdered his wife and innocent children? He has cost the county thousands of dollars and has been instrumental in bringing about a false denunciation of as good a people as live on earth. How easy it would be for these good people to be misjudged as they are too modest to make a defense, and what in future generations would be prejudiced toward them in the manner that the present generation is prejudiced against the great religion that has ever preserved the idea of one God. Moser should be hung four times if such a thing were possible. He took the life of four innocent beings, and there should be an eye for an eye and a tooth for a tooth. Moser had murder in his heart for five years, as was shown by testimony; and if the defendant is not hung, God save the wives from the cowardly hands of brutes like Moser.

* * * * *

A lady subscriber has written us a letter requesting that we stop her paper. She said some very harsh and foolish things, among them being that she would never take a paper that would call Moser a cold-blooded murderer. For anyone to stop a paper is laughable. We prefer sensible subscribers. Many women are sympathetic in nature, but they are not foolish enough to say that Moser should go free. We repeat it. Moser is a cold-blooded murderer and should be hung four times if that were possible.

* * * * *

On the Other Side—

Correspondent Thinks That There
Is a Screw Loose Somewhere

Editor Star: Dear sir—I want to call the attention of your readers to the article entitled "The Amish People," which appeared in Saturday's *Star*, February 23. I presume some generous-hearted, devout Amish with their usual benevolence put his hand down in his jeans in the region of a fat pocketbook and gave our Pekin correspondent some of the "genuine persuader," for we do not think that anything but the glitter of the "almighty dollar" could have persuaded him to take such a bold stand after firmly and emphatically stating in those same columns at the outset that his readers should have an unbiased, nonprejudiced report of the Moser case. I advise him to look up those words in his dictionary. No doubt Mr. Green appreciated the "soft soap on the side" delivered for his benefit, but a man of his ability and discretion would scarcely notice the criticism, so our correspondent should not have marred the harmony and unison of his song by these grace notes.

I quote from his article: "If all the people in this country were as good as the Amish, we would need no laws, and this nation would be as near perfect as it is possible to be on earth." To uphold a sect of people as models for the American nation, who will not become citizens, who are clannish, prejudiced, not neighborly, who screen the crimes of their members till the outer world learns and then throws them out like a viper (good enough to associate with Americans then) that they may appear as godly through their sanctimonious screen, is wholly unpatriotic, ought to be classed with anarchy, and is little short of blasphemy. This nation has progressed in all lines of national progression for a century before Pekin correspondent gave us the Amish for a model and, from present tendencies, can pursue the same progress without his new ideal. Again I quote, "Nowhere in this country can a more virtuous people be found." Indeed! This is rather contradictory as about a week or two ago, this same correspondent chronicled the shameful, disgusting affair (the participants all being Amish) that occurred near Tremont. When the facts became known, the man (who is the acknowledged and confessed seducer of his wife's sister, who lived with them) was "turned out" of the church, and there it ended. That was all! And that's the kind of law that is held up for our nation to copy!

"We would need no laws were we as pure as they!" God pity our country and pity our daughters then!

An Amish preacher that once lived in that same place showed a "virtuous trait" also when, because his horse balked one day, he hitched another horse to a chain, which he secured to the balky horse's tongue and pulled it out by the roots. If I remember rightly, he was not even "turned out of church." Glorious examples, indeed, to hold up for ideal American citizens. I have lived among the Amish for over thirty years and could tell numerous other cases of similar and worse conduct. I am not upholding Moser for his murdering, but I can readily believe he thought his little ones and wife were better off in the future land with His little ones than to be raised up in the way of the Amish church, which had so mistreated their father and where he had repeatedly seen lust and crime. That he is demented, we do not see how any sane person can doubt. We are glad to note that the lady who discontinued her paper because she didn't like the piece referred to has resubscribed, for the *Star* is all right, the best paper in Central Illinois, the paper for the freeman and patriot, and so she must remember that the Pekin correspondent is not the whole thing; he fills only a small corner, but we are sorry that he was so ungallant as to print the gentleman's laudatory letter and omit her scathing one. When he joins the Amish church, we hope he will let us all know so that we can go and see him kiss the brethren. "Did Moser show mercy?" He thought he did in putting his children beyond the reach of his tormentors. We suppose that it is part of the model Amish Christianity that the correspondent advocates when he says "show him no mercy," "hang him four times," "an eye for an eye," etc. That is Old Testament law, but even there it says, "Thou shalt not kill." Turn over a few pages in His word. He spoke, "Love your enemies," "Bless them that despitefully use you," "Forgive as you would be forgiven." Lastly, and most important, "Vengeance is mine, I will repay, saith the Lord."

In conclusion, let me rearrange his closing words by saying, our country would be much safer with Moser running at large that such men as are at large as mentioned in the two preceding instances, who do not kill physical bodies but killed the mortality, virtue, honesty, and all true sentiment that govern them, so I say God save our wives and sisters from the cowardly hands of brutes like these. I have no poetry to quote but have confined myself to prose and facts.

RR

* * * * *

Editor Star: I noticed in last evening's *Star* an article signed "Subscriber," Tremont, Illinois, in which he said that the government ought to keep the Amish out of the country. I'm sure that Subscriber does not know what he is talking about, and all his statements are false. I have worked among Amish farmers and always found them ready to help anyone, using the very best up-to-date machinery. They are the only God-loving people on the face of the earth—honest, sober, economical, and kind. Now, Mr. Subscriber, what more do you want? Remember this: you can see a straw in your neighbor's eye but cannot see the log in your own. Maybe Subscriber's brains are affected with a

peculiar disease known in our business
as Wingbagia Liarum Tiemontir. The
only cure for that is to go West and, for
God's sake, keep your fingers off the
press, or you are liable to get pinched.

Hoping Subscriber will not fail to
read this.

I am yours, come again,
Fluctuat Neg Mergiture,

* * * * *

The Moser Case—Blind Devotion of the Amish to Their Religion

Expert Testimony Introduced Today

If the Amish were greater in number,
history, no doubt, would record them as
a great religious people. It is strange
that no reference books or magazines
dwell on the lives of these peculiar
people. They put the Scriptures above
everything else and are constantly
afraid that they will go to hell if they
do not obey the Bible. The majority of
the Amish are ignorant, and the older
members of the church are content to
remain so; and for this reason, they
often put a wrong construction and
some of the things which they read in
the inspired book and induce a false or
rather incorrect meaning such as was
brought out during the trial that no

one is permitted to shake hands worried at the same table with the person who is been drawn out of the church. It is utterly impossible to convince them that they are wrong. We challenge anyone to point out to us a more peculiar and religious people in this country.

The Bible is first with them, their money next, and their own flesh and blood third. Talk about sending correspondents to Africa and South America for facts concerning strange people—why, we have the most peculiar and devout set of people that are to be found anywhere right here in our very midst. As we stated in article on the homage, we believe that they are a good people and honest in every way, but they have their faults, and we are not a bit backward in pointing them out: one is their blind devotion to their religion.

It is all right to be religious, but who in this civilized world being a father a mother or sister of a man accused of murder would walk by him and look down into his face without shaking his hand or at least speak a word or two with him? It may not seem strange to the Amish, but it certainly does to those who are educated. If the Amish would only expunge certain parts of their religion, what a perfect system it would be. But strange to say, every religion seems to have some objectionable feature in it. One would think that the Amish would become alarmed as we are of the opinion that the religion of the strange people will be but short-lived.

* * * * *

Plea in Moser's Defense:

In Which the Amish Church Will
Be Severely Arraigned

Whether Sam Moser, quadruple murderer, is sent to the gibbet or to the steel-barred cells of the madhouse, a mighty effort to connect the alleged evils of the Amish church in the United States will be made.

This is the ultimatum issued by the friends of Moser on the outside of the church, and if their present determination shows no waning, the fight will be waged to the bitter end, not alone for the purpose of avenging the wrongs that are said to have been done to Moser but for the purpose of correcting the franchise of evils that exists under the tents of the church.

The first point of attack will be the rule that revokes a member's franchise. It will be argued that every freeholder, living under the broad flag of Uncle

Sam, cannot be bound by religious ties that prevent him from exercising the greatest gift of the citizen of a republic: that of voicing his opinion at the polls. In support of this argument, it will be shown that an Amish cannot hold office, cannot express his belief as to the merits of a prospective officeholder, in public or in private, and cannot fight for the flag under whose beneficent influences he is deriving a living and a being.

These rules, it will be charged, are in direct conflict with the Constitution of the United States and that, therefore, their enforcement in Amish colonies denies to the colonists the protection that comes to everybody who abides by and lives up to the amendments and the laws.

The peculiarities of the defense are gradually being evolved. It will be set forth that while Moser may not be insane now, he was temporarily deprived of his mental faculties by the iron-bound rules that prevented him from showing that devotion to his family that his saner instincts and desires might have prompted. Continued enforcement of these rules, it will be claimed, so unbalanced the mind of Moser that—believing at that time, as he did in the Amish precepts, he had forever lost those nearest and dearest to him—it were best to kill them and himself.

The Amish rules say that when a husband and father sins, the sin is visited upon the wife and children. Moser sinned in displaying openly and without restriction affection for the children; therefore, according to the teaching, his wife and children had sinned and were consequently dead to him and the world forever. This fact, added to his expulsion, it will be argued, so preyed upon the man's mind that he decided it would be better for all to be dead. The quadruple murder followed in this alleged line of reasoning and that the murderer failed in his attempts to kill himself will be laid at the door of unsteadiness of hand and mind and not to genuine desire of heart to spare himself.

The rules of the Amish church are severely strict. So severe, in fact, that the defense's claim that they can unsettle the mind of a person of only "reading" intelligence, may not be without foundation. For instance, the education of the children of colonists is restricted to such an extent, and their general knowledge of the world is so limited that the outer world and its customs are as Greek is to the longshoreman.

Two former members of the church voice in the following the virtual keystone of the defense, as showing the punishment meted out to a member who had violated the church rules and which is calculated to unsettle his reasons:

"Neither the voice of nature nor the ties of blood are allowed to plead in their behalf or to procure them the slightest degree of indulgence. In such a case, the exchange of good offices, the sweets of friendly conversation, the natural effusions of tenderness and love, are cruelly suspended, even between parents and children, husbands and wives, and also in all the other endearing relations of human life."

This was speculated to be the main drift of the defense, and its details would be carefully arranged. In explaining the cause of the shooting, a resident of Morton said, "She went to church against his wishes and left him alone with the devil all day."

Court convened at 9:30 a.m. on Monday, and Attorneys Cunningham, Black, and Green held a consultation with the judge regarding what action should be taken. Cunningham and Black asked for an adjournment for several days until Miller would be able to resume his duties as a juror as the expense of securing another jury would be enormous, and all the witnesses would have to come back again to testify. They argued that it would be an imposition on the people of Tazewell County to have the trial thrown over at this time, when, after a reasonable wait, it could be continued with the twelve jurors as originally selected. Everyone knew it would be hard work to obtain another jury in Tazewell County.

Attorney Green wished to have the defendant discharged. He did not believe that Miller will be ready to go on with the case at all in his present condition as he could not stand the strain. He wanted the case postponed until next term and begun all over again. The state resisted, saying that Green was exaggerating the juror's condition, grasping at straws in the hope of saving Moser's life.

Judge Puterbaugh listened to the arguments and the report from the doctor, which seemed to indicate that the juror was possibly not as ill as was first thought. He was doing well and was well cared for by the doctor overseeing his treatment. He had gotten up and was dressed today and walked about his room a bit.

Finally, Puterbaugh rendered his decision. He ruled that court would be adjourned until Miller was able to attend. The case would go on where it was left off. That is, the defense would continue their examination of witnesses. If he was able to go on with the case Thursday, the witnesses would be notified Wednesday. All witnesses were told to come when notified and at once left for their homes.

It was reported that Moser looked quite refreshed that morning and had a week's crop of whiskers on his face. He seemed somewhat encouraged and was more talkative. He had a long talk with his attorney about the decision; after which, he seemed greatly relieved. Sheriff Mount bought him a new shirt and a necktie and collar. Moser put everything on but the necktie. The Amish never wore ties, and probably Moser was not in the habit of having one on. After the ruling of the court, he was taken back to his cell.

During the progress of the trial, Moser received many letters from all over the country. They were mostly in regard to certain parts of the Scriptures which Moser was said to read. One letter, from a preacher in Ohio, explained the lines which it was alleged that Moser put special strain on and told him to pray to God. The letter was such as any preacher would write and was of little interest to the accused as he had received so many of that nature.

Moser had received many letters of sympathy from people outside of Pekin. This was probably due to the fact that a number of reporters who were here from Chicago sent exaggerated accounts to their papers and took the part of Moser. All the letters which he received were first read by the sheriff as he did not wish to give Moser unnecessary pain by leaving him to read a letter of censure.

The adjournment of court gave opportunity for a general discussion among the gathered farmers and neighbors of the defendant on the progress of the trial as far as it had gone and their thoughts about the probable outcome. The defense, so far, had not made much progress, the witnesses with whom Mr. Green wished to lay the foundation for his insanity evidence having left the courtroom on Thursday, believing they would not be needed.

The papers throughout Central Illinois were discussing the case, and nearly all the outside papers were of the opinion that Moser was insane at the time he committed the terrible deed. They were all praising Attorney Green, and he deserved it; but at the same time, they did not overlook the splendid efforts of the prosecution. Most of the papers were against the prosecution, but that was partly because that side was giving nothing for publication for fear of revealing their plans. Mr. Green was very friendly to all the newspapers, regardless of whether they were for or against him.

It remained to be seen how Mr. Green would surmount the difficulties attending his conduct of the defense. The case for the state also was incomplete as much valuable testimony was expected to be given in rebuttal. It was not only difficult to say which side had the best of the legal contest so far, but it was quite out of all human possibility to say what the jury would do, which certainly didn't keep anyone from speculating.

If Moser had pled guilty, an expensive and vexatious matter to all concerned would have been quickly disposed of, and it was thought that he would likely have fared as well. It was hardly credible that Mr. Green would be able to make such a showing of the extenuating circumstances in this case as to liberate the defendant. His insanity, if established, would result in his incarceration at Jacksonville; and in case the jury was not convinced of his irresponsibility at the time the crime was committed, his sentence would likely to be a heavy one.

The opinion as to what would be done with Sam was divided. Some thought the jury would return a verdict of life sentence, but those who had studied the jury closely and have followed the case were of the opinion that the verdict would be death. Little evidence had been introduced so far in favor of Moser while, on the other hand, Attorneys Cunningham and Black had proven beyond the shadow of a doubt that Sam Moser did kill his family. It remained for the defense to show that Sam Moser was insane when he committed the act.

On Tuesday, Benedict Moser came to see his son Sam at the county jail. He did not object to the presence of the *Star* reporter but shed bitter tears at the sight of his son. Sam sat reading a German history of the United States. He put down his book and just looked at his father and two sisters. One of the sisters completely ignored Sam and just looked around in wonder. Apparently, she had never been in such a place before. The other was in tears and looked at her brother with pity plainly depicted on her face.

The father spoke quietly, "Sam, I know you're my son. Mr. Green thinks awful hard of me because I won't help you, but you know, Sam, it is against the Scriptures, and I know you don't want my soul cast into damnation. You know I can't go against the Scriptures, Sam. The crime is terrible, and I think the jury and judge and the court know best what to do. If I could do anything for you, I would, but I can't risk my soul to damnation. You had your troubles in your school days like all boys, but the main trouble was at Gridley [where he quarreled with the minister over bouncing his baby on his knee]. I wish something could be done, but the Holy Scriptures forbid me. Is there anything we can do for you, Sam?"

Sam leaned forward with tears in his eyes.

Then the father said in German, "Sam, you know I am right, don't you? Can I do anything for you?"

Sam replied in German also, "I can't say anything, for the reporters are there."

Even the reporters that felt that Sam should have no mercy and deserved the rope could not help feeling sorry for him. He stared at his father, with tears running down his cheeks. They later wrote that the scene would have touched the hardest heart.

After several minutes, the father drew nearer to the son, said his goodbyes, and left. The cell doors closed, and Sam really began to sob. The reporters wrote of the meeting and explained their reactions:

> Some cannot understand how the father can help from assisting his own son. What sort of heart has he, they say? Is he shut against pity, charity, and parental love? It is difficult to com-

prehend how the father can stand by the side of his son and not be touched by the sad, poignant face of his own flesh and blood. But the father said the Scriptures forbid him, and he is afraid of "damnation." He believes, so he says, that the law is just and should take its course. Can it be possible that it is all acting and that Benedict Moser is really assisting his son?

On Tuesday, February 26, 1901, there was another news story to focus on. The infamous Carrie Nation, famous for attacking alcohol-serving establishments with a hatchet, had come from Kansas for a visit in nearby Peoria. The newspaper report gives an interesting glimpse into the views of religion and morality of the time.

Mrs. Nation Has a Busy Day

Gets Out an Edition of a Local Paper, Lectures, and Visits Saloons and Dives—Makes Profound Impression—Exhorts Women to Use Hatchets, if Denied Votes, and Begs Dancing Girls at Variety Theater to Lead Better Lives

Feb. 26—Carrie Nation has been in Peoria today, and the town has been hers. She has edited a newspaper, made half a dozen speeches, and visited some of the notorious saloons. She has done no smashing. Her work has been with pen, Bible, and words of mouth, but is has been done in the true Carrie Nation style.

She says it is hard work being an editor, and she does not think that was just the work she was chosen by God to do. Yet her edition of the *Peoria Journal* was unique and successful. It was the talk of the town. Carrie Nation's name is on every tongue.

In Peoria, the world's center of distillation, the world's greatest whisky town, the "Kansas Cyclone" has aroused a sentiment never before experienced. At eleven o'clock tonight, this little gray-haired crusader is making her way through alleys and along dark paths, among the saloons and theaters, along the principal streets—everywhere, imploring men to leave their sin and wretchedness to take up the life as taught by the Nazarene.

She is doing this, moreover, in spite of protests of the city's leading temperance workers, who implored her to go to her hotel and rest. Mrs. Nation got up early this morning and was busy with writing all the morning and up to two o'clock this afternoon. She did not go down to the *Journal* office until later in the afternoon, preferring to do her work in the quiet of her room. She allowed no one to see her except W. A. Brubaker, the Prohibition lecturer and former secretary of the Peoria YMCA, who assisted her in getting out the editorial page of the paper.

Later in the afternoon, Mrs. Nation went to the office, chatted with the regular editorial staff, saw the foreman make up some of the pages, watched the presses run, and then returned to the hotel to rest.

Tonight at Rouse's Hall, she addressed several hundred persons and talked earnestly. After denouncing the saloons in her usual style, Mrs. Nation went on to defend the hatchet crusade. "I've worked for years and years without seeing any fruits of my labor, but since I have taken to smashing, the fruits can be seen everywhere. Men and women are being saved from death, and the keepers of hellholes are leaving their damnable business. People talk to me about the legalized saloon. Might as well say legalized hell. Shall we legalize murder? I'll show 'em that a hatchet and a little woman are legalized too. People ask me why I don't attack all the other vices of the world. I can only answer that I am attacking the fountainhead of all. I am killing the hen that lays the egg.

"I am going to stay in Kansas until I get my own house cleaned, and then I will help other people clean their houses. I've got plenty of hatchets and plenty of strength in this good right arm. You men say we women shan't have a vote, but thank God, we've got hatchets, and we will use them. Our hatchets in Kansas have done more than all the men's votes. Arouse yourselves, women. Fight for your homes and your babies. Save them from hell. So many women are mere mannequins on which are hung the fashions.

"Some people think I'm kind of crazy, but they don't know. I have the spirit of God. People said Jesus was crazy and that John the Baptist had devils. They're good enough company for me. A selfish and hypocritical church is meaner than a saloon," cried Mrs. Nation. "Organize and agitate, women. Your salvation and the sanctity of your homes lie in your own hand. If pleading will not save you, try hatchets."

Hundreds of people crowded up around the platform when Mrs. Nation had concluded, all wanting to shake the hand of this woman and get a "home defender" button. Mrs. Nation insisted on going out to visit the "joints" of the town, accompanied by two reporters. At the first place visited, she created much excitement. A reporter introduced Mrs. Nation to the proprietor of the place, and a lively scene followed. The little crusader pleaded with the men at the bar to throw away their drinks and cigars and lead different lives. She threw up her arms in horror at a large painting of women in the nude which hung on the wall.

"Take it down, take it down, or I will smash it! Think of it, men, as the form of your mother. Don't your hearts cry with the shame of it?" Mrs. Nation waved her arms and pleaded. Here an officer, in citizen's clothes, took a hand in the proceedings and talked rather insultingly to the crusader, only to bring down upon him some of the choice terms she recently applied to Governor Stanley.

"Perjurer, liar!" she cried, shaking her fist at the officer, "I'll show you that Carrie Nation is as good as her word." Mr. Weast and the reporters led Mrs. Nation through the hallway into the variety theater attached to the place, and trouble was averted. Here, she spoke for a couple of minutes and then went on to other places.

Several hundred men were in the theater; and a song-and-dance turn, marked by scanty attire, was in progress. Mrs. Nation sat down with Mr. Weast and watched the performers. Then she addressed the crowd from the platform, urging them to give up drink and lead better lives. Kissing the dancing girls goodbye, shaking hands with the men performers, and bestowing a "God bless you" upon them all, she made her way down an alley to the Alcazar saloon, the finest barroom in Peoria.

At the auditorium theater, she spoke to one thousand people. Mrs. Nation retired shortly before midnight. Tomorrow she will visit some of Peoria's great distilleries. When about to make her speech in Weast's place, Mrs. Nation was approached by the manager under whose contract she had spoken at Rouse's Hall and informed her that her contract did not permit her to make any other speech than the one at that hall, and that if she did so, she would not get her money.

"Well, I'll speak to these men if I have to walk back home," said Mrs. Nation, and she spoke to them.

In her salutatory in today's issue of the *Journal*, Ms. Nation related the story of "one precious boy," who was leaving the saloon business on her account and to whom she has promised financial aid. She states, "As God prospers me, it will be my joy to help in any way the poor in spirit, as well as in purse. Love is the one thing that gives us real happiness, and I am glad to be able to love the worst of men so much that I will dare to smash the thing that injures them. And the more I love them, the more I smash; and the more I smash, the more I love. And the more I love and smash, the more the people love me. Loving and smashing are two good yoke-fellows and should never be separated. And if any poor effort of mine shall hasten the day when all men shall be free from the slavery of drink, I count it a great privilege to give it—no matter what the cost."

On Wednesday, it was announced that the Moser trial would resume the next morning, Thursday, at nine o'clock. Juror Miller had almost entirely recovered and would be in the courtroom with the rest of the jurors. The measles was said to have entirely left him, and he'd been able to walk about the hotel. His recovery had been remarkably rapid, but this was said to be due in large measure to the constant attendance and great care that he had received. He had expressed himself to the bailiff and physician as feeling excellent and ready to resume the trial, which would be concluded in as short a manner as possible.

All the witnesses were notified and would be there when needed. It was expected that the same great crowds that have thronged the courtroom on previous days would be present at both sessions the next day.

Among them would be the mother of the accused. Her testimony would be very important, if it was allowed. An effort would probably be made to prove that her son had been men-tally weak since a boy. It was said that Mrs. Moser was a very nervous woman and might break down on the stand. Dan Moser, a brother of Sam, would also be among those called to testify. It seemed that his own story was one of a man pushed to the brink of insanity by church rules and regulations.

Chapter 12
The Defense

The justifications of men who
kill should always be heard with
skepticism, said the monster.

—Patrick Ness, *A
Monster Calls*

1901

When court convened at one o'clock, the first witness called for the defense was Christian Zehr Jr., who resided near Deer Creek. He formerly lived in Woodford County and had been acquainted with Sam Moser for four years. He knew his reputation as a law-abiding citizen to be good. He said that he did not believe him a man likely to commit murder while in his right mind. The witness was acquainted with Moser's family, having lived within three miles of them for a number of years. He had formerly belonged to the Amish church but was not currently a member.

Here followed a tilt between the attorneys on the introduction of testimony of several years ago, also in regard to insanity. Mr. Green asked that the jury be dismissed from the room during the argument of the attorneys as to the admission of this evidence, which was done.

Mr. Green stated that he wished to show the relation existing between Moser and his wife, as to whether they were friendly or otherwise, and how he treated his children. He also stated that he wished to go back to the birth of this man and show by physicians' testimony the mental condition of the brain of this man at the time of his birth and that he still had it.

Mr. Black objected on the grounds that if counsel wished to show insanity on the part of the defendant, he must show it at the time of the commission of the crime. As to the relations between the defendant and his wife, and the matter relating to the New Amish Church, he must show that the insanity was the result of this cause. He must remove by good evidence the presumption of sanity at the time the crime was committed. Proof of hereditary insanity can only be by cumulative evidence, which is not permissible unless proof of insanity at the time the crime was committed has been given. Mr. Black quoted several decisions in similar cases to prove his point.

The court sustained the defense, ruling that evidence of the nature at this time was not relevant if meant to show insanity. If, however, it was for the purpose of showing family relations between defendant and family, it was relevant. The jury was then recalled, and the testimony proceeded.

Mr. Zehr said that he had worked for Moser, shucking corn for two weeks in Woodford County about two years before. He slept and ate in the Moser house. While working for Moser, he observed that their family relations were friendly. Moser was always kind to his wife. He saw Moser helping his wife do the washing as she was not strong enough to do that work. He helped Hanna around the house when she needed it. He was kind and loving to the children; held them and kissed them. There was a New Amish Church three miles from their house. Mr. Green asked the witness as to the possession of an organ by the defendant, but the question was ruled out as immaterial.

On cross-examination by Mr. Black, the witness said he never heard any objection made to Moser's affection for his children. Moser helped to get breakfast. Witness said that he had heard about Moser's driving the Stoller family out of his house with a stick of wood. On redirect, Mr. Green asked the witness if the Stollers had not been ordered out of the house several times by Moser and if Mr. Stoller had not said he would stay as long as he pleased. This evidence was not admitted by the court.

Dr. J. A. Taylor, MD, was called to the stand and testified that he resided in Gridley and had practiced medicine there for twenty-five years. He confirmed that he knew Samuel Moser and Rudolph Witzig, the New Amish preacher. He was then asked about attending the child of Witzig, who was said to have been injured in the hayfield. Objections to the questions were sustained, but Mr. Green persisted in his questions, and the story was told. There was an accident involving Witzig's daughter, who was injured while at work in the field for her father. A runaway team of horses caused the child to be thrown from a hay rake against a barbed-wire fence, her throat being frightfully lacerated and one side of her face torn off, in which condition she remained without medical attendance until the protest of the neighbors caused the doctor to be sent for. "The child died from the effects of the injuries sustained." The state objected to this. Court held that testimony was not relevant, and the witness was excused.

Peter Rinkenberger said that he lived in Gridley and was a farmer, owning his own land. He answered that he was a citizen of this country, was married, and had five children. He testified that Moser was a law-abiding citizen and said that he did not think that Moser would commit murder. Witness was a former member of the New Amish Church but withdrew fourteen years ago. He had assisted Moser in threshing for part of three days during the busy season. He took his meals at Moser's house at that time. He said that Moser treated his wife and children kindly. He was also acquainted with Reverend Witzig. Mr. Green asked him about the Amish doctrine and whether or not Amish children were permitted to attend a school over which floated the American flag. This was objected to, and the court sustained the objection.

Mr. Rinkenberger was asked if the reason he'd left the Apostolic Christian Church was because they had encouraged his wife to divorce him. The question was ruled out. "In regards to the rules and discipline of the New Amish Church, you have spoken of and its teachings. Can you state what that church teaches as to the treatment of sinners who have been put out of that church as to eating and drinking with them? Does that include the father and mother of a member of the church who has been put out for having any dealings with the son? When you were a member of the church, did you have the privilege of voting? While you were a member, did you have the right under the rules, discipline, and regulations of that church to hold office? Has a member of the New Amish Church a right to send his children to a school which permits the American flag to float over the schoolhouse? Has a member of this church a right to volunteer as a soldier in the event of this country being at war?"

These and a number of similar questions were objected to and the objections sustained. Mr. Rinkenberger was handed a paper by Mr. Green and asked to state whether he had received that paper from the New Amish Church of which he was a member. The witness identified the letter and said he received it some years ago. "Did you receive it from the church I have been asking you about?" asked Mr. Green. Objection was made and sustained.

It was expected that Mr. Rinkenberger would expose the behind the scenes of the Amish church: their laws, whether they could vote, hold office, or assist an ousted member of the church. He was not allowed to testify to such questions, objections having been made by the prosecution and sustained by the court. But his story came out in the newspaper the next day.

Scores of Homes Broken Up by the New Amish Church

Facts and data will be introduced by the defense in the trial of Sam Moser, charged with a quadruple murder, to prove that the New Amish Church has broken up scores of homes in Tazewell and McLean Counties.

This morning, one of the strongest witnesses for the defense came to Pekin and told a story of unrelenting and terrible prosecution on the part of the Amishites. His statement seems to bear out the claims of Moser that he was driven to commit murder by the Amish religion. Peter Rinkenberger, living near Gridley, McLean County, is the witness by whom Attorney Green proposes to prove to the jury that Moser was driven insane by the strange religious sect. Rinkenberger is a well-to-do farmer, about fifty-five years old, and tells his story in a straightforward manner.

"My home has been broken, my life made a hell, and the love of my wife taken away from me by the New Amish Church," he said. "I have been a member of the church since I was a boy. I was taught to believe in the rules of the church and accept without question the word of our preacher. I was well satisfied without voting or associating with the outside world until over a year ago.

"I had married, and I don't believe a happier man or woman could be found in all this world. I made money, and I had a certain influence among the members of the church and the preachers, owing to this fact. The preachers had never entered my home as they did and do with other members of the church.

"One day they came, or rather, one of the preachers did. I was away, or a murder would have been done that day. Mind, a member of the church must never question what a preacher may do. I was not the narrow-minded, crawling dog like other Amishites. I came out before the world and denounced the preacher for his attempting to enter my home. I said I would resent any such actions. That was a bombshell in our circles. I had sinned. I was not of God. I was dead in the New Amish Church.

"My wife was bound with fetters of steel in that church. She sided with me, but she dared not give up the church. She could not see beyond the limited world of the life she had always lived. I tried to explain. I pleaded with her in our love, but no, the poor woman could not give up the church, for she feared the hereafter.

"Then came the revenge of the New Amish. I could not trade with my neighbors. I could not talk with them. I was cut off from them. I have lived in and around McLean all my life. I have been a farmer, and I am too old to go out into the world and make a new home. There is nothing for me to do but live on and on, only hoping and praying that my wife will see as she should."

This is a partial statement given by Rinkenberger, and before the famous trial is at an end, others will be put on the stand to tell how their homes were broken up by the New Amish Church.

Joseph Rinehart testified that he was sixty-one years old and a first cousin of Benedict Moser. A native of Alsace, France, he had come to this country when he was seventeen years old. His mother and Benedict Moser's mother were sisters. He was asked to state whether or not there was insanity in that family and, after objection, was permitted to do so. He said that Benedict Moser's mother had a brother who was insane. Andrew (possibly, Adam) Roth was crazy in the old country. He saw a carriage with lighted candles coming down the road and thought an enemy was coming. Took a club and smashed both lanterns. He was later found in a creek, nearly dead and without clothing. He was locked in the cellar to prevent him from doing mischief and later died in an insane asylum.

He testified that he also knew Daniel Moser, brother of Sam. He'd known him well since boyhood but did not know he was insane. He said the reputation of Sam Moser was good and that he was not a man likely to commit a murder. But on cross-examination, Rinehart said he had not seen Moser from the time Moser was seventeen years old until he came to Tremont last spring.

A number of character witnesses from Gridley were placed on the stand and testified that Moser's general reputation was good while he was there:

- M. C. Drum, resided at Gridley for the last thirty-five years and was a farmer and painter. Knew Sam Moser while there about a year ago (five years ago), had dealings with him. Moser had a good reputation, not likely to commit murder.

- G. A. Frank(s), lived at Gridley, had resided there for twenty-six years. The general reputation of Sam Moser was good while there. Knew Moser very well, reputation was good in community in which he lived, did not think Moser likely to commit murder.

- John Neuhauser, resident of Gridley for the last thirty years. Knew Sam; his general reputation was good.

- Daniel Augspurger, Gridley, dealer in general merchandise. Sam's general reputation was good. Did not think that Moser was likely to commit murder.

- John Surch, resident of Gridley for twenty years, knew Samuel Moser; his general reputation good.

- Samuel Kurth, Gridley farmer, cousin. Moser's general reputation was good as far as he knew. Treated his wife all right, never saw Moser kiss his children but knew he loved them. Was a member of New Amish Church, was sent by the Amish church with a notice to Moser to appear at church and confess his sin.

At this point, an objection was made, and the jury again retired from the room. Mr. Green stated what he wished to show by this evidence. The court decided that the testimony was not competent at this time, and the witness was dismissed.

The next witness, Jacob Yergler, lived close to the church at Gridley and said that he knew Moser. Moser was good to his family; his wife was good to him. He did not eat with Moser because he was expelled from the Amish church. Sam was good to his family, but he was a bad boy.

He incidentally remarked, "He did not come much to my house."

"Why did he not?" asked Mr. Green.

"Probably," was the characteristically Amish reply, "because if he had acted like a good child, he would not be in the case he is now."

Otto V. Siebenhal resided at Peoria and was formerly a member of the New Amish Church. Mr. Green asked questions touching on the peculiarities of the Amish sect and his reasons for leaving it. Objections were made to him testifying about the church, which were sustained. He did not know Sam Moser.

Many church members would not be silenced, however. They'd looked forward to their day in court, and once they were denied this, they turned to the newspaper reporters who swarmed the courthouse. The next day, an article ran in the Peoria newspaper entitled "Five Funny Mustaches."

> According to statements made by O. V. Siebenthal, who reportedly lived on the corner of Wayne and Washington Streets, five distinguished elders of the Amish church had been expected to visit the Central Illinois churches almost three months prior. They were traveling from the old country and held a rank similar to that of bishops. They were to be distributed among those states in which the Amish church is particularly strong and growing stronger.
>
> Announcements had been made of their coming, and their arrival was anticipated with a calm and holy joy. As the church in Central Illinois was the most flourishing, as it is also among the oldest of that sect in the United States, they were to make it their first visit; and at a conference to be held here, the matter of distribution was to be arranged.

The five bishops arrived, and as soon as their faces were seen by the faithful, there was trouble at once.

"The poet hath said that when Satan entered the Garden of Eden, a shiver of horror shook all its roses. It was the same here. A shiver of horror shook all the Amish, or at least all the strictly orthodox, for each of their bishops wore a mustache. Had each bishop been another Moser, with a smoking revolver in his hand and four gory corpses at his feet, he could not have created a greater feeling of revulsion. The laws of the Amish are as exacting as those of Leviticus to the Orthodox Jew. One of them declares that no adult male member of the church shall wear hair on his upper lip. He may wear a beard like that of a patriarch, clear up to the back of his ears or sweeping down to his waistband, but his upper lip must be clean-shaven.

These good brethren had come from a part of Europe in which this law of the church had become a dead letter, or for some special purpose, had been revoked, and so no part of their faces had ever known a razor."

The weary travelers were not officially received by the local church officers, and the church members were instructed to have nothing to do with the mustached men until their case had been passed upon by a church council called to be held at Morton. In the meantime, they were strangers in a strange land and did not know its language. Several members were mortified at how these men were treated and couldn't bear to see them left to fend for themselves so far from their homes. Many of the local church members were recent immigrants themselves and knew well the difficulties of finding lodging and provisions when unfamiliar with the language and terrain. They disobeyed the instructions of their leaders and took in the visiting elders, keeping them in their homes, feeding them, and making them comfortable.

There followed a stormy session at which the five bishops from Europe were called upon to confess that they had violated a solemn canon of the church. They were instructed to show penitence by denuding themselves of their offending mustaches. The bishops made a stout defense, but it was said that they might just as well have talked to stone walls. The Amish of Peoria and Tazewell Counties would have none of the unshaven ministering among them, and finding that they had come among a fanatical and unreasoning people, the five bishops girded up their loins and went right back to the old country, taking their mustaches with them.

Having gotten rid of the unshaven visitors, the officers of the church turned their attention to those who had provided for them, pending the Morton conference. All who had talked with them, fed them, and lodged them were called upon to confess their sin before the congregation.

The accused declared that they had done nothing more than their solemn duty, as defined by the Scriptures. They found the visiting missionaries hungry, and they fed them. They had no place to lay their heads, and they took them in and ministered unto them. They refused to apologize for what they'd done. Not one responded as they were directed, and their consequences were announced.

They would still be allowed to attend the religious services held in the sanctuary on Green Street, but they were denied the communion and the holy kiss. In the course of their devotional exercises, the members of the congregation salute one another with a chaste kiss, and this ceremony is revered as second only in solemnity to the holy sacrament. To be denied this holy kiss and the communion is to be denied the highest and holiest offices of the church, so that those who have been placed under the ban are still in that condition until they show symptoms of penitence and, standing up before the congregation, confess that they were wrong and that they are sorry for it. Then they would be received again into full fellowship.

The twenty or so members who were disciplined were all from Peoria. They included Mr. Siebenthal's mother, who was seventy-two years old at the time; Mr. and Mrs. Baer; Mrs.

Binkele; Mrs. Sommers, wife of one of the pro-
prietors of the Keystone Wire Fenceworks in
the south end of the city; Mrs. Stahl; Messrs.
Schultz and Mathis; and perhaps most interesting, a man named Witzig, whose brother
was the preacher in the Moser case—Rudolph
Witzig.

This incident was, of course, of more than
usual interest at this time, when the Amish
church was practically on trial in connection
with the Moser murders. The court could rule
against the testimonies of those who wanted
to testify against the church, but stories such
as this spoke volumes.

Chapter 13
The Family
Testifies

Every journey into the past is
complicated by delusions, false
memories, false naming of real events.

—Adrienne Rich

Thursday
February 28,
1901

The Moser case was resumed at nine o'clock that Thursday morning, after a lapse of five days. The jury, the defendant, and everyone else appeared better for having a week's rest. Sam had been shaved but looked downhearted about getting back to the business of the trial. The usual crowd was in attendance, and all the seats in the courthouse were filled.

The roll of jurors was called, and all responded. They had scarcely settled themselves in their chairs when they were then ordered into the jury room as the attorneys had something to say which they did not desire the jury to hear. Attorney Green laid a complaint before the court to the effect that the Moser family resisted his efforts to have them appear as witnesses. He had experienced great difficulty in obtaining anything from either the father or mother or the two sisters of the defendant, with regard to evidence for Sam Moser.

The father, Benedict Moser, had refused to allow the mother or sisters to answer questions. Mr. Green said that his repeated efforts to see Mrs. Moser and her daughters had been frustrated by the command of the father that they should not go to Mr. Green's office. If he wished to talk with them, he was told that he must do so in the office and presence of the state's attorney, Mr. Cunningham, or his assistant, Mr. Black. At Mr. Green's request, Mrs. Moser and the girls did finally come to his office but declined to say what they knew on the subject he wished to ask them about—one of the girls treading on her mother's toes whenever the old lady began to speak. The charges were denied by Attorney Cunningham. Mr. Green wanted Benedict Moser fined or put in jail for contempt of court.

The attorneys on both sides argued this point relative to the duties of Benedict Moser, and the court said that he would do what was consistent and proper in law; and that if Benedict Moser and his daughters were wanted, they would have to testify. The court stated that Mr. Green had the right to summon his witnesses by due process of law. The court would see that such process was served and that the witnesses on the stand answered all proper questions. Further than this, the court was without jurisdiction. The jury was then brought back to their seats, and the case proceeded.

Mr. Green then began to swear in his witnesses. At that time, the Reverend Witzig, the Amish preacher of whom so much had been said, was present. As the witnesses began to take their oath, an Amish gentleman sitting by the side of Reverend Witzig stood up and said, to the surprise of everyone, "Reverend Witzig does not swear."

The clerk continued reading the usual words to which the witnesses were required to swear and attest while the Reverend Witzig stood up. He was about sixty-five years of age, with white hair and a snowy-white beard. The preacher did not raise his hand but simply nodded his head. When he stood up to take the oath, his eyes were turned to the floor and were partly closed. He sat down quickly and remained in the rear of the courthouse throughout the morning session.

Nearly the entire Moser family was there to testify. It was the first time any of them had appeared in court, and the spectators and jurymen were fascinated. They also refused to swear in taking the oath but simply affirmed.

Daniel Moser took the stand first and said that he was thirty-eight years old. He was born in Morton Township, the son of Benedict Moser and a brother to Sam Moser, the defendant. He had a meager education, as did his brother Sam. They did not study geography, grammar, or history, only the basics: reading, writing, and arithmetic.

His brother John Moser acted strangely at times and one time even jumped into a well. He was not injured but climbed out without assistance and returned to the house. Another brother, Christian Moser, who lived near Wing, Illinois, was not like other men and once jumped out of a second-story window in his night-shirt in the springtime. He was sixteen years old at the time.

Daniel said that he was a member of the New Amish Church but was not now part of the flock of Brother Witzig. Two years before, he had been at an asylum at Mount Pleasant, Iowa, for nine months. His mind was affected, making life burdensome, and so he'd been sent to the asylum. When asked what had caused these troubles, Daniel replied that it was the members of the church. Mr. Black made an objection to this and the objection was sustained. He then said that he was overcome by the heat while working in a grain bin in Iowa. He was in the wire fence business and was worried as the business was failing. He was taken to the county court at Mount Pleasant and put in an asylum. After some months, he was discharged and returned to Morton. He was currently selling books in Chicago at his place of business—148 Dearborn Street. His family lived in Morton; he had ten children.

It was already eleven thirty in the morning when Sarah Moser took the stand. She said that she was a daughter of Mr. and Mrs. Benedict Moser and resided with them near Morton. Her father and mother called on Sam's family and would have dinner with Hanna and the kids, but not with Sam. Sam would eat alone by himself. His father and mother were always good and kind to Sam's wife, but did not shake hands with Sam, for he was put out of the church. Sam was good and kind to his children and had numerous playthings, including an organ and music box.

She appeared to the spectators to be somewhat weak-minded. She admitted that she'd attended school for only five or six years and had only gone to the third room at the school in Morton. She did not belong to the New Amish Church and so spoke about it freely. She seemed to take pleasure in telling how Sam had been persecuted.

The next brother to testify was thirty-five-year-old John Moser. He had many of the characteristics of his father, but did not resemble the other brothers as much. John was a member of the Evangelical Christian Church (or New Amish Church) and so did not shake hands with his brother Sam when they met. He had not shaken hands or eaten with Sam for the past five years because of his expulsion from the church. John went to school for ten or twelve years, and when he was not at school, he was working on the farm.

He also worked for his brother Daniel Moser up in Woodford County about ten years ago. He had mental trouble while there and jumped in a well, later crawling out without assistance. He returned to the house at that time and had had no further problem with dementia. He said that the cause of the trouble was that he wasn't living according to the Holy Scriptures. He was plainly troubled by the questions of counsel and seemed not to be able to recall much of what led him to the well. It did not seem to have been a deliberate attempt to commit suicide since it was not dangerously deep nor full of water. The irresponsible act of a temporarily disorganized mind seemed to have shocked him, restoring his balance. He went on to become a steadfast member of the church and a prosperous farmer, managing 160 acres of land.

John was the favorite brother of Sam. The two played hour after hour as children and were very close until Sam's split with the church. At one point in his questioning, he clearly hesitated when he had the opportunity to say a good word for his brother. It seemed that he believed that he would be punished if he lent any aid to Sam. Sam wept aloud at this change of heart.

Court was adjourned until 1:30 p.m.

At the start of the afternoon session, Lydia Moser took the stand, wearing her black dress and hood. She was a sister of Sam Moser and lived with her parents, Mr. and Mrs. Benedict Moser.

She affirmed, as did all the Amish people, rather than swear an oath. She was apparently unable to comprehend the simple queries of counsel. She had reached the third reader before leaving school. She was asked whether she knew where Indiana was, and she replied *no*.

She said that she didn't eat at the same table with her brother Sam as she was not allowed to do so, according to the Bible. Sam would eat alone when at his father's house, and she would eat before or after him. She did not have any dealings with her brother after he was put out of the church. When asked why he was put out of the church, she didn't know.

Green asked whether or not she was permitted to shake her brother's hand. She didn't respond, so Mr. Green turned to the defendant and said, "Sam, let's see if your sister will shake your hand." Lydia shook her head and turned deadly white. Sam looked up as if he did not comprehend what his attorney wanted him to do. But before he could do anything, Judge Puterbaugh interjected that the court would allow no such dramatic episodes.

Next on the witness stand was Sam's brother Christian Moser. He resided in a small town called Forrest, which was in Livingston County. This was roughly seventy miles northeast, along Route 24. He actually lived in the country between Forrest and Wing—an even smaller village. He had moved there about eight years earlier with his wife, Lydia Yoder Moser. They now had five children. He belonged to the New Amish Church and had for the past ten years.

His brother Sam used to be a member until four or five years previous. Christian had no dealings with his brother since he'd been out of the church because he did not belong to the church. The witness had never had any mental trouble. He said that he'd never jumped out of the second-story window as described by his brother Daniel but had only let himself down with caution.

He was ill with a high fever at the time. He did not fall, was not injured, went back into the house, and recovered fully. He had not been in the home of his brother Sam at a mealtime since he had been put out of the church and didn't shake hands with him because it was against the rules of the church. Christian was very matter-of-fact about the church situation, as if it was a given—he had no hard feelings against his brother.

Mrs. Benedict Moser took the stand after affirming her intention to speak the truth. She began by saying she did not understand English except plain talk but seemed to have very little difficulty either in understanding what was said to her or in making herself understood. She stated that her name was Fanny Moser. Her given name was Verena Steiner. She was raised in the church in Wayne County, Ohio. She had married Benedict Moser there thirty-seven or thirty-eight years ago. They had moved to Morton, Illinois, about twenty years before.

Mrs. Moser said that she was a member of the New Amish Church. Her son Samuel once belonged to that church, but he had been expelled from the church by the preacher. Mrs. Moser did not know why Samuel was put out of the church, because it was in Gridley and not at Morton where Mrs. Moser and her husband attend.

She wouldn't eat with Samuel because he was "away from God," nor could she shake hands with him. She explained that when Samuel's family had visited at her home, Samuel's wife could eat with him there if she chose. She preferred to eat with the family as they had prayers, and Samuel was left to eat alone. He was invited to eat first but said he would wait. Mrs. Moser could eat at the table with his wife, but not at the same table with Sam. He could eat first or afterward. They could not buy a horse or trade with him after he had been put out of the church. Mr. Green asked Samuel's mother if she would give twenty-five cents of her money if it would save Sam from death. She replied that she would not give it, for that "would be a sin against God and the church." They could not even touch him, for he was "possessed of the devil."

Mrs. Moser testified that Sam had always been good to his wife and children. She said that Samuel had an organ and music box, but did not play them when she was there. Asked if she objected, she said she had no right to object to anything he had in his own home. He was a good husband. She went on to say, "He was the kindest man to his family. I never saw a man help his wife so much." Hanna had told her that she "could not have a better man, only he was not satisfied with the church." This mention of his wife moved the prisoner to tears again, and he covered his twitching face with his hand. His mother saw this but showed no emotion. It was difficult for the jurors to watch.

Mr. Green then turned the line of questioning toward Mrs. Moser's family history. She confirmed that she had three brothers: Dan, Levi, and Jacob. Her brother Jacob Steiner, who lived in Morton, was sometimes called "Cedar Rapids." Mr. Green had long endeavored to get Mr. Steiner into the records and at last succeeded. Mrs. Moser spoiled the effect by remarking that Steiner had been all right until a colt kicked him in the head, rendering him unconscious for some hours. Since then, he had been demented, thus destroying the hereditary value of "Cedar Rapids."

She testified that she had a brother Eli in Ohio, of whose four children two could not walk nor talk; but on cross-examination, she admitted that she had not seen one of these babies since it was a year old, and the other not at all.

On cross-examination, Mr. Black showed that Samuel rented his father's farm after being put out of the church and paid his father rent for the same. Mr. Green made a point to show that the father went to the same grain dealer where Samuel sold his crop, but the distinction was made to seem trivial.

The reporters covering the trial described Mrs. Moser as a woman of considerable energy. They thought she would have liked to talk with greater freedom than the considerations of the church and the constant objections of counsel permitted. The reporters also noted that not a single one of Moser's family, "however weak-minded," failed to stop at the county clerk's desk and receive their fees as witnesses.

Sam's Music Box

What could seem more harmless than a music box? A tiny, little wooden box that plays music when you open the lid—a gentle faint tinkling of notes that makes a child's eyes light up with wonder, makes one lean in closer to hear the melody more clearly. So simple and serene.

For the children, it was an object of absolute wonder. Just turning the little wind-up key was fascinating to them. There was a feeling of anticipation as they turned it; everyone gathered around watching them. To be the turner of the key was something special in itself. You could hear the little key affecting the parts inside—winding them up, getting all the players of the notes into place. How did the song get in there? What made it go?

Once it started, you could see the tiny mechanism working. The song played, and all the little pieces moved, working together to pour out the notes. It only played for a short bit, but while it lasted, it was truly magical. Everyone hushed their breath and just listened.

Sam loved to watch them. The children would get so excited. Their eyes shown with the fascination of it. They loved to show it to someone who had not seen it before. If they had a new hired girl or someone was staying with them while they helped with the farming, the children would drag them over and show them how the little box was played.

Hanna didn't mind usually. She enjoyed the children's reaction, he could tell. Her own father played the organ and the violin. She'd grown up with music. But she also knew that it was forbidden. She was much more thoughtful about who was shown the little box. She would warn the children sometimes when certain people were coming over. The box must be hidden away. They wouldn't understand.

Sam thought it silly. It was just a little music box. If someone didn't approve, it was their own problem, not his. Knowing that someone might not approve made him want to get it out and display it all the more. Let them know he didn't care what they thought of it. The fact that Hanna cared so much annoyed him. Why did she always seek to please them?

It was a reminder to her. She knew he'd brought it with him from his time of running around. Before they'd married, he'd gone north to the city to get away from his family. He'd gone to find out what all the talk was about. He'd been gone, and he'd come back with the music box.

The next witness was Mr. L. C. Hoyt of Eureka in Woodford County. He was a twenty-six-year-old farmer who bought and sold stock. He said that he had known Sam Moser for four years and was a neighbor of Moser's when he lived in Woodford County. He worked on the Simpson farm that Moser rented in 1896. He testified as to Moser's kindly treatment of his wife and children at that time. He said that Moser humored his children in every shape and form that he could, often taking them to town with him and buying them candy, bananas, and little playthings. He held the children on his lap and caressed his children; the witness never heard him reproved for doing so. He had an organ and a music box, which he played for the children's amusement, and the witness never heard any complaint made about this. The witness said that he had boarded with the Moser family for four months in the spring of 1899 and saw Moser assist in the housework and the washing. When his wife was busy cooking the meals, Sam would set the table. All of them ate at the same table during his stay at Moser's home. There was nothing wrong, in his memory. Benedict Moser, the father of Sam, was at the house once but did not eat at the table with him.

On cross-examination, the witness admitted that Moser sometimes acted strangely. He often seemed moody and sat with his head in his hands, as if he was in distress. Mr. Hoyt said that he thought it nothing unusual for a father to love his children, and nobody objected to it. Moser also helped the hired girl when she was there. He raised good crops and conducted the farm like any other good farmer. He attended to his own business. He thought that Sam knew the difference between right and wrong.

Jacob Barkdoll, who had a store in Tremont, testified that the defendant came to his store for a seeder in March 1900. He thought Moser at that time seemed "a little bit kind of funny." In fact, he did not seem to be "right." On cross-examination, the witness said he talked with him only a few minutes but thought a man queer who wanted to sow oats in March on the snow.

Twenty-six-year-old Reuben Moser, who was not a member of the New Amish Church, said that he had visited his uncle Levi Steiner last winter in Ohio. He clarified that three of the five children were affected; two could not talk and had to be fed. The youngest, who was about eight years old, could not walk. He saw his father's sister, who had been confined in an asylum in Ohio for six months. He explained that C. R. King, who would next testify, was his first cousin on his father's side.

C. R. King, from German Township, Ohio, was the nephew of Benedict Moser. He testified that he saw his aunt Lizzie Schrock in the asylum at Toledo, Ohio.

Ms. Lizzie Metz was the next witness. She lived near Eureka in Woodford County and was acquainted with Sam Moser and family when they lived on the Hoyt farm. She worked for them for three weeks after the youngest child was born at their residence in October. Dr. Crawford of Eureka was called there on professional business. Benedict Moser and his wife called at the Moser residence and were friendly, but did not shake hands with Sam.

She testified that Moser did considerable work about the house—washed the dishes and hung up the clothes. He had an organ and also a music box in the house to amuse the children. He played the organ and would wind up the music box, and the children would listen to the music. Ms. Metz was described as a bright-faced girl and an intelligent witness. She made a strong impression on the jury.

A number of citizens of Eureka/Woodford County also testified to the general reputation of Samuel Moser while he lived near there. The first was W. R. Simpson, who spoke of Sam's good reputation. George and Frank Dorward knew Sam; Frank helped Sam on the farm. They agreed that he was a peaceable citizen. Peter Garber had boarded with Sam and his wife for two weeks. He said that he treated his wife and children "splendidly," helping his wife with the household duties. On cross-examination, he clarified that Mrs. Moser did most of the housework and washing.

John Finley resided at Eureka and had been a farmer there. He was acquainted with Sam Moser in Woodford County when he lived on an adjoining farm. He said that Sam treated his children well, that his general reputation was good, and he that he did not think him likely to commit the crime of murder. Under cross-examination, Mr. Finley admitted that he didn't know anything more about Sam since 1898, when he had been a neighbor. John's brother George testified that he'd done some hauling at corn-shelling time with Sam. Moser's reputation was good, as far as he knew.

Mr. Black grew rather sarcastic during this whitewashing process and, taking a leaf from Mr. Green's book on cross-examination, proceeded to ask a few questions of each one. Regardless of objections sustained by the court, he asked whether they were aware that Samuel Moser had purchased a .32 caliber revolver for the purpose of killing his wife and that he had chased his brother-in law Mr. Stoller out of the house and upstairs with an ax. Also, that while he was supposed to have been so wonderfully kind and thoughtful of his wife, he had locked her into her room during an illness and refused to let her sister Mrs. Stoller in to see her while his wife wept. The witnesses assured Mr. Black that they had not known these things, but of course, his points were made.

Rudolph Witzig was called to the stand, and as he did not speak English, Mr. Velde was sworn in as an interpreter. Mr. Witzig was the minister of the Morton congregation and farmed a section of land in that vicinity. He was sixty-eight years old, was born in Switzerland, and lived there until 1883, when he came to Gridley. Objections to questions concerning his education and citizenship were sustained by the court, and the witness was excused.

Sign directed immigrants

By DON THOMPSON
Pantagraph staff

GRIDLEY — When immigrants to the United States got off the ship in New York City about 1885, one of the first things they saw on the wharf was a 3- by 20-foot sign painted black with large white letters "This way to Gridley, Illinois."

A huge white hand pointed the direction.

The sign was placed on the wharf by Rudolph Witzig, an elder in what is now the Apostolic Christian Church. Witzig came to Gridley from Zurich, Switzerland, in 1883 and left the sign in New York to direct those who came to America at Witzig's urging.

Dr. J.A. Taylor of Gridley and Dr. S.A. Dunham of Kansas City, Mo., spotted the sign on a tour of the docks while they were attending post-graduate courses at Bellevue Hospital in New York City, according to a pamphlet written by J. Earl Taylor in 1959.

Chapter 14
Expert Testimony

Nothing is easier than denouncing
the evildoer. Nothing more difficult
than understanding him.

—Dostoyevsky

1901

W. L. Foster was the next witness called. He formerly was an attorney and clerk of the court in the town of Eureka and now resided at Toledo, Illinois. He met Samuel Moser in November of 1897 when he consulted him professionally at his office. Mr. Green endeavored to bring out that Moser seemed mentally impaired at that time, and after many objections and exceptions, Mr. Foster was permitted to state only his own observations. He was asked, "Did you observe the mental condition of the man?"

"I did."

"How did the mental condition manifest itself?"

"My impression is that he was mentally deranged on some points. He spoke incoherently and was emotional. He cried and seemed very nervous." Questions as to the knowledge of the witness in the matter of Moser's relations with his wife and his children were objected to by the state and the objections sustained, as it was evident that Mr. Foster only knew what had been related to him by the defendant at that time. On cross-examination, Mr. Foster said that Moser was worried when last at his office.

"Did you advise with him in regard to his going to Minnesota?" (This was objected to and sustained.)

The witness was dismissed.

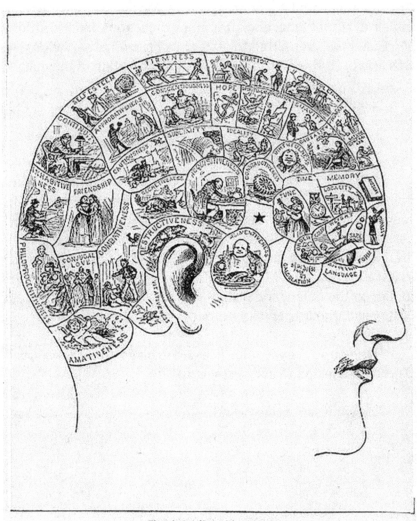

Phrenological Chart of the Faculties.

The next witness to be put on the stand for the purpose of showing Moser's insanity was Dr. Napoleon B. Crawford of Eureka. The doctor's testimony carried considerable weight from his experience and study, as well as the fact that he had been consulted as long as eight years ago by Moser and his father.

He was a well-known physician, who had been practicing for thirty-seven years. He testified that he knew Benedict Moser and had treated the family. He was consulted before Samuel Moser's marriage by the boy and his father and made an examination at that time as to the mental condition of the defendant. At the time, Benedict Moser had just returned from Ohio with Samuel, who seemed to have run away to his Ohio relatives. The visit to Dr. Crawford was made in the belief that he had a physical ailment.

He was in good physical condition, except for the sluggish conditions of the organs. As a result, his mental condition was not good: he seemed depressed and melancholy. The doctor explained that melancholy was usually a product of heredity. His judgment was that Sam's brain was not in a normal condition. He was morose, sullen, and would not answer questions. The doctor considered his intellect as hardly medium. When his father was informing the doctor of Sam's troubles, Moser would cry. The doctor was not able to get much out of him but monosyllabic answers to questions. He was, in no uncertain terms, said Dr. Crawford, morose and melancholy—an irritable man with an inherited tendency to insanity. He gave him a prescription (probably laudanum, a mixture of opium and alcohol) and considered him much improved upon meeting him subsequently.

In Dr. Crawford's opinion, the mental condition that Moser was in was brought by the trouble he had with his church. He would weep and was in a bad state of mind. It was the doctor's opinion that Sam was insane at the time he killed his family.

Dr. Crawford later attended Mrs. Moser during her last confinement. Samuel consulted the doctor as to his troubles, asking not for professional advice but for friendly counsel. At this visit, the witness said Moser wept when speaking of his family. Questioned as to his professional opinion as to Moser's sanity at this time, the physician said, "He was in a bad state of mind, not in a normal condition. It is my opinion that his troubles with the church produced it, from what was related to me."

Dr. Crawford was referred to in the letter written by Samuel Moser in Salt Lake City, in which he said, "What is this life worth if there is no pleasure in it? I had no good or enjoyment of wife or children, and they had no good of me. Whoever says it is all my fault, why did you backslide? I wish to say the Lord will judge. That man at Gridley and those who agree with him are perhaps some cause. I have talked with Dr. Crawford, an old experienced man, but they expressed themselves as not feeling able to step between family affairs and are the worst or baddest thing in this world. Husbands should respect their wives and know they are the weaker," etc.

Mr. Green propounded the hypothetical question permitted by law in such cases, covering the facts developed by evidence as completely as possible, closing with, "In your professional judgment, was or was not Samuel Moser at the time of the crime sane or insane?"

The answer was, "My judgment is that he was not sane."

"Why?"

"It was the act of an insane man. I can understand how a man can become angry with his wife or his brother or his father and, in passion of anger, seek their lives, but I cannot understand how a man can murder his little ones and be sane." From this, it would appear that the physician was arguing backward from the crime rather than from the circumstances toward it.

"Was he capable of understanding right from wrong?"

"I think not."

Asked what tendency religious troubles would have on a mind like Moser's, the witness said the natural tendency would be to break down and destroy the reasoning powers and that his people being precluded from eating with him would have a detrimental effect. Testifying as an expert on insanity (having read several medical books on the subject), Dr. Crawford testified that he considered Moser irresponsible at the time of the commission of the crime.

At the beginning of the cross-examination, Mr. Black propounded a hypothetical question, which was objected to on the grounds that it included certain statements that had not been developed in the evidence. Mr. Black believed that a basis for everything connected could be found in the testimony of the witness, Edward Rollins, and the stenographer was asked to turn to this testimony and ascertain exactly what had been said.

It was now five o'clock. Juror Miller sat in the corner of the jury box, looking rather wan. He seemed to bear the fatigue of the days' session very well, giving close attention to the evidence. But as it got later and the evidence dragged on, his fatigue was more and more evident. The court was moved to adjourn until Friday morning, when Dr. Crawford would be cross-examined.

On Friday, March 1, 1901, there were fewer women on hand in the crowded courtroom. It was thought that they had been drawn in the day before by the testimony of Samuel's mother. The Moser family was not in attendance, but there were many Amish there, including Reverend Witzig.

The professional testimony was continued, beginning with the cross-examination of Dr. Crawford. He testified that melancholy and mania are both subject to outbreak and excitement. There is a state of excitement in mania and in melancholy, and it is impossible to distinguish one from the other. If a person goes into one of these fits of mania, he is apt to commit murder and not know what he has done after it is over. The doctor was asked, if a man kills his wife, is he necessarily insane? The doctor answered no. Then he was asked whether he thought that Sam Moser was insane at the time he shot his wife, and to the surprise of everyone, he said yes. Attorney Black got the doctor at close quarters, and for a time, he had to think several minutes before answering. Mr. Black was very persistent and asked the doctor if he believed that Sam Moser knew the consequences of this act when Moser wrote it in his letter, "I know I deserve the rope." The doctor said he believed that Moser did have the knowledge of right and wrong then and knew what he was doing.

Dr. Crawford said the memory is not always affected by insanity. Chronic mania is opposed to melancholia. When acts are committed in a frenzy, the recollection is likely to be dim and disordered. Melancholics have these outbreaks, as well as persons afflicted with acute mania. Terror or fear usually superinduce these frenzied periods, and suicide or homicide is the usual result. After the frenzy passes, he will not likely have a clear recollection but may run away, as self-preservation seems to survive everything else. In other cases, no attempt at concealment or fight is made. Dr. Crawford says a man may not be insane if he kills his wife, but if he kills his children, it is much stronger evidence of insanity. He did not, however, wish to be understood as stating that he must necessarily be so.

Mr. Black stated this hypothetical question covering the incidents of the murder. It was objected to by Mr. Green on the grounds that the facts introduced in evidence were not sufficiently brought out in the question. Judge Puterbaugh stated that while the questions must not contain facts not adduced in evidence, they need not explicitly state every point brought out in the evidence.

"I think it was the act of an insane man."

"You think any man who will kill another man is not in a normal state of mind?"

"I think not, unless in self-defense." The doctor explained that a man afflicted with melancholia might commit acts of violence without being in a frenzy.

Mr. Black propounded another hypothetical question covering the details of Moser's flight from the scene of the murder and Moser's action in Salt Lake City, asking as to the knowledge of Moser as to the consequences of his act. Dr. Crawford answered that Sam might "not necessarily" be cognizant of the consequences of his crime.

Mr. Green read letters written by Moser at Salt Lake City. Was the man sane or insane at the time he penned the letters? "I think he was insane." From the letter in which Moser said, "I know I deserve the rope," Dr. Crawford thought he knew the consequences at that time and that he knew he had done wrong when the letters were written.

Dr. Crawford made an excellent witness for the defense. His high standing as a physician and his evident earnestness of belief in the mental irresponsibility of Moser made a strong impression with the jury.

The next witness was Dr. Cody of Tremont, who was put on the stand at ten thirty. He had practiced medicine in Tremont for ten years. He testified that on the first of May 1900, the defendant had called at his office, but not for professional advice. Asked if he was able to state what Moser was affected with at that time, the witness said he had formed the opinion that the man was insane. He could not define the form of insanity, except in the light of the events that followed two weeks later.

To the hypothetical question propounded by Mr. Green, the witness said he had an opinion that such a man as indicated would be an insane man. That his affliction was paranoia—a form of insanity hereditary, chronic, and incurable. He was possessed of fixed delusions and, while generally rational, was a dangerous man to be at large. The paranoiac usually has a delusion that he is being persecuted by his friends and that they are conspiring against him. Moser might have been irresistibly drawn to deeds of violence by the delusion he was possessed of.

Under cross-examination, the witness was led into the mazes of definitions of *delusion*, *illustration*, *hallucination*, and other technical expressions. The fine distinction between these terms were explained in classic language by Dr. Cody, who was perfectly willing to display his erudition but opposed to the efforts of the counsel to pin him down to the point in hand. He persisted in making diffuse and discursive replies and was evidently more anxious to preserve the integrity of his opinion that the man was insane than to assist the counsel in determining his qualifications as an expert insanity witness. Dr. Cody endeavored questions propounded by himself but was continuously told by the court that the court would rule on this point. Another remarkable feature of the testimony of both Dr. Crawford and Dr. Cody was that they did not seem able to get away from their previous acquaintance with Moser and their preconceived opinions as to his mental condition and answer the hypothetical questions fairly upon the facts of the question, although repeatedly advised by both counsel and court to do so.

Dr. Cody said that the paranoiac always considers himself right and his deeds justified—but that the letters of Moser written at Salt Lake City, in which he alluded to his crime and said he "deserves the rope," and otherwise referred to the penalty, need not necessarily indicate that he was not a paranoiac as they have intervals of lucidity or apparent sanity. To the hypothetical question of Mr. Black, Dr. Cody would not reply without explanations, which he seemed grieved to learn were not proper responses to direct questions. He would say, however, that such a case as indicated by Mr. Black's representation of the facts adduced to evidence: the man might be insane and might not be, which seemed to sum up the value of expert insanity testimony very neatly.

Dr. Amos Crook arrived just in time to appear in court at the convening of the afternoon session. Placed on the stand by Mr. Green as an expert witness, he qualified himself as able to form a professional opinion as to a man's sanity or insanity. He was currently practicing medicine in St. Louis, Missouri, but had lived for two years in Morton and treated Mrs. Moser professionally. He observed the defendant on these occasions and noticed that he seemed very solicitous.

Mr. Green then spent some time covering the evidence as to Samuel's inherited mental taint, the trouble in the church, the various removing and wanderings of the Moser family, the incidence of the crime in minute detail, the subsequent actions of the murder, the reading of the letters written in Salt Lake City, and everything else that could be construed into a bearing on the case—framed-up as hypothetical questions as to Samuel Moser's mental state at the time of the crime. Dr. Crook replied, without consideration, that the man indicated was a paranoiac.

On cross-examination, the doctor stated that he was twenty-nine years old and had practiced medicine for only three years. He had studied the usual text books on insanity during his college years and seen many insane patients in the asylum. He understood the symptoms of paranoia to be melancholy delusions, stupidity, moroseness, and unsociability. As to the form the delusion might take, much depended on the education and environment of the patient. In paranoia, the memory is affected. Sometimes acts of violence are committed.

Mr. Black demonstrated to him in something less than a few minutes that his qualifications were not sufficient. Mr. Black had learned something from his discussion of the symptoms and indications and effects of paranoia with Dr. Crawford and Dr. Cody and floored Dr. Crook with an innocent request for a definition of delusion as used by the witness. The technical meaning of *delusion* in this connection is to the effect that the delusion is a belief that no rational person would entertain, but the expert witness said, "It is where person who believes that the act committed by another individual or any individual to be other than an act that the same individual would supposed to know be an act of a sane person."

Some more of the physician's testimony was almost as obscure, and finally on being asked by Mr. Black how he could go from listening to the hypothetical question put his finger immediately on the very particular form of insanity that the man was afflicted with, he replied that he was judging from his own observations and knowledge of the defendant at a previous time. As this is exactly what the witness was supposed not to do, and as Dr. Crook had been instructed by the court in the first place that the hypothetical question must be answered on the facts of the question without consideration of any extraneous matters coming within his knowledge, Mr. Black asked to have the testimony stricken out. His testimony as to Moser's insanity was stricken out and the witness excused.

Dr. Schenk of Pekin said he conducted a professional examination of Sam Moser upon his return from Salt Lake and found no symptoms of insanity at all. From the manner in which he had gone about the deed, the deliberation and preparation upon the crime, led him to believe Samuel Moser was in full possession of his mental faculties and was fully able to realize the enormity of and consequences of his crime. On the whole, he believed Samuel Moser planned and executed a deliberate murder. The most convincing fact that Moser was not insane was his trying to cover up his crime by tacking newspapers over the windows, locking the doors and pinning the curtains to the sashes. He attempted to escape by boarding a train on the blind side and paid cash fare to avoid knowledge of his destination being disclosed.

There was a growing feeling that in such cases so-called expert testimony was largely a waste of time—as many conflicting opinions can usually be gathered as there are witnesses. Most physicians seemed inclined to consider any man insane who does anything out of the ordinary. Dr. Crawford testified that he considered any man insane who committed murder unless in self-defense. Dr. Cody also testified that from the crime, the man must be insane. Dr. Cody testified that the paranoiac always considers himself right and his deeds justified and, a few minutes later, said that the fact that Moser seemed to realize fully his crime and admit that he deserved the rope did not necessarily indicate that he was not a paranoiac. The paranoiac has fixed delusions, says one expert. Another says he may appear rational to the ordinary observer and be a dangerous man to be at large at the same time.

This was further demonstrated by experts in religious insanity. Dr. Seldon H. Talcott, head of the Middletown, New York, Hospital for the Insane and one of the world's greatest alienists, said that the church aisle can be the high road to an insane asylum. In an article that ran in the Chicago, Illinois, *Inter-Ocean* newspaper on November 20, 1898, Dr. Talcott said that religion is frequently presented in such a way "that the shock of fear blights the forces of growing youth, and an agony of remorse for sin is allowed to produce worry by day and insomnia by night, until physical and mental development is effectually arrested, and insanity results."

Dr. D. R. Brower, of Chicago disagreed strongly, saying, "A man is a lunatic. He raves over religion, and the superficial observer at once says that is religious insanity. There never was a case of insanity developed in a single generation. The foundations for the mental disease were laid generations back. There was a hereditary predisposition to insanity in the victim and a great excitement over any cause—political, religious, literary, oratorical, or anything else will, when the time is ripe, send him to an asylum. But to call his disease political, or religious, or any other kind of insanity is the height of absurdity. It frequently occurs that insane patients constantly talk of religion after becoming mentally imbalanced, even though they never opened a Bible or heard a prayer in their lives. This peculiarity of the insane leads the physician who examines superficially and who knows but little of mental diseases to dub the trouble religious insanity."

Dr. H. W. Thomas of the People's Church, however, agreed with Dr. Talcott. "Every word that this New York physician has said is the eternal truth. The world does not know the mental and heart torture that came through religious teaching of the past. The old conceptions of God, not as a Father but as an arbitrary king, a conception of total depravity, penal atonement, of the judgment day, and of endless fiery torment, were enough to drive a world crazy. When the methods of teaching are employed so that fear instead of love is known, the seeds of insanity are sown. In my own experience, I have known almost hundreds of cases where minds were hurt by unhealthy religious excitement. One of the most sacred things is to unfold the great truths of religion to the minds of children and youths, and it should be done not dogmatically, but from the affectional—the heart side. In our own age of the world, it is positively wicked to bring before the rising generation the old and horrible views once taught in the name of religion."

Dr. S. V. Clevenger, for years the head of the Kankakee, Illinois, insane asylum responded to Talcott's theory with a passage from his own work: "Wars and political and religious excitement merely give color to preexisting insanity and are seldom causes in themselves. Practically, there is no religious insanity nor political insanity. People are weak-minded from causes occurring back through the generations. Some great excitement makes them crazy. Grant you, it may be a religious revival or religious teaching that causes them to fear the wrath of God, and they go insane. But mind you, also, their insanity came not because the cause was religious but because it was exciting."

"I suppose there are cases," said the Reverend R. A. Torrey of the Bible Institute, "where young people physically weak might be driven into insomnia and then into insanity by having hell preached to into them constantly. In other words, if God as a master instead of God as a Father was the aspect of the deity which they are taught, I believe in some cases lunacy might result. To this extent, I agree with the Eastern alienist. Let me change religion into irreligion and what he says is gospel truth itself. There are many people who are convinced of the truths of religion but who will not accept Christ. These people frequently go insane, and then in their insanity, they harp constantly upon religion. This leads the unthinking to say, 'That man was driven crazy by religion,' where, as a matter of fact, irreligion was at the root of his trouble."

He continued, "I know a man in Minneapolis who was irreligious inasmuch as he had not and would not accept Christ, yet peculiar as it may seem, he had an idea that he had committed the unpardonable sin. He went violently insane. The influences of religion were brought to bear on that man, and the seeds on insanity which were sown by irreligion were killed. He recovered fully and is a consistent believer today. Irreligion caused another man not far from here to be monomaniacal and to attempt suicide by morphine four times. Religion saved that man. Of course, I cannot give his name, but he is one of the great merchants of Chicago. Doubt, which led to his insanity and to his attempt on his life, has given place to that implicit belief which brings peace in its wake. Within the week, I have ministered to a man who was driven violently insane by irreligion. This man is now mentally restored and, in due time, will accept the Great Physician whose ministration preclude any thought of mental disturbance."

County physician E. A. Fortner, who was in charge of the detention hospital, had, in the course of a year, many insane patients temporarily under his care. "I am not an alienist," said Dr. Fortner, "and have never pretended to be, but I will say this: I don't agree with Dr. Talcott's idea that the church aisle is a much-trodden path to the madhouse. Insanity is, to the largest extent, a matter of heredity and environment. I suppose if a boy had a weak body and a predisposition to a weak mentality that the preaching of hellfire at him for a while would send him over to be placed temporarily under my care. People, preachers included, are getting more and more to believe that the basis of religion is love. I cannot see where Dr. Talcott gets his data for his observations on religion as a cause of insanity. I will say this, however, if it gives a crumb of comfort to any believer in his theory: that, while there are comparatively few Salvation Army soldiers in Chicago, I have had three of the members under my care suffering from acute mania. However, this doesn't prove a thing, except possibly that the Salvation Army services, being of an emotional character, produced the excitement which was necessary to bring out the insanity which had come down through generations."

The Reverend J. Q. A. Henry also agreed with Talcott. "I suppose insanity does spring sometimes from religion, but many more times, it springs from a want of religion. It is undoubtedly true that religious truth may be presented in such a way and under such circumstances as to produce a religious monomania. As a rule, however, it results from an unscriptural presentation of the truth. The scriptures do not lay chief emphasis on fear, but they appeal rather to the nobler motives of love and righteousness."

Rather than clarifying the issue, the experts were complicating it. Sam was the final witness to take the stand, but it was somewhat of a letdown. He told the story in his own words, but it had all been heard before. His testimony only confirmed what people already believed at this point—whether they'd been for or against him, they heard what they expected to hear.

SAM MOSER, THE SELF-CONFESSED MURDERER.

A belief is not merely an idea the mind possesses;
it is an idea that possesses the mind.
—Robert Oxton Bolt

REASONS FOR ADMISSION
1864 TO 1889

INTEMPERANCE & BUSINESS TROUBLE	DISSOLUTE HABITS
KICKED IN THE HEAD BY A HORSE	DOMESTIC AFFLICTION
HEREDITARY PREDISPOSITION	DOMESTIC TROUBLE
ILL TREATMENT BY HUSBAND	DROPSY
IMAGINARY FEMALE TROUBLE	EGOTISM
HYSTERIA	EPILEPTIC FITS
IMMORAL LIFE	EXCESSIVE SEXUAL ABUSE
IMPRISONMENT	EXCITEMENT AS OFFICER
JEALOUSY AND RELIGION	EXPOSURE AND HEREDITARY
LAZINESS	EXPOSURE AND QUACKERY
MARRIAGE OF SON	EXPOSURE IN ARMY
MASTURBATION & SYPHILIS	FEVER AND JEALOUSY
MASTURBATION FOR 30 YEARS	FIGHTING FIRE
MEDICINE TO PREVENT CONCEPTION	SUPPRESSED MASTURBATION
MENSTRUAL DERANGED	SUPPRESSION OF MENSES
MENTAL EXCITEMENT	THE WAR
NOVEL READING	TIME OF LIFE
NYMPHOMANIA	UTERINE DERANGEMENT
OPIUM HABIT	VENEREAL EXCESSES
OVER ACTION OF THE MIND	VICIOUS VICES
OVER STUDY OF RELIGION	WOMEN TROUBLE
OVER TAXING MENTAL POWERS	SUPERSTITION
PARENTS WERE COUSINS	SHOOTING OF DAUGHTER
PERIODICAL FITS.	SMALL POX
TOBACCO & MASTURBATION	SNUFF EATING FOR 2 YEARS
POLITICAL EXCITEMENT	SPINAL IRRITATION
POLITICS	GATHERING IN THE HEAD
RELIGIOUS ENTHUSIASM	GREEDINESS
FEVER AND LOSS OF LAW SUIT	GRIEF
FITS AND DESERTION OF HUSBAND	GUNSHOT WOUND
ASTHMA	HARD STUDY
BAD COMPANY	RUMOR OF HUSBAND MURDER
BAD HABITS & POLITICAL EXCITEMENT	SALVATION ARMY
BAD WHISKEY	SCARLATINA
BLOODY FLUX	SEDUCTION & DISAPPOINTMENT
BRAIN FEVER	SELF ABUSE
BUSINESS NERVES	SEXUAL ABUSE & STIMULANTS
CARBONIC ACID GAS	SEXUAL DERANGEMENT
CONGESTION OF BRAIN	FALSE CONFINEMENT
DEATH OF SONS IN WAR	FEEBLENESS OF INTELLECT
DECOYED INTO THE ARMY	FELL FROM HORSE IN WAR
DERANGED MASTURBATION	FEMALE DISEASE
DESERTION BY HUSBAND	DISSIPATION OF NERVES

TRANS-ALLEGHENY LUNATIC ASYLUM
WWW.TALAWV.COM 304-269-5070

Chapter 15
Closing Arguments

The dead cannot cry out for
justice. It is the duty of the
living to do so for them.

—Lois McAlister Bujold

Monday
March 4, 1901

At 9:15 a.m. on Monday, March 4, 1901, the Moser trial started into its third week. It had stormed overnight, but the muddy roads did not keep the people at home. It seemed that all of Pekin and people from the surrounding countryside were there. The morning trains brought large numbers from Peoria, Morton, Tremont, and other nearby towns. This was the day the attorneys would make their closing arguments. The life of Sam Moser literally hung in the balance, and before many hours had passed, his case would be decided by the jury.

State's attorney Jesse Black made the first closing speech. He began by assuring the jurors that the long and weary trial was almost over and congratulating the jury for paying close attention. "You were chosen after long and careful consideration," said Mr. Black, "and I believe you will keep the faith and not break that oath which you took. We accepted you men of the jury because we believed you to be good men and true and because we believed you would bring in a verdict according to the evidence in the case, according to the law. The truth is, we look to you now to do that. You must not shrink from that duty, however painful." He spoke of the indictment and said that no personal prejudice should interfere with the verdict.

He reminded them of the tone of the opening speeches of both counsels and said that what he had promised in his opening speech had been exactly what he had proven. He applauded the opposing attorney for the eloquent speech he'd made in his opening statement on behalf of his client. He then turned to the jury. He said that no man ever made a better speech in a poorer case in the state of Illinois than Mr. Green in opening this case. "I thought as I listened to his eloquent words of feeling and sarcasm and passion what could not Mr. Green do if he had facts to draw on rather than his imagination? Mr. Green told you that the Amish people live like hogs. Do you remember the sweet-faced sister of the deceased woman, Mrs. Julia Stoller? Do you remember the kindly and intelligent brother who appeared upon the witness stand here, Timothy Hohulin? Mr. Stoller, a typical farmer of the well-to-do class? Do you recall the rich father, Mr. Benedict Moser?" He painted a clear picture of the quiet manner of the Amish farmers that tended to their own business, then drove his point home, saying he wished that the world was fuller of that kind of "hogs."

He went on to show by testimony that Amish children did go to school, and each had a good education. While Green had told them that the Amish people "would not allow children to attend school where the American flag was floating," he certainly had not proven this. He reminded the jury that the indictment did not charge crime to Benedict Moser, but Attorney Green had tried to lead them to believe that he had conspired with the state in the prosecution. "Benedict Moser appeared before the grand jury because he was subpoenaed. He had no right to refuse to come. The defense tried to lay blame on Benedict Moser instead of his son, who committed the crime. The son is on trial here—not the church and not Benedict Moser."

He went on to discuss each of the indictments. He explained the duty of the jury regarding the verdict that should be brought in, saying that he had proven that the defendant committed the crime and must suffer accordingly. He reminded the jury that the counsel for the defense had said that "the state must prove beyond all reasonable doubt that every charge was true." Black clarified that the law did not require that, and that if it was the case, the country would be full of thieves and murderers.

He asked the pardon of jury that he would have to take time to explain the meaning of words *malice* and *insanity*. He gave the meaning of the word *malice* as regarded by the law and argued that the state had proven that Moser's crimes were deliberate and unprovoked—predominated by malice. "The word *malice* has been much used in this case," said Mr. Black. "The prosecution does not have to prove malice, though we have proven it beyond question of doubt. In a deliberate and unprovoked murder, gentleman, malice is assumed." A reasonable doubt must not be based on any particular of the evidence but upon all of it. It must be such as would cause a prudent man not to hesitate.

"It is true, gentleman, that insanity is a proper defense offered in good faith," continued the prosecutor. "But let us see what the law says about insanity as a defense." The question that they were to decide was, did the man know the consequences of his acts? "If you find that he knew the difference between right and wrong," Black explained, "you must find him guilty—even though you believe him not exactly sane, even if you have a reasonable doubt of his sanity." By their oaths, the jurymen were bound to find the man guilty unless they had a reasonable doubt as to his sanity at the time of committing the crime, and it must be a doubt of his sanity—not three years before, not six months before, but on the day of May 13, 1900, when his crime was committed.

The prosecutor poured out bitter ridicule against the defense's expert testimony, remarking that Dr. Crawford said Moser had melancholia. Dr. Cody said it was paranoia, and Mr. Black asserted that the forms of insanity with which Moser was inflicted were limited in number only by the number of experts examined. Yet in the case of paranoia, the intellect is not affected: the patient knows right from wrong. He argued that the plea of insanity was becoming too common in the courts. Spies, Fielden, Schwab, Prendergast, Piteau were paranoiacs, and they died on the gallows for murder. Mr. Black also insisted that proof of the insanity or imbecility of certain relatives of the defendant was not to be taken as proof of the insanity of the defendant. Mr. Black then spoke at length of the expert testimony offered by Dr. Schenk and Dr. Warren—witnesses of the state—and argued ably for a fair and honest consideration of the evidence offered by these witnesses.

The prosecutor next referred to the testimony of Dr. Crawford of Eureka, who had known Moser and testified that Moser had not been in a normal mental state and, after examination, testified that he believed Moser knew right from wrong and realized the consequences of his act. It was noticeable, however, that Mr. Black failed to refer to much of Dr. Crawford's testimony, for readers of the *Pantagraph* would remember that Dr. Crawford testified and remained unshaken in his testimonies that Moser was insane and had not been in a normal mental state for many years. Mr. Black passed briefly over the expert testimony of Dr. Cody of Tremont, who testified that Moser was a victim of the form of insanity known as paranoia, a form in which the sufferer is driven irresistibly to acts of violence. Attorney Black argued that expert testimony was of no more value than nonexpert testimony. In nine cases out of ten, the expert was either paid for his testimony or was on the witness stand with a biased opinion. Most expert witnesses came to the stand fully convinced, knowing precisely what they were to say, and usually the opinions of experts differed in essential particulars. Mr. Black insisted that the evidence given by the defense was remote and conflicting.

The nonexpert testimony put on by the state, consisting of the farmers and merchants of Tremont who were neighbors of Moser's during the last six months preceding the crime, and his relatives, every one of whom testified that they believed the defendant to be sane and rational at all times, was said to be of more weight than the expert testimony of men who had seen Moser only a few times at infrequent intervals.

Mr. Black spoke of the character witnesses, most of whom were acquainted with Moser several years before the murder. He said that much of this testimony was valueless for the reason that every man had a good reputation until he committed a felony. "There are Sunday school superintendents in the penitentiary today," said Mr. Black, "who could have furnished hundreds of good-character witnesses as to their reputation several years before the crime." He reminded them of the testimony of Attorney Foster of Eureka, whose office Moser had visited more than three years before the commission of the crime. Mr. Foster testified that Moser seemed strange. Mr. Black contended that men were generally in trouble when they visited lawyers and were often depressed and acted strange. He had seen the defendant but once, and that was three years before the commission of the crime. Mr. Hoyt had lived with the defendant but a week but said that "some men are different from other men at home." His testimony was worth nothing.

Attorney Black gave Green credit for having "eloquent lips" and told the jury that the defense witnesses had testified that Moser was kind to children, but what man isn't? He went back to several years ago, showing that even then Moser loved his children, but Green had denied that the rules of the church would allow it. Three years before the commission of the crime, he'd treated all with due respect. Mr. Black argued that such conduct was not that of an insane man. The letters Moser written at Salt Lake City were read and analyzed, with particular attention being called to such phrases as "If I could have got around the penalty of death, I would have tried to live here in Salt Lake City, as these people I like." "For love of reason, lay not that flattering unction to your soul, that not his trespass but his madness speaks."

The state had shown conclusively that there had been trouble between Moser and his wife. As evidence of this, he read one of the letters written by Moser at Salt Lake City in which the defendant said "in this final days of ours, we have had more and more trouble or disagreement." Mr. Black declared that this was evidence of the trouble which existed between Moser and his wife, which had been omitted by Mr. Green in every hypothetical question asked of the expert witnesses. Mr. Black dwelt upon the fact that Dr. Crawford had testified that Moser was conscious of the consequences of his act and knew right from wrong. He eloquently declared that if this testimony of the defense's own expert was true, then Sam Moser didn't know right from wrong and did know the consequences of his act, then it was the sworn duty of the street to bring in a verdict of guilty.

In his conclusion, Mr. Black pleaded eloquently for the honor of Tazewell County, the peace of the state, and justice between man and man. "Why, gentlemen, this man should suffer the penalty of his acts. This man, who militates against the church of which he was a member, this church that attempts to follow the teachings of the Bible, and the teaching of the Lord Jesus Christ, and the law of Moses. Why, men, more than six thousand years ago, amid smoke and thunder around old Sinai's head, the Lord God of Hosts handed down to Moses that law which has been the law of all mankind since, 'Thou shalt not kill.' If a man smite another, that he die, he shall surely be put to death. If any mischief follow, thou shalt give life for life, eye for eye, tooth for tooth, hand for hand, foot for foot, burning for burning, wound for wound, stripe for stripe.' And the Lord Jesus Christ Himself said to the rich man, who said to him, 'Good master, what shall I do to inherit eternal life?' Jesus Christ said, 'Thou knowest the commandments: Thou shall not commit adultery, thou shalt not lie, thou shalt not steal, thou shalt not kill.'

"It is the law yet, gentlemen, the law of Moses and the law of Jesus Christ. It is the law of the state of Illinois. On the thirteenth day of May 1900, the birds were singing in glee and in happiness. The sun was shining as it had shone on a day in May for six thousand years. The wife and the children of this defendant were in health and in happiness. They went to church, never dreaming that it was the last Sunday on earth that they should walk together and worship God. They came home, and there sits the man with the same revolver in his pocket that he had purchased three years before in Minnesota to kill them. There goes the wife into the cellar, there follows the man whom Mr. Green says reminded him of Christ before Pilate. Oh God!

"The brute and the assassin steps up to the right of her and shoots the wife of his youth, the mother of his children, dead. She falls back and dies. And this Christ before Pilate, as his wife lay upon her back, with the unhealthy light struggling in from the cellar window in order to avoid the glance of her ghastly eyes as they looked up at him in death, covers the face of his dead wife and conceals the windows. He went upstairs, gentlemen, and in succession kills his family and flees. Oh, what a scene was there— wife, sons, and baby—something like the picture drawn by the myriad minded bard in which Macbeth slays the king. And as he steals into the king's chamber in the darkness of the night to commit the deed, he passes there the sleeping watchman at the door. He tells his wife about it. 'There's one did laugh in sleep and one cried murder, that they did wake each other. I stood and heard them, but they did say their prayers and addressed them again to sleep. One cried, God bless us, and amen, the other, as they had seen me with these hangman's hangs, listening their fear, I could not say amen when they did say, God bless us.'"

Mr. Green was unfortunate in his opening statement to say that Moser reminded him of Jesus Christ before Pilate. This comparison was made the most of by Mr. Black, who said eloquently, "Jesus Christ was the Savior of the world. He bore upon his shoulders the sorrows of the world. He stood before Pilate a just and upright man. He said, 'Let the little children come unto me and forbid them not, for such is the kingdom of heaven.' If Moser reminds me of anyone between the lids of the Bible, it is Herod, who ordered the massacre of the innocents.

"And this man, gentlemen of the jury, with the blood of his wife, with the blood of his children upon his hands, ought not to be able to sleep. For this man to go free—write it down, gentlemen of the jury—publish it, broadcast that in Tazewell County, men can kill, and kill, and kill, and kill and go scot free. I want you in deliberating upon this question to think of the safety of your own children. I want you to think of your own wives and babies.

God knows at what time, at what hour, some man may do as this man has done and come into this court and put up the defense that he was insane.

"When you go into the jury box to deliberate, before you bring in a verdict, I want you to remember the night of the thirteenth of May. I want you to remember in the darkness of the cellar, the dead staring face of the woman, with no company but the rats, as they clamored over her dead body. I want you to remember the faces of those children looking up to that God who gave them life, giving up their lives at the hand of a monster, whom Mr. Green tells you should walk forth a free man. God pity you, gentlemen, God pity the state of Illinois, if justice in Tazewell County is to be a mockery and a byword, and crime and killing and murder go unpunished forever. I believe, gentlemen of the jury, in the light of the evidence, in the light of the facts, you will stand for the peace of the state, the safety of society and justice between man and man. I thank you for your patient and kind attention."

Black had spoken for two hours. This young man, just thirty years old and with a record of only three jury trials, had been pitted against a much more seasoned defense lawyer, whose reputation was already established. But he had clearly demonstrated that he had the concentration, the earnestness, and the ability to make a famous criminal lawyer. He had given a concise, logical analysis of the evidence as it had been presented. He had spoken with an eloquence and fire seldom surpassed in a courtroom—holding the rapt attention of the jury and courtroom.

By all accounts, it was a masterful and eloquent speech, such as was never before heard in the circuit court. "It was a forceful, eloquent masterpiece of oratory and held jury and audience spellbound in admiration with his flow of silvery words and rhetoric." Black's speech made such an impression on the jury that some of them were crying at its close. People later wrote to the newspapers asking that the speech be reprinted in its entirety.

Congratulations were poured upon the young man by all his friends.

It would certainly have been a hard act to follow, but there was little choice. Attorney T. N. Green began his closing remarks at one thirty that afternoon. The courtroom was again packed. Everyone paid the closest attention to Mr. Green when he commenced his argument. He began by saying that it was impossible to try this man unless you try the Amish church. Speaking of Preacher Witzig, he said, "Did you ever see such a face? He can't talk the language and has only been a citizen for the past seven years. Benedict Moser, the father of the defendant, would not give assistance to his own flesh and blood...and just so with his mother—because Sam was thrown out of the New Amish Church."

He spoke of the relatives of the defendant, many of whom were of unsound mind. "Dan was driven crazy and was sent to an asylum at Mount Pleasant, Iowa, and his brother John jumped into a well—they're all weak-minded." Green continued by saying that the Benedict Moser family were all troubled with insanity. Every one of them. In the old country, a brother of his, a maniac, was chained in a cellar. John Moser, Chris, Lydia, Dan, all "intellectual giants," said Mr. Green sarcastically. "These are the kind of people Mr. Black wishes there were more of."

"The Amish people have married and intermarried to their detriment—until they are paralytics, and God has brought this disaster of the Moser murder about to instruct the people of this county that if they fail to counteract this influence, it will be to the detriment of the entire county."

Mr. Green said that he had a bitter feeling in the case. The only protectors that Moser had were the laws of the land and his lawyer. Moser was deserted by his father and mother and everyone else, with the exception of one insane brother. The Amish haunted the life out of Samuel Moser. They would not trade with him, nor would they help him in any manner. The attitude of the father and mother of the defendant was scored by the attorney, who said if they believed all the things they were taught by the church, still no power should keep that mother from the side of her boy nor prevent her from rendering him what assistance she could. The father and mother refused to shake hands with their son, the defendant, nor even put their hands on him by the rules of the church, and it was just so with his sister. "We don't want that kind of people or cattle in this country," Mr. Green said. There was a burst of laughter at this, and the court ordered the sheriff to put out any in the courtroom who again laughed out loud.

"Drive the Amish into the sea. It is in your power, gentlemen of the jury, and you have the opportunity to assist mankind to give these vipers to understand that they can't deprive him of his reason, his wife, and his children. What sort of citizens will they ever make? Do you want more of them? If you do carry out their wishes and their doctrines, you have your victim. And if you want to visit the punishment that they deserve on him, you can do it, but I believe you will not."

The testimony tending to remove the presumption of sanity was reviewed by Mr. Green: the hereditary tendency, the environment, and the specific acts of persecution by the church. The incident that resulted in Moser's expulsion from the church was dwelt upon and the attitude of the man—who, to reenter the church, would have to admit that he did wrong when he did not believe that he had and to apologize to Witzig—justified. "Still," said Mr. Green, "you cannot get them away from the church" Samuel Moser is as big a fool as he ever was. Didn't you see him affirm when he took the stand?" Mr. Green alluded to Witzig as "that gorilla-faced individual" and said he would as soon repent to a mummy. The testimony of Moser that he could not work while in Minnesota after his wife left him, that he was sad and sorrowful, and that he bought the revolver to end his own life was emphasized.

The details of the murder were reviewed by Mr. Green as showing Moser's irresponsibility. When Attorney Green described the killing of Mrs. Moser and the children by the father, it brought tears to the eyes of many in the audience, but the defendant kept his face covered and shed no tears. "Murder must be willful, felonious, and malicious," explained Mr. Green, "but there is no evidence that Moser had malice toward his wife." Volitional insanity, the irresistible impulse to destroy or kill, was explained. The various confessions of Moser in his interviews with reporters and others were somewhat discredited by Mr. Green, who said he had been unable to get Moser to talk to him, his client seeming to think he was inquiring into things that were none of his business. Mr. Rollins got more information from Moser in fifty minutes than anyone else had since. Mr. Green considered Moser a man cruelly wronged and said if he did not earnestly believe the man to be insane, he would not be arrayed in this case against such odds and talent. The incoherency of the letters was pointed out and the fact that they stated the case of the trouble.

Mr. Green made an eloquent plea for Moser, stating that the man had been deserted by all his friends and relatives and that in all the world, he had but two protectors: the law of the land and his counsel. "Thwarted at every step by the father and mother of that man in procuring testimony on his behalf, deserted by his family with the exception of the insane brother and of the other brother Reuben, absolutely deserted, absolutely alone—on trial for one of the most infamous crimes, if he was a sane man, that was ever committed in any country. I simply ask you, gentlemen, on his behalf, in passing upon the questions of fact involved in this case, keep in mind the evidence, all the evidence that has been introduced before you. Bear in mind the promises that you made in regard to the degree of proof that you would require at the hands of the people in this case, and in my judgment, your path to a verdict in this case is an easy one. You cannot help but say in your own conscience, guided by this evidence, governed by the law, that, that man under the evidence in this case at your hands is entitled to an acquittal, and I ask you for that kind of a verdict."

The arguments were confined strictly to such facts as were contained in the records, and Mr. Green acknowledged with some signs of discouragement that he had been under a particularly heavy disadvantage, his client refusing to talk and many of the witnesses appearing only with the greatest reluctance and saying as little as they possibly could. Green talked for three hours.

He was followed by the state's attorney J. W. Cunningham, who talked for forty-five minutes. He started by explaining that it was the duty of the state's attorney to see that the laws were upheld. He said the case had been a great burden for three weeks, but there had been the kindliest feelings between court and counsel and everyone generally. He had no feeling against any church, and every word that had been uttered against the Amish church had been done for a purpose. The counsel for the state had tried to divert the minds of the jurors from the real issue of the case. He believed the world is better for the churches and that the jury would rather see a Bible in the house than a revolver.

Every witness who took the stand was satisfied Moser knew right from wrong and that the law should hold such a man accountable for his acts. As to character witnesses, every man had a good character until he committed some felonious act. Mr. Cunningham followed the flight of the horror-stricken murderer: "He reached Salt Lake City. His physical condition is weak. His mind is weak—whose would not be? He goes out and buys a paper and looks for the account of his crime. Then he decides to kill himself and writes the letters, showing the man was not right, was no doubt in mental distress, and had remorse."

He alluded to Dr. Warren's testimony that Moser's acts were too deliberate to be those of an insane man. "There was system and deliberation in his actions. His brain was probably not in a normal condition, but he tried to cover up his crime and effect his flight. Mr. Green asked you what the motive was. It was to bring down public disgrace and calamity on the church, to get rid of his wife because he could not rule her. In one letter, he says, 'Before I would be ruled by my wife, I choose to die.'

"Moser says he would have tried to 'pull through' if he could have 'got around the penalty of death.' He went down in the River Jordan and hid around in the bushes, he says, until the people stopped passing. But wasn't it because he was a coward and lacked the nerve to do what he knew he ought to do? He has killed four different people. You can only hang him once, but if the law is to be upheld, Moser should suffer for his crime.

"The testimony of these two physicians had a telling effect and greatly strengthened the case of the prosecution. This insanity dodge is the last resort of every murderer. When anyone commits a rash act, such as killing a man, that person is partially insane. Most anyone has at one time or other felt insane promptings, and mad impulses have arisen in the mind, prompting one to do some foolish act. Because Moser was ignorant, because he was thrown out of the church, and even though he had insane tendencies, is no justification for him taking the lives of innocent children. What a fine example he would present to the world were he to be set free and allowed to be at large, for if he is found not guilty, that is what it will mean."

The court then read the instructions to the jury. The instructions of the court covered the technical meaning of *murder, reasonable doubt*, etc., and the law on all material points that the jury would need to consider in its deliberations.

Later that day, state's attorney Cunningham was asked by a *Star* reporter what would be done in case that Sam Moser would be found not guilty. Mr. Cunningham said that it would liberate Sam. He explained that Sam was currently being tried for the murder of his wife, Hanna Moser. While there were three more indictments to which he must answer, Moser had already cost the county several thousand dollars. If he was found not guilty of Hanna's murder, it was doubtful that he would be tried again as a similar trial and outcome might be expected.

Chapter 16
The Verdict

It costs a lot more than your
life. To murder innocent people?
It costs everything you are.

—Suzanne Collins

Tuesday
March 5, 1901

Moser's fate was now in the hands of the twelve men who had been sworn to judge him according to the law and the evidence. Thousands of people all over the country waited to hear the results. Moser didn't talk to anyone. He just waited.

Judge Puterbaugh finished instructing the jury at 6:20 p.m., and the jury was sent out. They first went to the Tazewell hotel where they took supper in the private dining room in which they had taken their meals during the trial. At 7:20 p.m., they were marched to the courthouse where they took their first informal vote. Three were for hanging, two for acquittal, and seven for a prison sentence. The discussion began. Judge Puterbaugh left the courthouse about 9:50 p.m. but would return early the next morning in the hope that a verdict might be reached. The sheriff's office was open, and a few court attachés remained there.

A cold wave swooped down in the evening, causing the streets to be deserted to a great extent, but groups of people gathered in the stores and talked over the probable outcome of the case. Those who had been in the courtroom most of the time looked for a penitentiary sentence. A story circulated that the jury at the time of their retirement stood ten to two for conviction, but no one seemed to know how this information had come to them. The jury was closely guarded. There were many who believed the statement while there were many others inclined to doubt its authenticity.

By the seventh ballot, it was found that the two would not agree to the death penalty; they agreed to recede from their position if the two would agree to a long-term on imprisonment. By four o'clock in the morning, on the ninth and tenth ballots, the figures were changed to eleven to one. It's easy to imagine a tired and frustrated jury working to persuade the last remaining holdout to switch sides. An hour later, he did. After a night of discussion and balloting, the compromise was reached at 5:10 a.m.

The jury went to the hotel and partook of breakfast. When breakfast was cleared away, they spent the time until nine, smoking and congratulating themselves that the long siege had been raised. Liberty after twenty-two days of imprisonment was gladly welcomed.

Judge Puterbaugh was notified and left as soon as possible, taking an early train to Pekin. He arrived at nine o'clock, and after court convened, Moser was brought in. As they waited for the jury, Sam told his lawyer that he didn't think they'd hang him. He would be satisfied with a penitentiary sentence. The jurymen filed in one by one into the courtroom to take their places. They seemed greatly relieved. It was not generally known that a verdict had been reached, so the courtroom was only half filled.

The judge addressed them, "Gentlemen, have you agreed on a verdict?"

The foreman, Abe Thornton, replied, "We have." The verdict was handed to the judge. The crowd was silent, on the edge of their seats. On March 5, 1901, in the Tazewell County circuit court at Pekin, Illinois, the verdict was read by Judge Leslie Puterbaugh in a strong clear voice:

"We, the jury, find the defendant, Samuel Moser, guilty of the crime of murder, in manner and form as charged in the indictment."

Moser sat, unmoving—his face resting on his left hand, eyes turned to the floor. He did not seem to hear the verdict. It was said later that had the verdict been that of death, he would have remained as immovable as though it had been acquittal. Some were reminded of his words from before the trial: "I don't care what they do with me."

State's Attorney Cunningham asked that the prisoner's age be inserted in the verdict, but Attorney Green at once jumped up and said it made no difference whether it was in or not and asked for a new trial. He stated that he had only the night before learned some new facts that he wished to bring out, and the judge said he would give him a chance to do so. Mr. Green asked that the jury be polled, and each one declared that the verdict was his. Sam's eyes were fixed on each juror. The judge then discharged the jury, and they slowly filed out, some of them stopping to shake hands with the lawyers and court attachés.

As Sam was led to an anteroom to consult with his attorney, he said, "I am satisfied." After a brief consultation, Sam was taken back to the jail. He repeated that he was satisfied to Sheriff Mount as they walked back to the jail. A reporter apparently misunderstood him and wrote that he said, "It ain't right." Others reported that "a smile crept over his countenance" at the reading of the verdict and that "his face showed more signs of intelligence than had been visible during the entire trial," insinuating that he'd been manipulating the jury. In general, though, people seemed to be in agreement with the verdict. The verdict quickly became known all over town and was the sole topic of conversation. Both sides were congratulated, the prosecution because they had secured a conviction and the defense because the prisoner's life had been saved.

Sam was told he would be taken to Joliet probably sometime the next week. People speculated that if Moser was sent to the penitentiary, he would live only a short time. It already appeared that the trial had taken a great toll on him. It was felt that he wouldn't be able to do the hard work required behind prison doors.

Sheriff Mount reported that Moser had nothing to say. He acted exactly as he did before the trial, and the verdict did not seem to have affected him at all. He expressed neither joy nor regret and was busy reading his German history. The Moser family was evidently pleased that Sam would not be hung. It was said that they expected a jail sentence. Some, however, were still of the opinion that Benedict Moser had given financial aid. If the case would be taken to a higher court, this theory would be generally accepted. The jurors had departed, only too glad to return to their homes and families.

State's Attorney Cunningham received many callers in his office the next morning. Several congratulatory telegrams were also received from newspaper people and others in outside cities who had followed the progress of the trial. "Well, you can say for me that I am satisfied," said Mr. Cunningham. "I am satisfied because I have to be, and because the verdict is about all that the state could hope for. The plea of insanity and the alleged church persecution were the two elements that saved Moser's neck. It was a hard fight, harder than people realize, and we consider the result a victory."

Jesse Black, who had assisted him, was likewise pleased. He said that it was a big victory. He felt that the verdict vindicated the law. It was Attorney Black's first great criminal case, and he had made a good reputation for himself. He was evidently very pleased with the verdict and spoke enthusiastically of the result. He and Attorney Cunningham had done all that was within their power to see that justice was done.

The newspapers reported that arguments for a new trial in the Moser case would be held on Friday. Some startling disclosures would be made. It was said that affidavits would be presented showing that one of the jurors said on three different occasions that he would like to get on the jury and hang Moser. Another had expressed an opinion that he ought to be convicted. But the most important piece of evidence was a sheet of instruction that had not been given by the judge. The paper had been printed at a job printing office and had original instructions in typewriting.

It was not favorable to the defendant and had not been given to the jurymen by the court. They had used it as scratch paper, and five of them had scribbled their names on the back. Mr. Green proposed to find out how it got into the jury's hands.

He stated that he had sufficient grounds for a new trial and that he would push his claims to the utmost. There seemed little on which to base expectation of a new trial, but Green expressed confidence that the judge would rule in his favor and said that he was going to fight the case to the finish. Even those who disagreed with Mr. Green had to admire him. He was the only protector Moser had, and it was due to his efforts that Sam's neck was saved. A lot of people sympathized with Moser, even if they thought he was guilty.

Mr. Cunningham and Deputy Ball said that the instructions in question were there for years. There was a table in the jury room, and in the drawer of the table there were old instructions. The jurors opened the drawer and took out one of the sheets to write on. The jurors would make affidavits that they did not even read them but used the back of the old instructions for writing paper.

The state's attorney said the prosecution would resist the application for a new trial with all the force at their command. A new trial would come as a calamity to the people of the county. Tazewell was already weighed down with debt brought on by the various murder trials. The Moser trial had cost the county between six and seven thousand dollars, and a second trial would cost far more. Everyone knew that it would be impossible to retry the case there anyway. The general opinion was that Moser gotten off easy and should serve his sentence. They asserted that the defendant should be satisfied.

To this, Mr. Green responded, "Indeed I am not satisfied. People are saying that I got Moser out of it easily, but that isn't the way I look at it. If he is guilty of murder, this is no punishment, and if he isn't guilty, he deserves acquittal. There can be no just compromise in a case like this. There are only two possibilities, and the verdict comes within neither of them."

Mr. Cunningham, when discussing the matter, said that at the last trial, Mr. Green tried the Reverend Witzig and not the defendant. But at the next trial, if he were to secure one, he would be compelled to try the defendant and the defendant alone.

At 3:30 p.m. on Friday, the circuit court was convened. But to everyone's surprise, Attorney Green, for Samuel Moser, stated that he wished to withdraw his notification for a new trial. This being granted, Judge Puterbaugh commanded Moser to stand while sentence was passed upon him. When asked if he had anything to say, Moser simply shook his head no. Judge Puterbaugh sentenced him to twenty-one years in the penitentiary at Joliet, in accordance with the verdict. The first day was to be passed in solitary confinement and the remainder of his term to be spent at hard labor. If Moser was an obedient prisoner, he could earn his release in eleven years and nine months, which would make him forty-five years old at the expiration of his term.

After the adjournment of court, state's attorney Cunningham asked permission to speak to the prisoner. Cunningham approached Moser, who suddenly jumped up and struck him in the face. Moser's face was flushed with anger, and he looked surprised at the reactions around him, asking "Did you say you wanted to fight?" Moser was hustled out of the courtroom by the sheriff, and the attorney went looking for a hydrant.

After Sam had calmed down, he asked Sheriff Mount to have Mr. Cunningham to come to the jail. The state's attorney went over to the jail, and Sam apologized to him for the wrong he had done. He was under the impression that Cunningham was trying to tease him. "A few days ago, I heard you say you wanted to fight me, and I thought that was what you said to Mr. Green just now," Moser explained.

Mr. Cunningham replied, "Why, Sam, I said nothing about fighting you. I simply desired to talk with you."

Matters were again explained to him, and he was finally quieted. Cunningham asked him if he did not think he got off pretty easy, but Moser made no response. He would be taken to Joliet on Wednesday. The struggle was over. It had been a long and weary trial; and the jurymen, lawyers, and court officials rejoiced that it was finally at an end.

Just before the jury was secured for the Moser trial, T.N. Green's father, Judge Nathaniel W. Green, began complaining of respiratory distress. He'd had a cough for a few days before that, he'd said, but now he tired easily, felt poorly, and was achy. They'd agreed that he'd have to stay close to the house on South Fourth Street in Pekin and try to head it off.

The elder Judge Green was considered one of the most able jurists in Illinois, but his son worried that this trial was causing him stress. He'd always taken on the weight of the cases his son was handling. They'd discussed his cases, and his father felt useful in advising his son on the details of the trial. But this case was different—it was so public, so controversial, so draining. His father knew better than anyone how difficult it was for him and the toll it took on his family.

He'd seemed better. They'd both had a break from the trial while the sick juror, Roy Miller, was recuperating. He'd been his old self and seemed more rested. But then he'd insisted on getting back to work. Too soon, obviously. The very day that the trial had resumed, he'd gone to Peoria to take depositions. He was taken in a faint and had to be brought home. Such a blow to his ego to have to be brought home like an old feeble man. He'd complained, but it had obviously scared him. He'd stayed around home since then.

On Sunday, March 10th, the judge ate Sunday dinner with his family. At three o'clock that afternoon, he was seated in the parlor talking to his daughter, Miss Lillian, and his son Don. He arose from his chair and started to walk across the parlor to the settee. He began to falter, and his children, observing this, tried to catch him, but he went down, clutching his chest. Medical aid was summoned, but the spirit had departed. Two days after the close of the trial, T. N. Green's father, Judge N. W. Green, was dead.

Chapter 17
Joliet Penitentiary

I believe in two things:
discipline and the Bible.
Here you'll receive both.
Put your trust in the Lord;
your ass belongs to me.
Welcome to Shawshank.

—Warden Samuel Norton, in
The Shawshank Redemption

Wednesday
March 13, 1901

In his 1853 inaugural speech, Governor Joel Matteson told his constituents that a new penitentiary was needed in Northern Illinois. With the population of Illinois quickly expanding, the crime rate was increasing rapidly, and it was expensive to transport prisoners downstate to the outdated prison at Alton. The location suggested was Joliet, Illinois.

Seventy-two acres were purchased along Collins Street, two miles north of the city for about $100 an acre. Ground was broken, and preparations begun in the late summer of 1857. There would be a staggering 1,100 cells, with 100 for solitary confinement and 100 for women, with two wings of cells on each side of the warden's quarters.

The first thirty-three inmates arrived from Alton to begin construction in May of 1858. Eventually, 160 prisoners would supply the labor force, with more inmates arriving as cells were completed. The use of convict labor kept costs low, with the total price tag for the project estimated at $75,000. The prison would be the largest in the country, and its design would become a model for United States prisons.

The last prisoners were transferred in July of 1860. When the Civil War broke out less than a year later, 800 convicts were serving time in Joliet. For the next four years, both criminal prisoners and prisoners of war were kept there. The population had reached 1,239 by 1872—a record number for a single prison.

Though it was birthed with an eye toward reform, Joliet prison was still a very primitive, difficult environment for the men who lived there. In 1877, a commission was appointed to investigate reports of brutality in the disciplining of prisoners in "solitary confinement." Whipping and gagging were said to be standard punishment, and prisoners were routinely tied to the iron doors of the cell. A prison physician recommended that "sound-deadened" walls be installed in the solitary quarters. The report complained that prisoners feigned insanity hoping to be removed from the prison. In 1898, there were thirty-two deaths from tuberculosis.

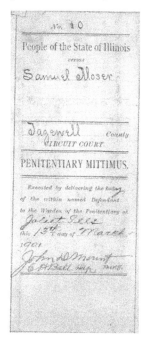

Samuel Moser arrived at Joliet Penitentiary on March 13 of 1901. Deputy Ball and Sheriff John D. Mount signed the body receipt, showing that he'd been delivered as promised. He went through the usual routine: bath, shave, haircut, and then a night in the solitary cell. They also took the series of measurements that had become known as Bertillon measurements. This precursor to fingerprinting consisted of five identifying measurements—head length, head breadth, length of middle finger, length of the left foot, and length of the forearm. Joliet prison was a pioneer in this new scientific system.

Sam was measured and weighed. He answered questions and followed orders, and finally he slept. He almost wished he could stay in solitary. He almost wished he had hanged.

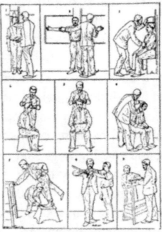

RELEVÉ
DU
SIGNALEMENT ANTHROPOMÉTRIQUE

1. Taille. — 2. Envergure. — 3. Buste. —
4. Longueur de la tête. — 5. Largeur de la tête. — 6. Oreille droite. —
7. Pied gauche. — 8. Médius gauche. — 9. Coudée gauche.

No. 7342　　Samuel Moser　　ASSIGNED TO

Received March 13th 1901　　Ratian #2
Sentence 21 years　　Mar 16/01 Hosp
Mar 27/01 Ratian 2
May 1/25 Chair 3

County Tazewell　　Term of Court February
Crime Murder

Color White　　Age 32
Hair ch dk　or　Eyes dk red Nativity Illinois
Height 5' 3¾" Build med　Weight 130
Religion Eumanish　　Education Com. school
Profanity yes　　Drink yes
Smoke no　　Chew no
Shoe #6　　Associates good
Parents Living yes　　Father Born in Switzerland
Left Home What Age 21　　Mother " " Ohio
Married yes　　Children
Wife Living no　　Where
Heriditary Disease none
Condition of Heart normal　　Lungs normal
Arrested Before no　　Crime
Occupation Farmer
Working When Arrested on Present Charge yes
How Long Before, if not
Name and Address of } Father Mrs. B. Moser,
Parents and Family, or }　　Morton,
Correspondents }　　Illinois

Remarks:

Life went on for those left in the wake of the trial. Though they were relieved that the chaos had quieted, there were matters to attend to and decisions to make.

There was a quantity of grain stored on Samuel Moser's farm. The family decided that it would be sinful for them to touch the grain, but instead hired men who were not members of the church to haul the grain to market and divided the money among themselves. It was reported in the papers that the church members had "plundered" Moser's farm.

On Tuesday, March 12, 1901, which would have been Ezra Moser's eighth birthday, an article ran in the newspapers called "Farmers to Move."

> There is now a well-grounded statement made in circles directly concerned that the trial of Sam Moser in Pekin is to be followed by widespread results in the Amish community, of which he was a member. Men who reside in the locality say that the Amish people are exceedingly cast down. The court revelations of their church discipline has touched them to the quick. Some of their most important men are now advocating a general removal, and the changes seem to be that this policy will be gradually carried out.

> The first step to be taken is the sending of agents to Dakota to look up a suitable farming location for the colony. If this prospecting proves encouraging, the Amish farms in Tazewell County will be thrown on the market,

and there will be a general exodus. Their religion is more to these people than life itself, and they cannot bear the opprobrium which they imagine follows the developments in the case of Samuel Moser.

It is, of course, a fact that, in its essence, their creed is unpatriotic. That much was revealed in this city some time ago in matters electoral. But the spirit of drastic discipline applied to those who fail in observing the Puritanic rules of the church was not understood by the mass of the people here. Now that the facts are fairly well known, there is more or less outspoken hostility to the New Amish Church, and those responsible for its policy seem to think that it will be best for all hands to pull up stakes and seek a new community location.

This defense had created a great stir in Illinois, and many Amish farmers felt that it would be best to seek a new location for the colony. It was suggested that they relocate somewhere in the state of North Dakota. The colony, which occupies the greater part of the counties of Tazewell and McLean, is wealthy, and its farms are among the best improved and most valuable in the state. The members of the community are almost without exception well-to-do, and from a financial point of view, it will be a fine thing for this state if real estate dealers succeed in interesting them in North Dakota lands.

It is understood that it is desired to close the deal as soon as possible as to longer remain in Illinois will be unpleasant owing to recent events. During the recent trial, all the fanatical teachings of the New Amish Church were exposed. There is a large community of wealthy Amish farmers in Tazewell and McLean counties, and they are greatly downcast by the revelations of their creed. It is announced today that they will probably give up their rich farms in this state and seek a new location in the northwest for their colony. Agents will be sent to Dakota for prospecting purposes.

Speaking of the matter yesterday, a man who is interested in inducing the Amish farmers to locate here said, "I consider that it will be a big thing to get the Illinois farmers here. They are all well-off, and will bring a great deal of property to the state. They are good, thrifty farmers, as has been proven from the condition of their farms in Illinois."

An article in the *Minneapolis Journal* confirmed the news on March 16:

> One of the big real estate firms of Grand Forks, North Dakota, has received several letters from representatives of a community of rich Amish farmers who, at present, reside in Tazewell and McLean Counties in Illinois. Negotiations have been opened for the purchase of large tracts of land in this state, and it is thought the deal will be closed in the near future. The negotiations have progressed so far that a representative of the prospective purchasers will be here within a few days and look the situation over. [The Samuel Moser trial] has created a great stir in Illinois, and the Amish farmers have decided that it would be best to seek a new location for the colony somewhere in North Dakota. The colony, which occupies the greater parts of the counties of Tazewell and McLean, is immensely wealthy, and the farms are among the best improved and most valuable in the state. The members of the community are almost without exception very wealthy; and from a financial point of view, it will be a very fine thing for this state if the real estate dealers here succeed in interesting them in North Dakota lands.

On the first of October 1901, a national conference was held at the old Amish church, five miles south of Gridley on the line of the TP&W Railroad. The newspaper reported that one thousand delegates were present from Kansas, Missouri, Illinois, Iowa, Nebraska, Ohio, Indiana, and even Utah (which was likely the Tremonton settlement). Records of these gatherings, found as early as 1869 in newspapers, indicate that they were held regularly before and were common practice among the Amish and the Mennonite as well. But this particular gathering was surely held, at least in some measure, to address the crisis the church had faced as a result of the expulsion of Samuel Moser. One newspaper pointed out that "every state where the sect is numerically strong has showed the effects of the quadruple murder and the revelations concerning the faith that followed when the trial was held."

Headlines blared "Shots Shook the Church," and "Sam Moser's Revolver Revolutionizes the Amish." Though the elders may have disagreed with the reporters who wrote that they were meeting to "revise their rigid laws and tone down their religious austerities, so as to make their creed and condition conform more closely to society as it is found in a civilized society," it is likely that there were discussions of damage control and public perceptions as the church had spent the last year and a half fighting off "attacks upon the sect, prompted by the crime."

"The desire for the revision has been brought about by the scathing arraignment to which they were subjected at the trial of Samuel Moser last March for the murder of his wife and children." While reporters may have exaggerated the goals of the conference, it is also possible that the group of elders gave them a statement as one report said that "it was given out that the principal object of this conference is to revise their religious laws." All the proceedings were carried on in the German tongue, and great secrecy prevailed.

It was said that since the trial, the young Amish had shown an inclination to break away from the church, owing to its religious rules. For this reason the conference was called, that more privileges may be granted to preserve and increase the faith.

The world moves, and religious conditions
are compelled to move with it.

In November of 1902, the National Apostolic Convention of the New Amish Church held its sessions in Pekin, Illinois. There were reportedly nine hundred delegates present from various parts of the United States, Germany, France, and Canada. The sessions were conducted with the greatest secrecy, none being admitted to the church except those who were known to be members. Those of the New Amish faith were bitterly opposed to publicity of their proceedings in church or convention, and also comments upon their peculiar religious beliefs. The report was that some of the members were reprimanded for having speculated in land in Missouri and Mississippi, the board of elders arguing that it was simply a form of gambling. Several years ago, the church conducted an insurance department on the mutual plan; but during the last year, it was dropped. Since then, the members had been insuring their buildings in the regular companies. At the convention, it was decided to again engage in the fire insurance business on the mutual plan, and all members were instructed to cancel the policies now held by them and insure in the church association. None of the members were permitted to take out life insurance policies.

On December 16, 1902, the news broke that Daniel Moser had threatened his father unless he was given money.

Dan lives at Wheaton, IL, but refuses to work. He has a family of eleven children. His father, Benedict Moser, has given him money, and Dan Moser's wife is compelled to take in washing. The other day, Dan went to the home

288

of his father. He claims his father owes him $300. He went to Benedict Moser's home near Pekin Friday evening and threatened the family if the money was not turned over to him. Benedict Moser, fearing his life, went there and swore out a state's warrant for the arrest of his son. He was brought there late Saturday evening by Sheriff Clay and is in the county jail. He has his hearing today, and Attorney Frings has been retained to defend him. There is something wrong with the Moser family.

On December 31, 1902, a report titled "Troubles of the Moser Family" was run in the papers:

Benedict Moser of Morton filed a petition in the county court asking that his son Daniel, brother of Sam Moser, murderer of his wife and three children, be tried for insanity. Daniel Moser claims the constant nagging of his father, who endeavored to convert him to the new Amish religion, has driven him insane.

From there, Sam's story goes quiet for some time—until another man tells a similar story and Moser is asked to testify as a witness.

Chapter 18
The Isch Trial

Meekness: Uncommon patience in planning
a revenge that is worthwhile.

—Ambrose Bierce

1907

On October 7, 1907, a prominent Peoria businessman (vice president of a large implement firm in Peoria, Illinois) and former member of the Amish community in Tazewell County, Rudolph Isch, brought suit in the circuit court for $50,000 against Elder Rudolph Witzig, alleging conspiracy. Samuel Moser was to be brought from Joliet Prison to testify in the trial.

Sixteen years before, Isch was punished after breaking one of the rules of the church, which specified that no member of the religious sect shall be weighed. After engaging in a game of pool, he was refused permission to engage in church conferences.

When the elder learned that he had participated in a game of cards, Isch alleged that he was excommunicated. His wife and children were forbidden to eat at the same table with him or have anything else to do with him. (It was later reported that his banishment was a result of casting a ballot in an election, which was also taboo.)

Newspapers reported that Isch "charged that a wholesale plot was concocted, resulting in a systematic persecution of himself and family and the ruination of a once profitable business." He was driven from his employment in an Indiana town through the power of the church and hounded from place to place.

Isch described being separated from his family, his savings dissipated, and his means of subsistence taken from him—all because he was charged with behaviors that were contrary to the rules of the Amish church.

Newspaper articles covering the hearing described the elder Rudolph Witzig as a wealthy farmer from Metamora, owning several farms and worth a reported $200,000. Witzig's jurisdiction as an elder reportedly extended over the states of Illinois, Indiana, Kansas, Iowa, and Minnesota.

On January 4, 1908, a declaration of ten thousand words was filed in the circuit court. The plaintiff charged that because he had the temerity to express his views on the rules of the church, Elder

Witzig conspired with practically all the preachers and members of the Amish church to drive him out of business and that the members of his own church hounded him from state to state until his reputation was ruined. Isch charged that Witzig issued edicts which drove the plaintiff's own family to turn against him through fear of excommunication. The elder was also accused of saying publicly that Isch was the devil's own child.

On Friday May 8, 1908, the *Peoria Star* printed a massive several-page article summarizing the lawsuit:

Law Invoked to End Relentless Rule of Czar of the New Amish Church:

Persecuted by Elder Witzig, Rudolph Isch Appeals to the Court

Expelled Members Hounded for Years by Mandates of the Church

W. W. Robinson's dramatic retelling of Isch's persecution included a reminder to the public of Witzig's role in the Moser trial. Illustrated with ominous pen drawings of the elders looking downright evil, the article began with a comparison to the Catholic church:

Around her form I draw the sacred circle of our most solemn church. Step but one foot within that holy ground and upon thy head, yea though it wear a crown, will I launch the curse of Rome.

—Richelieu

So in olden times did Richelieu threaten with the thunderbolts of the most mighty religious organization the world has ever known, the audacity of the most powerful monarch in existence.

Since that day, the son of liberty but then rising above the eastern horizon has touched the zenith, but still there remains in the hands of the mother church this most dreaded of weapons to bring to terms those who rebel against the mandates of its spiritual and temporal head.

Having painted a clear picture in the minds of his readers of the very kind of controlling religion they despised, Robinson then sets the stage to tell the backstory:

Let us turn back a space of thirty years, and we shall see the curtain rung up on as strange a drama as was ever enacted, a drama that is now drawing to a close.

The scene is a rough, unpretentious building in the little town of Roanoke in the state of Illinois. It is near evening. A score of persons have gathered there to worship their Creator according to their strange creed. The service is drawing to a close; the voice of the minister is stilled.

It is not an ordinary congregation that waits the minister's word of dismissal. A majority of them are men and women past the prime of life, men and women who are clad in somber garments: sad-faced men and women.

The seating arrangements too are out of the ordinary. On the one side are the men, on the other the women. The elders occupy the front chairs, the younger members those in the rear.

Certain peculiarities of features and dress may be noted. The men are heavily bearded, the upper lip alone being shaved. Articles of adornment, such as neckties, watch chains, rings are missing. The women are attired in extremely plain dresses, hats guiltless of ribbon or feathers, their hair caught in a fine net.

Moments drag by without a sound to break the silence. Rigid as a statue the minister stands. The shadows deepen, and the light grows fainter.

A heavily shod foot grates on the floor. At the sound, the minister opens his eyes and, with a single word, makes it known that the service is completed. The younger worshipers in the rear arise and slowly file out. As they pass through the door, one of the elders who has opened it touches a young man on the shoulder and bids him remain. As he turns and retraces his footsteps, he is led to the space before the platform and faces the minister.

There is no mercy in the eyes that the minister directs toward the youth that stands before him. In cold, even tones, he speaks. "Rudolph Isch, you are accused of willfully violating the rules of the one true church. You are accused of worldly practices, practices forbidden members of our faith, practices that will corrupt your associates and bring disgrace and dishonor to your parents. Have you or have you not transgressed our rules?"

There is no reply from the accused. Directing his gaze toward the congregation, the minister singles out one after the other, and in turn, they arise and bear witness against the youth. Each charge is repeated by the minister, and to each charge there is entered no denial.

With the conclusion of the testimony, there is a summing up by the judge, and then, without a pause, comes the sentence of excommunication, a sentence received in silence by all except one woman as the dreaded ban is placed on her son.

Rudolph Isch is banished from the church of his fathers. The gates of heaven have been closed against him. This was thirty years ago. The minister who inflicted the punishment upon the youth is still living, an old man, still supreme head of his church, still armed with the same weapon. The youth has grown into a man, now in the prime of his life, still outside the pale of the church, determined at last to obtain redress for the wrongs inflicted upon him.

It was a simple matter for Rudolph Witzig, ruling elder of the New Amish Church to expel Rudolph Isch, a mere youth, from the church, to cause him to leave home, to hound him from place to place, to forbid members of the church from giving him shelter or food, to place a boycott against him from gaining a livelihood, to cause him sleepless nights and days of anguish. All this was easy for a man so firmly entrenched in power that none dare question his motives.

But there comes a time when justice seeks her own, when the victim rebels against ceaseless persecution and, with all his strength, turns and defends himself. And that day, after thirty years, has arrived.

Banished from the church, with the knowledge that its laws no longer hold him, Rudolph Isch has appealed to the laws of his country, the laws—ought at naught by the elder and his followers—and in the circuit court of Peoria County during the present month, he will seek redress the law affords him, monetary compensation for the evil done him. Above and beyond the thought of whatever amount of money he can obtain as damages, however, is the knowledge that the exposure of the man who has pursued him so relentlessly for thirty years is to be accomplished at last, that Witzig is to be unmasked before the community, that in open court his stewardship is to be questioned.

The trial of the suit bids fair to be one of the most notable in the annals of the courts of Illinois and to rank second in interest only to the criminal case in Pekin several years ago when Samuel Moser, a member of the New Amish Church, expelled by this same Witzig, forbidden to associate with his wife and children, driven temporarily insane, murdered his wife and three children, and was sentenced to the penitentiary at Joliet.

For the thirty years that he has been hounded from pillar to post, Isch has never once dismissed from his memory the thought that someday he might strike back at the hand which had smitten him. For thirty years he has planned his revenge, and when he appears in court, it is said that the story he will tell and the evidence of the witnesses who will support him will be of such a nature as to shock the community. The events of the last thirty years will be laid bare before the jury.

At the time that Rudolph Isch was thrust from the church, his father was absent from home. His mother's pleas that action be delayed until her husband returned met with refusal from Witzig. The elder informed her he has evidence that her boy had indulged in sinful practices. At the hearing in the church, it developed that the boy had played a game of pool one day and that, on another day, he had weighed himself. These two ridiculous charges formed the basis for the accusations, and they were sufficient for Witzig to pronounce the sentences of expulsion from which there was no appeal.

Isch's parents and his brothers and sisters belonged to the New Amish Church. They protested against his expulsion but were warned to desist under threat of a similar fate. According to the rules of the church, a member is not allowed to eat or to sleep under the same roof with a person who has been expelled. There was but one thing for Rudolph to do: he left home. The first place he went was to Metamora, where he obtained employment in a grain office conducted by a member of the church. He had been there a short time when his employer was told by Witzig to discharge him under penalty of boycott. After trying to make a living in Illinois and failing because Witzig's influence was too great, the young man went to Minnesota, where he remained for several years. In the meantime, the father was growing old; and anxious to be near his parents, Isch came to Peoria and obtained a position with a Peoria implement company as a traveling salesman.

Assigned a territory near this city, Isch soon discovered that Witzig had not forgotten him. Members of the New Amish Church were warned not to purchase goods of any house that dealt with the firm for which Isch was working. He was a good salesman, and the Peoria firm did not desire to lose his services. In the hope that he could escape from Witzig, he was sent to Indiana. It happened, however, that at the time, the New Amish were starting several settlements in Indiana, and after a few months, Isch found the same condition confronting him. Witzig's influence had been brought to bear on the small dealers, and Isch could sell no goods.

The boycott was complete. In the meantime, the father and mother were having trouble. Some of the young sons, alarmed by the fate that had overtaken their brother, had refused to join the church. Witzig blamed the parents for the attitude of the children and subjected them to hundreds of trifling annoyances. Another brother left home. Rudolph was urged to take some steps to insure himself from the repeated attacks of the vicious elder, but whenever this was brought to his mind, he was reminded that it would cause additional trouble to his parents. He vowed that he would suffer in silence as long as his father lived.

Years passed by, and in the end, the father, worn out by trouble, finally passed away. Then came another difficulty. Witzig insisted that the body be interred in the Amish cemetery and according to the Amish rites. This would have barred the sons from attendance. Taking matters in his own hands, however, Rudolph brought his father's remains to Peoria, and the funeral was conducted in this city. Witzig and several of his associates refused to attend.

Having remained true to his vow not to seek revenge as long as his father lived, Isch began the work of collecting evidence against his persecutor. The case was placed in the hands of an able attorney, and suit was instituted. At this point, Isch received unexpected help. He had not been the only mark for Witzig's arrows. Emboldened by the knowledge that one man had dared to protest against the injustice done him, others who had been expelled came forward and offered Isch their aid. Dozens declared their willingness to testify in court as to Witzig's actions. The story got to the newspapers, and members of the church who had long chafed under Witzig's iron rule began to mutter and complain.

A few of the bolder men declared that they would no longer submit to the rules so rigidly enforced by this self-appointed czar. They were joined by numbers of the younger men who, by contact with Americans, had gained some idea of the blessedness of religious freedom and the curse of religious tyranny. In several places, new churches were formed, and everywhere could be heard words of condemnation of Witzig as the details of his curse became known.

Today Witzig's position is in peril. He knows that Isch is determined to press the suit to the utmost. He knows the nature of the evidence that will be produced in court. He knows that if he enters no defense, he can expect no mercy at the hands of the man he has so cruelly wronged. He also knows that if he does make a defense, he is violating a rule of his own church, a rule that he has enforced in the past to the letter. For it is forbidden for a member of the New Amish Church to appear in court as witness, juror, plaintiff, or defendant.

It is this last named condition that is causing Witzig a great deal of trouble. Time after time, he has compelled members of the church to settle suits brought against them by outsiders. He has warned them never to appeal to the law, never to allow themselves to be brought before the court. He has instructed them that it is a rule that must never be violated under any circumstances. And now he is in a position where he must appear as a defendant in a suit where his past will be revealed, a past that is black indeed.

* * * * *

Some Rules of the New Amish Church (Inset in the Newspaper)

- No member of the sect shall have his or her photograph taken.

- There shall be no sumptuous furnishing of homes. Wallpaper with figures on it and pictures on the walls are strictly forbidden.

- No carpets are allowed on the floors, unless homemade.

- The church must be a plain building and must be furnished plainly.

- Hooks and eyes are not allowed on the clothes; buttons are not allowed or articles of personal wear for ornament.

- All members are forbidden to go to law in any form and are not allowed to vote.

- Bearing arms, tale bearing, and taking of oaths are strictly forbidden.

- Courtship and marriage are provided for by the elders and ministers of the church.

- A man or woman must allow the church community to select a wife or husband.

- After the marriage ceremony has been performed, the couple are not allowed to take a wedding trip but must at once settle down as they are not allowed to have a wedding dinner or supper.

- No one may be admitted to the church until he or she has confessed their sins, with bowed heads and weeping, every Sunday for not less than six to eight weeks.

- Bishops, preachers, and elders are chosen by lot, and they are not allowed to accept any pay whatever for their services.

- It is prohibited that any man shall kiss or fondle his wife or children in public.

- Any member may be expelled providing the bishop or any elder or minister sees fit.

The Church Elders on Trial

Fairbury Blade

May 29, 1908

The Amish People

The much advertised suit, *Isch vs. Witzig,* which it was given out in the Peoria papers, was sure to be this term of court, has again failed to material-ize. The suit was brought by Rudolph Isch against Rev. Witzig of the Amish church. Isch claimed he had been put out of the church by Witzig and after-ward prevented from earning his liv-ing by the persecutions of Witzig and a number of elders of the German Apostolic Church. Last week, a page article appeared in the *Peoria Star* dealing with the matter in part and with the Amish people: their beliefs and personal life in general.

What the personal habits of the Amish have to do with the lawsuit of *Isch vs. Witzig*, it is difficult to determine. The suit will be decided according to its merits if it is ever brought to trial, and it is merely a matter between Messrs. Witzig and Isch. The article in question was a reflection upon the church and upon some of the church members.

In this country, man is permitted to worship God as he sees fit, and there is perhaps no more devout Christians in America than the Amish people. It is doubtful if there could be found a church of any denomination in the country every member of which is perfect, but no church is more strict in enforcing its discipline than the German Apostolic Church. If a member of the church is found unworthy and persists in doing the things he should not do, after he has been warned sufficiently, then he is dropped from the church membership. If he repents and proves his repentance is sincere, he is taken back into the church. And what good are church rules if they are not to be obeyed? And what good could churches accomplish upon the habits and acts of their members?

There are a large number of Amish people in this locality. They have a large church here and also one south of town. They are a law-abiding, peace-loving people who will go out of their way to avoid trouble. Many of these people have lived among us for over a quarter of a century—honest, hardworking, frugal people, liberal in their charities and helping one another whenever help is needed. They do not believe in living beyond their means or income, but when they have arrived, permit they desire. Many of them live in beautiful homes with surroundings as well kept as any in the city. As citizens, they, by their private and public acts, make themselves desirable to any community in which they live. We know but little of their church rules, but we do know that the members of the German Apostolic Church in this city are honest and capable citizens and consistent Christians. Any attempt to smirch them as a people and a church because one man is claimed to have injured another by overzealous efforts in church work is an injustice.

Almost a year later, on March 24, 1909, the newspaper reported that the jury had been secured in the case of *Rudolph Isch vs. Elder Witzig* and five other defendants prominent in the Amish church. Attorneys had made their opening speeches, and the taking of evidence had begun.

While this report claimed that Isch's expulsion from the Amish church took place twenty-five years before, Isch said that for the past ten years, he had been followed by Elder Witzig wherever he had attempted to do business throughout the Central West, and that the persecution of this aged elder, now seventy-five years old, and his brother—leaders of the German Apostolic Church—had caused him much personal suffering, as well as much loss in a business and financial way.

Judge Puterbaugh, who was again presiding over the trial, was having trouble with the witnesses, however. Over three hundred witnesses from throughout the central part of the state had been subpoenaed. The Amish, who were averse to going into court anyway, had apparently strategized since Samuel's trial. They presented certificates, stating that on account of their health, they were not able to attend court. But Judge Puterbaugh had gained some experience through his last go-round with the church as well. He responded by ruling that unless the certificate in each case was sworn to, it would be of no force, and the witness would be summarily brought before the court and dealt with as the case seemed to demand. "Owing to the fact that it is against the laws of the Amish church to take an oath, interest in the probable conduct of the witnesses for the defense is great," it was reported. "Tazewell, Woodford, and McLean Counties are well populated with members of the cult."

It was said that Sam Moser would be brought from the penitentiary to Peoria to testify.

Newspapers further reported that "the entire church membership has taken sides and is involved in a factional fight reaching to the borders of the church diocese. Open opposition through sympathy for Isch and rebellion against the stern measures of the German Apostolic Church has been aroused, and in the territory surrounding the seat of war, the feeling is most bitter. Wildest interest is being taken in the case, and Isch is receiving encouragement from dissatisfied members of the church from neighboring states."

On the second day of the trial, much time was taken in objections and arguments of the attorneys. No one seemed to mind this, however, as they were so interested in the other goings-on. It was said that nearly the entire population of Morton was in the courtroom. The line of seven elders was almost startling in appearance. "They are all so serious, so generous as to whiskers and hair, and their garments are so uniformly of the glacial period that their appearance behind any footlights as they appear in the courtroom would make their fortunes. Elder Witzig, the man against whom the brunt of the prosecution is leveled, is white-haired and bearded. He looks profoundly sorry that the case is in court and did not, on any occasion yesterday, permit himself the luxury of a smile, even at those times when the bailiff had to rap for order. The line of defendants is imposing and interesting."

Behind the defendants sat the others from the Amish church. "You can tell them at a glance. They are all of the same mold; and the entire crowd in the courtroom, with the exception of the attorneys and newspaper people, were strictly Amish and looked not unlike old pictures of the days of Miles Standish and his friends."

The women were present in large numbers, all wearing black and reportedly without smiles. They wore small black hats or black "fascinators" over their heads.

The first witness was Otto Seegar, who was at one time a minister of the old Amish church. He was now the founder of the New Amish Church on Hamilton Street and Knoxville Avenue at Peoria. He was described as "slowness personified" in his answers. "With great deliberation and hesitancy, he answered the questions that counsel on the other side would allow him to answer without objection."

Seegar said that he was formerly a clerk in one of the dry goods stores in Peoria, and the proprietor of the store was noti-fied that Seegar must be let out, or the Amish would transfer their trade. Seegar went out and was now employed by the Keystone

Steel & Wire Company. He stated that there was a "rule of the Amish church to restrain members from buying from a merchant who had been expelled from the church ad also a rule that members should not buy from a merchant who bought goods from a man who had been expelled from the church."

On Friday, March 26, Fred and Emil Isch testified. Rudolph's two brothers were strong witnesses, strengthening the case for the plaintiff. It was reported that the attention of the federal government had been called to the rules of the Amish religion as a result of testimony brought out in the suit of *Isch vs. Witzig et. al*, and that an investigation might result. "Plaintiff's counsel declare they have a trump card in the decision of the United States Supreme Court against the Mormon church rules." At this point, it was generally thought that the court, by his rulings on the admission of evidence, would place the suit in a position where it would be shut out of court.

News of the trial was spreading. In Iowa City, Iowa, on March 28, the headline read: "Sensational Suit Develops Peculiarities of Amish Faith." The writing was getting yet more dramatic: "Secrets of years of alleged religious oppression, dark and forbidden to the light, threaten to be revealed, and the power of the rules of the Amish church may be shaken in the trial of a sensational suit now pending in the circuit court of Peoria County."

On Monday the twenty-ninth, the rulings were announced. The two counts of the declaration alleging slander were dismissed by the court as to all six defendants. The charge of conspiracy and conspiracy to injure business were dismissed as to defendants Andrew Rapp, Christian Gerber, and John Schneider. The same charges were sustained and would go to the jury in the cases of Rudolph Witzig, Jacob Schmidt, and Michael Mangold. The plaintiff closed his case, and the defense commenced. Michael Mangold and Jacob Schmidt went on the stand. The line of defense was shown to be three passages of the Bible directing the faithful to withdraw from any who are ungodly or lawbreakers. Amish witnesses on the stand read the New Testament to the counsel.

Rudolph Witzig took the stand for two hours in the court Tuesday afternoon, March 30. He denied all statements made by Isch on the witness stand as to the persecution to which Isch claimed Witzig subjected him. John B. Niehaus acted as interpreter since Witzig spoke only German. He was scheduled to resume his testimony the next day and shortly after court convened. It was thought that he would probably be turned over to the counsel for the prosecution and would be subjected to a merciless cross-examination.

On Friday, April 2, Rudolph Isch was given a verdict of $1,000 in his case against the Amish elders. Only Rudolph Witzig and Michael Mangold were held, the jury finding that J. M. Schmidt was not guilty. It wasn't the $50,000 that he'd asked for, but it was something.

On April 15, it was announced that the Amish would appeal. Having discussed the subject with the members of the respective congregations of the German Christian Apostolic or Amish Church throughout Central Illinois, it was decided by Rudolph Witzig, the elder of the Gridley church, and Michael Mangold, elder of the church at Roanoke, to instruct their attorneys to enter a motion for a new trial of the suit brought against them by Rudolph Isch of Peoria and, in the event of it being denied, to carry the same to the appellate court.

But a follow-up article, dated May 5, said that the case had been closed. Following their time-honored custom, the Amish elders decided to settle this case rather than go on with further litigation; and the day before, John Schneider Jr. of Peoria handed a check for $1,000 to Joseph A. Well in the office of the circuit clerk and then paid the court costs, amounting to $261.93 in currency.

Officially it was over, but still more damage would be done to the reputation of the church before the week was out.

Fairbury Blade
May 7, 1909

Isch-Witzig Suit Settled

The Isch-Witzig lawsuit, which has attracted so much attention throughout the state of Illinois, and particularly in this section where all parties are known, has been settled. The case is a remarkable one. Rudolph Isch of Peoria was at one time a member of the German Apostolic Church at Morton. For some reason, he lost his membership in the church, and several years elapsed before he brought suit for damages against Elders Witzig, Mongold, Schneider, Gerber, Rapp, and Schmidt, of the German Apostolic Church for $50,000. The suit was filed two years ago, and Isch in his declaration alleged that the elders of the church had conspired to ruin his business and his trade. When the case went to trial on March 23, the judge knocked out several counts of the Isch declaration. The trial lasted several days, and when given to the jury, the judge in his instructions ordered the jury to bring in the verdicts of not guilty against Elders Gerber,

Rapp, and Schneider. The jury did this and also ignored Elder Schmidt in its finding, but they returned a verdict of $1,000 against Elder Witzig and Elder Mangold.

Arguments were made last Thursday for a new trial but were overruled by the judge, and preparations were being made by Mr. Cameron, attorney for Witzig, for an appeal. They, however, decided to settle the matter without further fighting in the courts; and Tuesday morning, John Schneider Jr. of Peoria handed Joseph A. Wiel, attorney for Isch, a check for $1,000 and also paid the court costs, amounting to $261.93.

In the opinion of many who heard the testimony in the trial, the elders had an excellent chance to win had they agreed to an appeal. But the Amish are of a peaceful disposition, and they probably figured that even if they beat Isch, it might amount to as much as the verdict.

Chapter 19
Monkey Hill

Where reporters cease from troubling
and typewriters are at rest...

1908

Most of what we know about the next chapter comes from the prison archives. One exception is a brief article in the *Peoria Star* from May 5, 1908. It reported the following:

> Moser has been an excellent prisoner at the penitentiary. By good conduct, he has reduced his term of imprisonment so that it will expire in about three years. He still broods over his troubles, however, and frequently expresses a desire to commit suicide.

On October 31, 1909, Sam wrote to the Honorable Governor C. S. Deneen:

> I take the liberty to inform you that I am incarcerated in penitentiary here at Joliet since March 1901. I believe I am held here not according to law. Is it or is it not illegal to commit a person in this institution without presentment of indictment? I have not seen nor received neither was informed of any. Is it legal to hold one under said circumstance? I have nobody to assist me to get my rights. Perhaps it is up to you my, dear sir, to make use of your power of pardonment and restore me to my legal rights. I cannot comply with law by publishing in newspaper and present a petition and what it all calls for. I have no money and no friend. Is there not provision in law for such are at hand? If you have no legal power (or for that matter any other methods or course) to restore me or cause me to

be restored to my legal right, please let
me know. I was sent from Pekin.

Yours truly,

Samuel Moser

He received a response on November 8, 1909:

Dear Sir,

I acknowledge the receipt of your
letter dated October 31 addressed to
Governor Deneen and have to state
that it has been referred to the State
Board of Pardons, who will communi-
cate with you directly.

Yours truly,

Secretary

On February 28, 1910, Benedict Moser wrote to the warden
of Joliet State Penitentiary:

Dear Sir:

Will you please kindly state to me
what day and what year Samuel Moser,
my son, will be released from the penitentiary under sentence he is now serving? Kindly send me another certificate
of his prison conduct that I may see
how he has been conducting himself
since you last made report tome. I am
sorry to say that I have lost or mislaid

the one you gave me a year or so ago
and greatly oblige.

Yours Truly,

Benedict Moser

Morton, Illinois

The warden responded later that day:

February 28, 1910

Mr. Benedict Moser

Morton, IL

Dear Sir:

Answering your inquiry of this
date, I would say that the term of your
son, Samuel Moser, No. 7342, is serving
the term of twenty-one years imprisonment in this institution on conviction
of murder. It will expire December 12,
1912, on his present record. I enclose
herein a certificate of conduct as
requested in your communication.

Yours respectfully,

Warden

For several months, Sam had been in feeble health. He was
subject to melancholy periods. The newspapers were reporting
that Halley's Comet would reappear soon, possibly snuffing out

all life on the planet. People began buying gas masks, "anticomet pills," and "anticomet umbrellas." Churches held all-night prayer vigils as doomsayers predicted that the comet would cause massive tides across the country.

It's hard to know what Samuel Moser feared most: the end of the world rushing to meet him or the possibility of parole. On March 14, he was found hanging from the window in his cell. He had made a rope from pieces of bed ticking during the night and had been dead for several hours when a guard found his body hanging from a nail.

Illinois State Penitentiary

Hospital *March 14* 19*10*

Convict *Samuel Moser* Reg. No. *7342*

Died at *5:55 A.M.* *March 14* 19*10*

Age *51*

Cause of Death *See coroner Verdict*

W. R. Fletcher
Physician.

In 1994, when I first met with Ben Hohulin about the murder of his aunt and cousins almost a hundred years before, he'd shared with me what he felt were the mysterious circumstances surrounding Sam's death. He believed that Sam did not die at Joliet Prison. This was his theory:

Samuel was due to get out of prison soon. His father had written to the warden to ask when Sam would be released. He had no wish for his son to come home and upset their lives all over again. Mr. Hohulin believed that Benedict had bribed the warden to fake Samuel's suicide. He then took Samuel out of the prison and helped him start a new life somewhere else.

Mr. Hohulin had spent a long time looking for Sam. He claimed that he'd checked burial records, talked to cemetery caretakers, and gone to genealogical societies. He was a member of the Apostolic Christian Church, so we can assume that he would have gotten the answers he was looking for if he'd asked the right people. But he'd found nothing.

Ben's theory is definitely intriguing. It's easy to imagine that times were much simpler than they are now and such a thing might be possible in 1910. It's even interesting to think that the Samuel Moser that many came to pity through his trial might have gotten a second chance to live away from the AC Church. It's not unthinkable that the warden, even beyond the temptation of a bribe, might want to help a man who lived quietly and respectfully within the prison—having served almost all his time anyway. Ben Hohulin was sure that was exactly what happened, and he was very convincing about it.

I started my own search by asking Ollie Moser Steidinger. She was Samuel Moser's niece, the daughter of his brother Christian Moser. She was also my husband's grandmother. Her sisters were "the elderly aunts" who had hung up on me when I first asked about the story years earlier. Ollie was now about eighty-eight years old and more curious about the story than her sisters had been. She wanted me to keep her informed of my progress in researching what happened. She had questions and opinions. She was a spunky old gal.

Ollie thought that Samuel was buried in an unmarked grave in an Apostolic cemetery near her parents, Christian and Lydia (Yoder) Moser. It was a quiet little country cemetery that was actually about three miles from my house. When I asked why she thought this, she could only say she had no idea. That was just the impression she had. She would have been eight years old when Samuel died.

While that doesn't give us a lot to go on, it is an interesting possibility. If you think of the logistics of the geography, it actually makes a lot of sense. If Benedict Moser traveled up to Joliet Prison to retrieve Samuel's body (as the telegrams suggest), he would have probably taken a horse and farm wagon. I would imagine that he would have had no desire to bring Sam back to Tremont or Morton. It was where the murders had taken place, and the community had been traumatized by it all. It was also just a really long trip to make at 130 miles, especially when transporting a body.

Christian, Benedict's son and Samuel's brother, lived near Wing, Illinois, about sixty miles southwest of Joliet. It was half the distance and a world away from Morton in terms of the impact that the crime had on the church community. It makes a lot of sense that Christian could have pulled strings or asked a favor that Samuel be buried in this small cemetery near his home. The Apostolic cemeteries only allow members to be buried there, but there are many examples of unmarked graves in the back, along the border—of those who have committed suicide. Samuel could be one of these.

For that matter, they could have buried Samuel on Christian Moser's property only a few miles east of the cemetery. This could have been done very quietly, without inquiry or the asking of favors.

The only thing that I found troubling about this theory is that Benedict Moser, who was now about seventy years old, would have had to hitch up a horse and wagon and drive 130 miles up to Joliet to deal with all this. It seems somewhat strange to me that he would not have just allowed him to be buried in the prison cemetery and not deal with it at all.

At that time, there was a cemetery east of the prison, near the quarry where inmates who died were buried. It was called

Monkey Hill. If Benedict got word that Samuel had committed suicide, he would have not only faced the impossibility of bringing him back home for burial but the "sin" as it was perceived of suicide on top of that. Why not just allow him to be buried there?

One possibility is that he just did not realize it was an option. The telegram just basically says, "Tell me what you want done." He may have thought it was his to figure out. The other possibility is that he did not want him buried up there. Maybe he considered it an embarrassment; maybe he thought he owed Samuel something. He either wanted him buried at home with family or wanted to bury the whole matter where he could make sure it was buried deep.

Then there is the third possibility—that he didn't realize the option of burial in Joliet until he got there, then made the arrangements and left for home without taking the body.

The first contact that I was able to make in researching Monkey Hill was a woman who had the role of reporting annually to the state on the condition of the cemetery. She described it as being remote and overgrown most of the year. She told me that the area is gated. When she goes to check on it, she is escorted by police officers as there are sometimes homeless people and junkies in the area. She seemed to think that gravestones that were that old had originally been wooden markers and were gone. She knew of no written records of the burials that had survived to the present.

My second contact was my brother, Adam, who is an amazing photographer. He enjoys taking pictures of abandoned places, cemeteries, and old haunts with interesting stories. He went in search of Monkey Hill a few times. The first, he was certain that a suburban neighborhood had been built over it, poltergeist-style. We decided this couldn't be true, based on the other contacts we'd made. He went back a few months later and was able to find it. His pictures show gravestones with names, but he said the older ones are impossible to read. While it is possible that old records will someday be digitized, Samuel's burial place may remain a mystery.

Fairbury Blade
Nov. 12, 1912

Rev. Witzig Dead

Rev. Rudolph Witzig, one of the most widely known ministers in Central Illinois, died at seven o'clock Monday morning at his home in Gridley. He had been ill for several months with kidney trouble, and for several weeks, his condition had been critical.

The deceased was born in Uhrziesen, Zurich, Switzerland, on September 13, 1833. He was married in Germany to Mary Huber, and to them seven children were born. Six of whom, with the widow, survive. They are Rudolph Jr., Emil, John, Fred, and Misses Lizzie and Sophia, at home. Mr. Witzig, for many years, has been pastor of the German Apostolic Church at Gridley and one of the prominent elders of the church in this country.

The funeral was held from the church Thursday at 10:00 a.m., and internment was made in the Gridley Cemetery. The services were attended by a large concourse of people, for the deceased was loved and respected. A large number went to Gridley from this city, and over three hundred came from Eureka, Morton, Roanoke, and other western points.

Chapter 20
After the Fire

After the fire, the fire still burns.
The heart grows older, but never,
ever learns. The memories smolder
and the soul always yearns... After
the fire, the fire still burns.

—Roger Daltry

2012

By the time I finished graduate school in 2010, I'd been work-ing on writing Sam's story for sixteen years. I wrote my master's thesis on the history of the Apostolic Church. I got back to work on Sam's story—with fresh eyes and a greater understanding of the times and the religious landscape on which the events took place. I was almost finished when the next turn of events took place.

On May 12, 2012, I was camping near El Paso, Illinois, with my husband and two of our four kids in a small family camp-ground called Hickory Hills. It was Mother's Day weekend, and we'd had company all day. It was about ten o'clock, and we were just getting ready for bed when the phone rang. It was my broth-er-in-law: "Amy, I don't know how to say this, but your house is on fire." The fire department had been called and were on the scene, but our house was so remote—miles out in the country. It had been burning for a while before it was discovered.

We scrambled to dress, and all piled into one car. Our two older boys weren't with us that weekend. We called them as we drove, praying desperately that they hadn't been home. We breathed a sigh of relief when they answered their cell phones. They had been out of town with friends and were headed home.

Soon my brother-in-law called back. "You need to prepare yourselves. There's nothing left." I've thought many times how important it was for us to hear that before we arrived on the scene. But we were still shocked when we got there. Fire trucks, emergency vehicles, and neighbors' cars and trucks were lined up on both sides of the road for half a mile. We couldn't get any closer, so we parked and gathered together, staring in disbelief. It was unreal. The flames shot into the night sky, but the house was gone. There was nothing left but basically one wall, which would soon come down as well. Tears coursed down our cheeks. We joined hands and walked down the country road toward the place we'd lived for almost twenty years.

Everything was gone. Much later, we were able to retrieve a black shiny door handle that had been in one of the upstairs bedrooms, but little else was even recognizable. Our friends, family, and neighbors were amazing. The testimonies from that time absolutely warm my heart. People came by the farm for days, like it was a visitation or a wake. They cried with us, held our hands, and helped us talk things out. Over and over again, we said how blessed we were—no one was home. No one was hurt. We had insurance. Ultimately, it was only stuff, and it could be replaced.

I knew this was true. I knew that my first and only thought had been my kids until I was sure that every one of them was safe. Next it was our pets: had they been let out when the boys left? The dogs were fine, and the cat eventually emerged from the barn. Next came the questions: Who needed to be contacted? What arrangements would need to be made? There were so many details, and so much of our lives had just literally gone up in smoke. You just simply cannot process it.

But right there in my mind—behind my husband, kids, and pets—was the awareness that all my stuff about Sam was gone. My research, my files, my newspaper articles, my contact information. Everything that I'd been putting together for literally more than a dozen years was gone. My children were safe, our animals had been outside and were unhurt; that was really all that mattered. But it was so many years of work, so many pages of information, so much progress lost. It was unfathomable.

I said something about my computer to my husband. I had left the case by the backdoor when we left for the campground, telling myself that it was Mother's Day weekend, and I shouldn't work; I should just enjoy my family. But now it was gone. He turned toward me. "I saw the case by the back door and thought you'd never leave it behind. It's in my truck at the campground." Some of my pictures and files were saved by this—they were saved on my laptop.

There had been two filing cabinets in our attic: one was filled with my files and research, the other with tax returns, receipts, and health-care forms. The one with my research was totally destroyed. Somehow, in the way the house went down, the drawers of the second cabinet must have fallen open, and the papers blew all over the farm. There were smoky seven-year-old bank statements blowing across the field, but nothing of my research. It was heartbreaking.

My mom took us in. The next morning after the fire, we drove to Walmart and bought six laundry baskets, one for each member of the family. We loaded them with everything each person would need to get us through the next couple of days. Each basket got a pair of jeans, a couple T-shirts, some socks and underwear, and so on. We would finally think we were done and realize that we needed a belt or more pillows. When we checked out, it was over $700 for those laundry baskets full of starter items. It's amazing really all the things that make up our lives—which we don't think about just being there, waiting for us each day.

The next morning, our family doctor's husband was on my mom's porch with a bag containing every single one of our prescriptions. They had paid for them personally. I hadn't even thought about them yet. The generosity and thoughtfulness expressed to us was so humbling. To this day, I work hard to live up to it and try to pay a fraction of it forward.

We got through the next few weeks before the end of the school year and my son's graduation from high school. His graduation gown had been hanging on the door in the laundry room. The invitations had been sent out for his party, which was going to be held at our house. Everything had to be replanned for the local fire-station community room; the school was able to get us another gown. People were so generous, so helpful, so kind. We have a lot of wonderful memories from that time. We lived with my mom for six months while the new house was being built.

Usually, I have a long list of things that I want to accomplish over the summer: remodeling projects, sorting, cleaning, organizing. That summer, there were literally none of those things to be done. I had things to do for insurance: lists to make, forms to fill out, calls to make, and so on. Some days, I just had to take kids to find some more clothes or get some more supplies to keep us all comfortable at Mom's or give us a break from one another. But it quickly became apparent that as much as I couldn't imagine recreating my work on the Sam book, I had to begin again. I couldn't let it go.

Along with my list of things lost in the fire that I was creating for the insurance company, I began a list of files, documents, and interviews. Things that I had put together over the years in researching Sam's story. Where had I gotten them before? Where could I get them now? Some things were simply lost. There are a few newspaper articles, pictures, and copies that I know are just lost—I have no idea now where I got them before, and there is nothing on the computer to help me replace them. There were notes from interviews that cannot be redone. The house where it happened had been torn down.

The most obvious thing that could not be replaced was the collection of articles that had been given to me by Ben Hohulin. I'd tried to find the originals years before and found that the newspapers they'd come from were not archived: they either came from a small now-defunct local paper, or they were destroyed in a fire years ago, or something. I found hundreds of articles later when searching the larger newspapers in Bloomington, Peoria, Chicago, and elsewhere, but many of these original clippings I had only ever seen in Ben's collection. I called his granddaughter and explained the situation. We made arrangements and met for lunch in Peoria at One World Cafe. We discussed many of the issues of the case. It was strange that after all these years, we were finally meeting. Sad that it took such extreme circumstances. Weird to hold the same laminated copies in my hand again after all these years. I agreed to return the copies to her office in a few hours.

I drove to a copy shop a few miles away. I settled in for a long afternoon at a machine. I chose one right by the door because it faced a window, had a table next to it where I could spread out my planned pages ahead, and got to work. I soon developed a routine and had piles spread all over the table. The laminated pages were huge, and so I had to scan a fourth of each page at a time, turning it awkwardly and double-checking to make sure they overlapped and I hadn't missed anything. It was time-consuming, and I was immersed in it.

At one point, I glanced up to find a woman standing next to me with an odd look on her face, as if she were waiting for me to notice her. She hated to interrupt, she said, but could I help her? She was trying to use another of the self-copy machines and having trouble. I helped her make a copy. She told me that she didn't usually come there, but a friend's beloved pet had died, and she wanted to share a poem about the rainbow bridge. She was lovely, and we talked for a few moments. She glanced down and seemed shocked by one of the headlines on my newspapers. I started to explain when she suddenly looked up and asked, "Did you just have lunch with Lynn?" Now it was my turn to be shocked. It turned out that this was her mother. She knew of the plans to meet, but not the copying-articles part of the plans. It was a total coincidence that we'd run into each other.

We talked for a while. She was Ben's daughter. I told her about my meeting with her parents so many years ago. She looked over the articles, and I explained my progress, my plans. We talked about the fire. She was so nice, so easy to talk to. Finally, she said, "Well, my daughter would never tell you this, but you need to meet Helen."

What?

She explained that there had been a falling out within the family over some of the things that were passed down after Ben's death. Ben wanted some things given to his granddaughter, who seemed the most interested in the case. This woman felt that they should not go to the next generation while she, who was of the older generation, was still interested in being the caretaker—something of that nature. They no longer spoke. Lynn's mother felt that it was sad that things had come between family. She gave me Helen's phone number.

Later, when I returned the articles to Lynn, she expressed her shock that I'd met up with her mother. Her mom had called and told her what happened—what a crazy coincidence it was. Lynn said, "Really, you have no idea. I would not even think my mother knew where a copy shop was. I'm surprised she didn't call and ask me." I thanked her profusely for sharing the copies and returned home, excited to get back to work.

Weeks later, my husband and I drove to Helen's house to meet her. She lived in a beautiful little cottage in a town about halfway from our house to Peoria. They had lived in this house for years, she said, but were moving soon and had just sold it. She was excited about moving on to the next phase of their lives but very sad to leave the house. We soon saw why. It was like a museum. Everywhere you looked were beautiful arrangements of antiques, most of which were meaningful to her family. Old memorabilia from the Hohulin Fence Company, an organ that had been in the family for years, gorgeous woven jacquards passed down from Gottlieb Hohulin, the master weaver, who was Hanna's father. One of the woven pieces, she said, was currently part of the art collection at the University of Illinois in Champaign.

There was a beautiful china cabinet filled with a pattern that seemed much older than dishes that you normally see on display. They were simple but very beautiful. It was the china that Sam and Hanna had received as a wedding gift. Such a normal thing for a couple to have. I thought of how it had been with them through their good times and bad. How it had been packed and taken with them through each of their moves: their attempts to make things work. The table would have been set with these dishes when Samuel ate separately from the family, when his brother came to pick up Hanna and the kids for church. If this stuff could talk! It had been there. It had seen it all.

She led us to a beautiful wicker baby stroller. Sunlight streamed through the window, bathing the room in evening light. It was lined with beautiful linens. It looked ancient but so elegant. It was absolutely pristine—spotless and without dust. It was obvious that Helen took excellent care of all these things. Beneath the linens, she carefully showed us, there was a bullet hole: the only reminder that Samuel Moser's child was murdered in this very buggy.

We talked about the plans for the book; she asked questions and answered others. She shared about their plans to move. I gave her copies of the articles that I had brought for her and hoped that there would be peace made within the family.

It was clear that the effort to start again after the fire was profitable. There almost seemed to be a blessing on this project, an anointing to see it through. I made trips to historical societies, research rooms—places I'd been before, but now they had more resources that were digital, files that were indexed. I'd often come home with most of the things on my list, but also a few things I'd never expected to find, things I didn't know existed. New details of the story emerged.

One day, I called the state prison archives in Springfield, Illinois. I explained that they'd sent me information on this story years earlier. A few weeks earlier, I'd called and requested replacements, which had just arrived in the mail. The problem was that I remembered it being around fourteen pages that they'd originally sent me, and now I'd only gotten three. Could they have overlooked something? The woman listened patiently to my questions, then explained that she'd sent everything that was in the file. I described my project again and explained how important this was. She promised to investigate and call me with her findings.

A few hours later, a phone call. She had talked to a colleague, who had directed her to another location of files. She had found the rest of the pages—and a bonus. The second file was a special kind of file that had an envelope built in (that she would not have noticed, she said). Her colleague opened the envelope to reveal a tin-type picture: Samuel's mug shot. I almost dropped the phone. There were pen drawings of Samuel in the newspapers. There were even places in articles that talked about a newspaperman having snapped Samuel's picture, but I'd never found a photograph. I couldn't believe it.

A few days later, the envelope arrived. I went and sat down at my mother's dining room table. I opened the envelope and slid out the pages. The first several were familiar, the ones I'd received before. Then...

It had been damaged, she'd told me. There had been some moisture in an old storage room. But there he was, wearing the tie that Sheriff Mount had purchased for him. Had this been taken when he was arrested, when he was brought back to Pekin? The tie is possibly the only clue. It's most likely that it was taken on his arrival at Joliet State Penitentiary.

I lined this photograph up next to the pen drawings that I'd assembled from the newspapers. Was my former impression of him still the same? Had these courtroom artists done him justice? It was interesting. Before, I'd seen him in a certain light (cast on him by the artist). In some, he looks so pathetic and sad—a victim of the abuses of the church, just as the article was implying. In others, he looks sort of dastardly, like a con man who had a plan all along.

This photograph takes all that away. He looks so human. It's easy to see why people were conflicted about him at the time. It's such a horrible story. What he did is so awful. But it's also easy to feel for him—to relate to his story, and to want him to be okay. Sheriff Mount, the very man who discussed the lynch mobs and likely hanging, bought him this tie.

I finished the first draft of this book in November of 2016. I made several copies and gave them to friends to read. I set a deadline of spring break to gather them back and process their edits and suggestions. In April, I got an e-mail from a Mark Hohulin. He was a relative and researching the story. We began to exchange information back and forth. He had pictures, family albums, stories. Even more pieces began to fit into the puzzle. Mark encouraged me to contact the archives in Tazewell County again. He thought there was more there than what they had sent to me.

When I drove to Tremont, the woman behind the desk retrieved the file for me. I hadn't really thought about it before, but I'd only seen copies. This time, she handed me the actual documents. The stack of documents contained the actual notes that Sam had handwritten. I didn't find a lot that day that I didn't already know, but it felt like that trip was important for me. It felt like I'd come full circle somehow—to be holding the actual papers in my hand, sitting in the courthouse in Pekin.

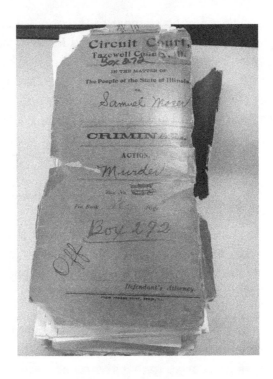

Mark and I still keep in contact. We've become friends. He once told me that he wasn't told much about what happened when he was growing up. The Hohulins didn't talk about it, not because it was hurtful for them but because they didn't want to bring up the pain and hurt that the Mosers would naturally feel because of the pain that their family member had caused others.

Now, all these years later, I feel like I've seen the story through to the end. I think back to the moment that I stood at the top of the stairs looking at the boys' tiny clothes hanging in the armoire. I felt then that Hanna wanted her story to be told. I hope I've done it justice. It became much more about telling Sam's story, but I think she'd be okay with that. She loved him once. Her children were his as well. What he did was horrible; what happened to them was tragic. But the events that led up to the murders was another thing altogether. It is a lesson to all of us: that religion and legalism can have very dark effects—where it becomes not about love and leading but about punishment and control.

I have always struggled with this story. It was important that I told it well, that I related it clearly. But I wanted to be neutral, to make sure that people walked away from it feeling that they'd been told the whole story and been allowed to draw their own conclusions. I didn't want to cast the church in a bad light or implicate anyone unfairly. I'm not sure that's completely possible, but ultimately what I've decided is that I hope people read this story and learn the lessons that history has to offer from it. Maybe that's the best we can do.

There are so many fragile things, after all.

People break so easily, and so do dreams and hearts.

—Neil Gaiman

About the Author

Amy Steidinger is hard at work on a follow-up book about the prisons in Joliet, Illinois. She has spent the last twenty-five years as a teacher and a genealogist. She went back to school and earned a master's degree in history from Illinois State University. She loves to travel and is always planning the next adventure. Her greatest joy is her family—her husband Jay and their four children, who have grown up to be amazing adults.

SSDGM.